Virginia Woolf and
Nineteenth-Century Women Writers

# Virginia Woolf and Nineteenth-Century Women Writers

Victorian Legacies and Literary Afterlives

Anne Reus

EDINBURGH
University Press

Edinburgh University Press is one of the leading university presses in the UK. We publish academic books and journals in our selected subject areas across the humanities and social sciences, combining cutting-edge scholarship with high editorial and production values to produce academic works of lasting importance. For more information visit our website: edinburghuniversitypress.com

© Anne Reus 2022

Edinburgh University Press Ltd
The Tun – Holyrood Road
12(2f) Jackson's Entry
Edinburgh EH8 8PJ

First published in hardback by Edinburgh University Press 2022

Typeset in 10.5/13 Adobe Sabon
by Manila Typesetting Company

A CIP record for this book is available from the British Library

ISBN 978 1 4744 8562 3 (hardback)
ISBN 978 1 4744 8563 0 (paperback)
ISBN 978 1 4744 8564 7 (webready PDF)
ISBN 978 1 4744 8565 4 (epub)

The right of Anne Reus to be identified as the author of this work has been asserted in accordance with the Copyright, Designs and Patents Act 1988, and the Copyright and Related Rights Regulations 2003 (SI No. 2498).

# Contents

| | | |
|---|---|---|
| *Acknowledgements* | | vi |
| *Abbreviations* | | vii |
| 1. | Introduction: Rainbow and Granite, Women and Biography | 1 |
| 2. | 'Vain are these speculations': Jane Austen and Female Perfection | 37 |
| 3. | 'Even a lady sometimes raises her voice': Mary Russell Mitford and Elizabeth Barrett Browning | 74 |
| 4. | 'That indefinable something': Charlotte Brontë and Protest | 108 |
| 5. | 'A gap in your library, Madam': The Lives of Professional Women | 137 |
| 6. | Writing Virginia Woolf: Autobiographical Fragments | 182 |
| *Bibliography* | | 199 |
| *Index* | | 211 |

## *Acknowledgements*

First and foremost, this book would not have been written without Jane de Gay. Jane's supervision, mentorship, and example have shaped my practice; in research, teaching and beyond. I have benefited immensely from the scholarly community at Leeds Trinity University and especially the Leeds Centre for Victorian Studies, and the supervision, support and mentorship provided by Juliette Taylor-Batty, Rosemary Mitchell and Helen Kingstone. I am grateful to Leeds Trinity University for sponsoring the PhD studentship that enabled me to undertake the initial research for this book; and to the PhD community at LTU, especially Tom Breckin and Ruth Clemens, for their stimulating company and collaboration. I have also benefited from the generosity of the academic community, through the advice and mentorship of colleagues, support in accessing resources, and through travel bursaries for the conferences 'Virginia Woolf and the Writing of History' (2018) in Rouen and 'Modernism in the Home' (2019) at the University of Birmingham.

I am very grateful to my parents for their encouragement and faith in me. My sister's unwavering support means the world to me. Finally, thank you to James and the hedgehogs for sharing this experience with me.

## *Abbreviations*

All texts are by Virginia Woolf, unless otherwise noted.

| | |
|---|---|
| 3G, AROO | *A Room of One's Own & Three Guineas*, ed. by Michèle Barrett (London: Penguin Books, 2000) |
| BTA | *Between the Acts,* ed. by Stella McNichol (London: Penguin Books, 2000) |
| CSF | *The Complete Shorter Fiction of Virginia Woolf*, ed. by Susan Dick (London: Harcourt, 1989) |
| D | *The Diary of Virginia Woolf*, ed. by Anne Olivier Bell and Andrew McNeillie, 5 vols (London: The Hogarth Press, 1977–82) |
| E | *The Essays of Virginia Woolf*, ed. by Andrew McNeillie and Stuart N. Clarke, 6 vols (London: Harcourt (vols 1–4) / The Hogarth Press (vols 5 and 6), 1986–2011) |
| F | *Flush*, ed. by Kate Flint (Oxford: Oxford UP, 2009) |
| JR | *Jacob's Room*, ed. by Kate Flint (Oxford: Oxford UP, 1999) |
| L | *The Letters of Virginia Woolf*, ed. by Nigel Nicolson, 6 vols (London: The Hogarth Press, 1975–80) |
| LS | *The London Scene* (London: Daunt Books, 2013) |
| MoB | *Moments of Being: Autobiographical Writings*, ed. by Jeanne Schulkind (London: Pimlico, 2002) |
| PA | *A Passionate Apprentice: The Early Journals 1897–1909*, ed. by Mitchell A. Leaska (London: Pimlico, 2004) |
| P | *The Pargiters*, ed. by Mitchell A. Leaska (London: The Hogarth Press, 1978) |
| TL | *To the Lighthouse*, ed. by Stella McNichol (London: Penguin Books, 2000) |

VO          *The Voyage Out* (London: Triad Grafton Books, 1978)
W&F         *Women & Fiction: The Manuscript Version of A Room of One's Own*, ed. by S. P. Rosenbaum (Oxford: Blackwell Publishers for Shakespeare Head Press, 1992)

# Chapter 1

# Introduction: Rainbow and Granite, Women and Biography

### 'Indiscretions': Virginia Woolf's Literary Biography

In the 1924 *Vogue* article 'Indiscretions', Virginia Woolf posits the existence of two different modes of reading: the literary critic engages with the text alone, while 'the rest of us' approach literature from a personal standpoint. Indiscreet and driven by affection, for these readers 'in every book there is something – sex, character, temperament – which, as in life, rouses affection or repulsion; and, as in life, sways and prejudices; and again, as in life, is hardly to be analysed by the reason' (*E* 3.460). These readers care for authors and not literature alone: they imagine the person behind the book, ascribe personalities and habits to their favourites, and banish disliked authors based on imaginary misconducts.

Virginia Woolf's decision to count herself as one of these readers may seem incongruous. In 1924, she was a leading literary critic who was able to 'extract the essence [of a book] and feast upon it undisturbed' (*E* 3.460), and a rising Modernist novelist who had perfected an impersonal mode of writing in her own fiction. However, this book will show that Woolf was often a personal and sometimes an indiscreet reader and writer, whose interest in the lives and personalities of authors fundamentally shapes her critical encounters with them. Much of Woolf's non-fiction intersperses literary criticism with biographical sketches and imaginary encounters: the demarcation between the literary critic and the indiscreetly affectionate reader is therefore much more porous than Woolf – however light-heartedly – suggests here. Woolf's responses to her literary predecessors also allow new insights into her self-positioning within the literary canon, her engagement with her predecessors and her responses to biographical traditions. Reading Woolf's non-fiction through the lens of literary biography therefore offers a new approach to the almost forty years of journalism she produced during her lifetime.

Mark Goldman's pioneering study *The Reader's Art: Virginia Woolf as Literary Critic* opened with the observation that 'Any study of Virginia Woolf's criticism must begin by pointing to the obvious but striking contrast between her stature as a novelist and her reputation as a literary critic'. Although few would nowadays dispute Goldman's assertion that read collectively, Woolf's essays set out her theories of reading, criticism and literary tradition, they continue to be a comparatively neglected body of work.[1] '[H]er literary and cultural journalism has consistently received less attention than her fiction', Alice Wood observes, yet as a large and heterogeneous body of work rarely studied on its own terms, its potential to '[generate] revisionary readings of both Virginia Woolf and Modernism' continues unbroken, as Leila Brosnan has productively shown.[2]

This revisionary potential is particularly prominent in essays like 'Indiscretions', which reveal the complex overlap of influences at work in Woolf's journalism. Woolf's distinction between professional and leisurely modes of reading is a timely intervention in contemporary debates about literary categorisation and the middlebrow that is echoed in Nicola Humble's pragmatic assertion that '[m]iddlebrow and highbrow books are distinguishable, fundamentally, not by any stable intrinsic differences, but by *how they are read*'.[3] As an experimental Modernist novelist writing for the fashionable and female mass readership of *Vogue*, Woolf straddles this cultural divide: while her novels lend themselves to the close reading and serious study associated with the literary critic and academic scholar, 'Indiscretions', with its confidential, gossipy tone and a strong interest in authorial personas behind the book, promotes a form of immersive, emotional reading more usually associated with the middlebrow.[4] The ideal readers of 'Indiscretions' therefore occupy 'a sort of third term, escaping the two extremes of either inaccessible scholarship or mindless consumption' as Elena Gualtieri notes of Woolf's Common Reader: they have 'managed to preserve that enthusiasm and personal involvement in the activity of reading which is often lacking in those who practise criticism as a profession'.[5] 'Indiscretions' therefore demonstrates clearly Woolf's position as a 'democratic highbrow', to use Melba Cuddy-Keane's term, and helps 'to locate both the person and her ideas in a different context – one that involves public debates about books, reading, and education'.[6]

Consequently, 'Indiscretions' does not require specialist knowledge from its readers. Moving from the 'attractions and repulsions of sex' which compel women readers to nod in bored agreement when men fall passionately in love with Byron, Woolf calls up a 'harem' of women writers for her readers' affectionate recollection:

> it is by no means certain that every woman is inspired by pure envy when she reads what another has written. More probably Emily Brontë was the passion of her youth; Charlotte even she loved with nervous affection; and cherished a quiet sisterly regard for Anne. [ . . . ] George Eliot is an Aunt, and, as an Aunt, inimitable. So treated she drops the apparatus of masculinity which Herbert Spencer necessitated; indulges herself in memory; and pours forth, no doubt with some rustic accent, the genial stores of her youth, the greatness and profundity of her soul. Jane Austen we needs must adore; but she does not want it; she wants nothing; our love is a by-product, an irrelevance; with that mist or without it her moon shines on. (*E* 3.462–3)

Woolf's literary family is as familiar as it is comforting: *Vogue*'s readers by no means needed an interest in contemporary or avant-garde literature to feel at home with this selection of nineteenth-century novelists, deeply familiar from adolescent reading. The vignettes are instantly recognisable: drawing on a strong biographical tradition, they combine familiarity with the New Biography's emphasis on brevity and scene-making over conventional long-form narratives.

As this book will show, such character sketches are a constant feature of Woolf's life writing. Yet the convenient shorthand of the passionate Brontës, profound George Eliot, and the distant perfection of Jane Austen also reveal the endurance of Victorian biographical narratives, each reflecting in different ways the lasting impact of competing constructions of female literary labour and changing modes of professionalism throughout the nineteenth century, as well as Woolf's responses to them. This familiar canonical assembly also fails to uncover forgotten foremothers of contemporary women's writing, as Woolf demands of her readers in *A Room of One's Own*: instead, as Alison Booth observes, Woolf limits herself to 'the well-lit corridors of history' in much of her female life writing. Booth provocatively asks of Woolf, 'Why did she ignore the hundreds of female prosopographies [that tried to recuperate neglected women writers' lives]?'[7] However, as ignorance is hard to prove, I will instead explore which Victorian biographies Woolf did read, and how they shaped her understanding of nineteenth-century women writers' professional and literary accomplishments. Works such as Elizabeth Gaskell's *Life of Charlotte Brontë* (1857) or James Edward Austen-Leigh's *A Memoir of Jane Austen* (1870) provide Woolf with influential narrative strategies and subtly shape her engagement with their subjects. Likewise, her habit of consulting Leslie Stephen's *Hours in a Library*, 'by way of filling out my ideas' (*MoB* 122), establishes an easy conduit for Victorian values and judgements, both literary and personal: as critics, both were 'predominantly biographical, or biographically oriented in their criticism', as Andrew McNeillie observes.[8] In contrast to the confident Modernism of her novels and select programmatic essays such as 'Modern Fiction' and 'The New Biography', Woolf's journalism therefore occupies a more complex territory. With strategies ranging from the deliberate deployment of outdated moral judgements to unwilling echoes of Victorian criticism, Woolf's essays and articles perpetuate, interrogate and re-contextualise Victorian verdicts on female professionalism and femininity, supporting Steve Ellis's conception of Woolf's 'post-Victorian' identity 'as a writer whose modern and innovatory practice coexists with a powerful nostalgia for various elements of Victorian culture'.[9]

To a modern reader, the 'harem' of women writers in 'Indiscretions' is furthermore eminently familiar from *A Room of One's Own* (1929). Targeting misogynist stereotyping, which views women as inherently hostile to each other, Woolf offers instead a supportive female community that effortlessly integrates *Vogue*'s predominantly female readership into its midst. This female genealogy points forwards to the collective analysis of women's lives that forms the basis of Woolf's feminist polemics *A Room of One's Own* and *Three Guineas* (1938), and foreshadows one of the central and most popular concepts of the former: 'we think back through our mothers if we are women' (*AROO* 69).[10] Here, Woolf asserts the fundamental importance of a distinctly female tradition of writing without which women cannot create a literature of their own: *A Room of One's Own* especially offers an anticipatory response to the anxiety of authorship with which Gilbert and Gubar diagnose nineteenth-century women's writing.[11] Although Woolf never proclaimed herself a feminist and famously cremated the word in *Three Guineas*, her undoubtedly feminist politics have driven her gradual transformation from a supposedly apolitical highbrow aesthete – 'the least political animal that has lived since Aristotle invented the definition' – into a modern feminist icon.[12] Brenda Silver, tracing this transformation, notes that 'American feminists in the 1970s subversively laid claim to Woolf's image – to her face and her name and her writings – to articulate a new social and cultural text [ . . . ] a feminist agenda.'[13] As part of this feminist reappraisal, 'texts such as *A Room* (1929) which had previously been confined to the niche dedicated to Woolf's "feminist pamphlets" and thus isolated from the rest of her writing' now occupy a central role in her oeuvre, '[carrying] with it the possibility of re-thinking from scratch the role of her non-fictional writings and their relation to her novels', as Gualtieri observes.[14] Today, the evocative title of *A Room of One's Own* appears on Penguin's branded mugs, bags and notebooks ('Intellectual women have their very own brand of commodity fetishism', Jane Marcus noted)[15] alongside the more traditional venue of introductory modules to literature and feminist criticism. 'The "thinking back through our mothers" that Woolf proposed in *A Room of One's Own* inspired the landmark feminist literary history on which we now depend; without it, countless projects recovering lost voices might not have been undertaken', Anne Fernald recaps.[16]

Fernald identifies a tension between Woolf's individual ambitions, her 'desire to be a great writer with no humiliating qualification of "for a woman"', and 'contemporary feminism's communitarian aspirations', often building on Woolf's ideas and concepts.[17] Although women's writing and the societal forces that shaped it are recurring interests in Woolf's essays and articles alike, closer analysis reveals that her 'thinking back' is not always as benign or inclusive as we may have come to expect it. Jane Marcus, making a forceful case for Woolf's feminism, socialism and artistry in *Art and Anger*, argued rather optimistically that

> 'Thinking back through our mothers,' a necessary act for all women writers, would afford one maternal protection for one's own raids on the patriarchy and simultaneously raise female consciousness. [ . . . ] [Woolf] expected that women artists would become feminists through this experience and also that they would make common cause with other oppressed groups.[18]

Consequently, Marcus easily accepts Woolf's attack on Charlotte Brontë in *A Room of One's Own* (to offer just one example of a less benign thinking back) as necessary to the text's internal logic. However, elsewhere Marcus also observes that '*Each history then is an act of erasure as well as an act of preservation. Each historian commits murder as well as resurrects the dead*'.[19] While Marion Dell's *Virginia Woolf's Influential Forebears: Julia Margaret Cameron, Anny Thackeray Ritchie and Julia Prinsep Stephen* traces Woolf's profoundly ambivalent responses to the achievements and legacies of these predecessors, Mary Jean Corbett's *Behind the Times: Virginia Woolf in Late-Victorian Contexts* sets the scene for multiple out-and-out murders. Corbett demonstrates that Woolf is highly selective in her engagement with her forebears and ignores, undermines and dismisses an entire generation of late-Victorian and Edwardian women writers, activists and philanthropists. However, where Corbett reads this act of disavowal as a strategy that allows Woolf to align herself more closely with an earlier, greater generation of Victorian writers, I seek to complicate this alignment with regard to women of letters.[20] Women's lives and personalities become particularly malleable in Woolf's skilful hands: as Janet Todd observes, they 'become what Virginia Woolf needs them to be, female heroes or distressed ladies of sensibility, and they write at her dictation'.[21] Thus, seeking to draw attention to women's suffering in patriarchal society, Woolf's feminism often works at the expense of individual writers. Naomi Black's *Virginia Woolf as Feminist* opens with the evocative anecdote of Mrs Green, apparently so annoying that Leslie Stephen point-blank banned women from joining the London Library Committee. Quite reasonably, Black notes that

> Feminists are more likely than other women to share Virginia Woolf's indignation, yet that episode can bring out feminist responses in women not previously radicalized. That is, it can make them angry at Mrs. Green's having been made the stand-in for a whole class of human beings who are seen as unfit to do what men do as a matter of course. *Three Guineas* is, among other things, an attempt to provoke in women just such an irritated awareness of the structures of sexist exclusion.[22]

Yet how will these readers, feminists or not, respond to Woolf's condemnation of Margaret Oliphant in the same text? Woolf 'deplore[s] the fact that Mrs Oliphant sold her brain, her very admirable brain, prostituted her culture and enslaved her intellectual liberty in order that she might earn her living' (3G 217), suggesting that Oliphant and countless nineteenth-century women of letters like her were entirely unfit to do what Virginia Woolf did as a matter of course: make her living as a professional author. As Emily Blair notes, Woolf's deployment of literary biography 'creates the same didactic tie between life and literature that conduct books and nineteenth-century anthologies established'.[23] This tendency is particularly pronounced in *A Room of One's Own* and *Three Guineas*, where women's lives, read collectively, highlight financial and social inequalities, patterns of abuse and fundamental biases in the structure of home and state. However, even when writing on individual writers, challenges like the aforementioned legacies of Victorian biography and Woolf's own desire for stylistic and biographical experimentation can sideline and overwhelm the nominal subjects of her essays, as I will explore in more detail in the chapters ahead.

The aim of this study is emphatically not to dismiss Woolf as a feminist critic altogether. Rather, I want to suggest that Woolf's feminism is not quite as monolithic as her most enthusiastic proponents believe: as Fernald notes, there is a

> branch of Woolf criticism [that] remains troublesome in its insistence on her radicalism in all things, her rightness, her anticipation of the most advanced views that we ourselves hold [ . . . ] For though all of these ideas exist in Woolf's writing, there is much else.[24]

While Fernald's own *Feminism and the Reader* traces developments in Woolf's feminism through criticism on heterogeneous figures, I focus on Woolf's engagement with those nineteenth-century women writers who might be considered her 'mothers' by virtue of their centrality to her writing, both in her journalism leading up to *A Room of One's Own* and *Three Guineas* and within these essays. My aim is to offer a detailed and nuanced analysis that allows us to fully appreciate the complexities and ambivalences of Woolf's feminism: instead of assessing it solely on the basis of her theories of women's writing, I also explore her writing on individual women. Elaine Showalter has warned of the dangers of the Room of One's Own as a withdrawal from the 'real' world of men, while Anna Snaith emphasises that it is 'a liberating private space, an active choice, and, importantly, it is from the room that the woman will gain access to the public sphere through writing'.[25] Katarina Koutsantoni counters critics of Woolf's self-censorship in *A Room of One's Own* by arguing for the superiority of a more conciliatory dialogic approach: 'She refused to maintain a selfish, stubbornly female and antagonistic position because she felt deep within her that art is for sharing with the public, and individualistic attitudes have no place in it'.[26] Victoria Rosner, on the other hand, reminds us of Victorian architectural practices by wondering

> [h]ow can anyone not think of their sex in a room like the study, a room dedicated to articulating masculinity through its furnishings, accessories, location, and solitude? How can the acquisition of a study make it possible for the woman writer to disengage from the separate spheres of gender that the study was built to secure?[27]

Like Rosner, I intend to return to the Victorian influences and legacies in Woolf's thinking to highlight instances in which they act as limitations on her thinking on women, literary traditions and female professionalism, as well as her feminist criticisms of them.

## 'A plague of essays': Virginia Woolf, Journalist

Unlike the female reader of 'Indiscretions', Virginia Woolf the literary critic, biographer and novelist does not easily fit into her imagined community of Victorian women writers. The harem setting of her imagined family of women writers evokes a secluded domestic setting, cut off from the public sphere, which encapsulates Woolf's preference for casting women as domestic amateur writers, thus undermining the achievements of mid- and late-Victorian female literary professionals who achieved financial independence through their writing, as I will argue in Chapter 5.[28] By 1924, Woolf herself, in contrast, could already look back on a twenty-year career in journalism, which had taken her from a modest beginning as reviewer for the women's pages of the clerical journal *Guardian* to a prominent position as literary critic in the leading journals of the day, which would be cemented the following year with the publication of the first *Common Reader* (1925).

Most importantly among these journalistic associations was undoubtedly the *Times Literary Supplement*, to which Woolf began contributing in 1905. Arguably, this is where Woolf learned the craft of a reviewer and critic. Although her relationship with its editor, Bruce Richmond, was sometimes contentious, she 'learnt a lot of my craft writing for him: how to compress; how to enliven; & also was made to read with a pen & notebook, seriously' (D 5.145). She also learned to work subversively within the limits of an often conservative periodical press.[29] In 'A Sketch of the Past', she traces the impact of a multi-generational Victorian education in femininity on her reviewing:

> When I read my old *Literary Supplement* articles, I lay the blame for their suavity, their politeness, their sidelong approach, to my tea-table training. I see myself, not reviewing a book, but handing plates of buns to shy young men and asking them: do they take cream and sugar? (*MoB* 152)

The explicitly female narrators of 'Indiscretions', *A Room of One's Own* and *Three Guineas* are an exception: frequently, Woolf obscures her own identity as a woman or assumes male pronouns as the norm, a practice further facilitated by the *TLS* policy of publishing articles unsigned. This habit is strong enough to emerge even in 'Professions for Women', an essay that explicitly addresses an audience of women and draws on her own experience of professional life: here, Woolf defaults to male pronouns in her exploration of the novelist's ideal state of mind in spite of the autobiographical nature of her discussion, demonstrating the truth of her assertion that '[i]t is far harder to kill a phantom than a reality' (*E* 6.481).[30] This Victorian legacy is further complicated by Woolf's nostalgic appreciation for the beauty of the 'civilized qualities' like 'restraint, sympathy, unselfishness' characteristic of idealised femininity, but also by her awareness of the subversive qualities inherent in this mode of expression: 'the surface manner allows one, as I have found, to slip in things that would be inaudible if one marched straight up and spoke out loud' (*MoB* 152). Her capacity for 'private thinking, tea-table thinking . . . thinking against the current, not with it' (*E* 6.242–3) was thus honed by decades of writing under an editor's nose.

Aside from a brief stint at the *Cornhill Magazine* (1905–9), where she contributed signed reviews in tandem with Lady Nelly Cecil to 'The Book on the Table', the *TLS* dominates and shapes Woolf's journalism until the early 1920s. That Woolf was an important contributor to the *TLS* is evident from her return to reviewing in full force, at high speeds and frequency, and in prominent positions, after a hiatus between 1913 and 1915. Woolf's introduction to the profession of reviewer thus happened firmly in the cultural mainstream. In *Fiction and the Reading Public* (1939), Q.D. Leavis classifies the *Times Literary Supplement* as a 'middlebrow' literary magazine with a large readership, which 'representing a safe academic attitude, will summarise and comment on the plot and merits of any work by a novelist of standing'; while Fernald observes that it 'had been concerned from the beginning with establishing itself as a guide for what the common reader should read, a project that has its roots in the criticism of Joseph Addison and Samuel Johnson'.[31] Thus, while a programmatic Modernist essay like 'Modern Novels' (1919) was not out of place in the *TLS*, Woolf also reviewed copious amounts of contemporary fiction and biography, and contributed leading articles that re-evaluated established canonical novelists, such as 'Jane Austen' (1913), 'Charlotte Brontë' (1916), and 'George Eliot' (1919), already familiar to her readership. Although it is difficult to generalise across such a large body of work as Woolf's non-fiction, there is a marked increase in her eloquence and skill as a reviewer around the 1910s. 'Her allusions and references confine themselves less to the works ostensibly under review than once they did and, ranging freely, reveal a wider and more fertile familiarity with her subjects, their works and lives', McNeillie summarises.[32]

In the 1920s, following her growing reputation as a writer of fiction, Woolf's journalistic reach considerably expanded. Thus she records in April 1925 that

> I'm out to make £300 this summer by writing [ . . . ]. But hush, hush – my books tremble on the verge of coming out, & my future is uncertain. As for forecasts – it's *just* on the cards Mrs Dalloway is a success (Harcourt thinks it 'wonderful'), & sells 2,000. I dont expect it: I expect a slow silent increase of fame, such as has come about, rather miraculously, since Js R. was published; my value mounting steadily as a journalist, though scarcely a copy sold. (D 3.9)

Woolf's reflection on the interdependence of her dual roles of critic and novelist is a useful reminder that her reputation as an essayist equalled, and for some even surpassed, that of her fiction. By 1924, she was regularly writing for publications as diverse as the *Athenaeum* (under the editorship of John Middleton Murry), later the *Nation & Athenaeum* (with Leonard Woolf as literary editor), T. S. Eliot's *Criterion* (undoubtedly highbrow),[33] the *New Statesman*, British *Vogue* (under the editorship of Dorothy Todd), but also the Labour-leaning *Daily Herald*, and increasingly reached an American audience. Crucially, this change of venue made Woolf a public figure in the world of journalism: in contrast, the overwhelming majority of her earlier non-fiction in the *Times Literary Supplement* had been published anonymously. Her increased fame allowed her to write more leaders and essays. However, even her nominal reviews now present themselves as stand-alone essays that needed little revision to be transformed into the first *Common Reader*: their relationship to the book under discussion is frequently so indiscernible as to depend mainly on paratextual clues, such as the header or footer with bibliographical information in the *TLS*, or the posthumous annotations in the *Collected Essays*. The *Common Reader* also confirmed Woolf's international fame, leading to an expansion of her North American market with articles now appearing in the *Atlantic Monthly*, *New York Herald Tribune* and *Yale Review* among others; while her regular contributions to the *Nation & Athenaeum*, *(New) Criterion*, *Vogue* and *Time and Tide* continued.

In fact, the only relationship that suffered from Woolf's wider journalistic reach was that with the *Times Literary Supplement*: McNeillie counts only seven *TLS* articles between 1925 and 1928, in contrast with almost seventy for 1919–24, and none after Richmond's retirement as editor in December 1937 (in spite of requests).[34] By the mid- to late 1920s, both Woolfs were successful journalists with a high income and the Hogarth Press was a successful business. This dropping-off therefore may have been financially motivated: in July 1927, Woolf notes that 'Bruce Richmond is coming to tea on Monday to discuss an article on Morgan; & I am going to convey to him the fact that I can't always refuse £60 in America for the Times' £10' (*D* 3.149).[35] Woolf's transformation into a cultural critic in her last decade, as traced by Alice Wood, thus happens against a backdrop of slowly decreasing literary criticism.[36] While the *Common Reader: Second Series* was celebrated enthusiastically by contemporary reviewers,[37] Woolf's focus shifted away from journalism and the attendant publicity. Thus, she notes in November 1936 that she had turned down a review for the BBC's *The Listener*:

> Joe [Ackerley, its literary editor] will only allow me 800 words of unsigned; 1500 of signed. An amusing illustration of the virtues of capitalism. Its the advertisement, not the article, they want. And its the advertisement I dont want. But anyhow the book is bad mostly; & to compress Miss W.[eeton: *Journal*

*of a Governess, 1807–1811*] into 800 words would not be worth doing. (*D* 5.32)

Only the war and its effect on their incomes made Woolf seriously consider a return to full-time journalism. By August 1939, she was noting of her efforts to place articles that '[m]y old age of independence is thus in danger. But in fact its hard to keep aloof & do my books. Theres a pressure about an article [ . . . ] that keeps one absorbed' (*D* 5.237).

Woolf's hesitant recognition of the allure of journalism confirms its central place in her oeuvre: in spite of its dreaded publicity and its competition with her books, journalism accounts for the majority of her non-fiction before the 1930s and thus was more than just a convenient form of income. The idea of Woolf actively managing her public image and her career sits rather uneasily with Modernism's image as an elite art form, yet reconceptualising Woolf as a prolific journalist and part-owner of a successful publishing house as well as an avant-garde novelist makes her close ties to the business of literature more visible. While Gualtieri and Koutsantoni's studies of Woolf's non-fiction focus on the genre of the essay, Brosnan emphasises her position 'between the "high" art of literary modernism and the "low" work of journalism'. Melba Cuddy-Keane reminds us that Woolf spent much of her writing life as a public intellectual 'outside of the borders that would limit her sphere to Bloomsbury, or to high modernism, or to feminism'; likewise, Claire Battershill argues that the Woolfs' Hogarth Press began with hand-prints in the spirit of a Modernist little magazine but quickly transformed into a regular business with commercial print runs in the tens of thousands.[38] Jane Garrity, Alice Wood and Lise Jaillant similarly read Woolf through the lens of her contributions to mass-market publications like *Vogue*, *Good Housekeeping*, and the Uniform Edition of her collected works, respectively, to present a writer who confidently and successfully negotiated popular markets to promote herself.[39] However, Virginia Woolf the journalist continues to be frequently absent from collections on Modernist print culture, while the (by and large) mainstream publications she favoured attract scholarly attention at much lower rates than little magazines or feminist publications like *Time and Tide*. Thus, *Women, Periodicals and Print Culture in Britain, 1890s–1920s* devotes a whole section to key literary figures such as Rebecca West, Dorothy Richardson, Katherine Mansfield and May Sinclair, yet Woolf only appears as a canonical touchstone that contextualises their work. Similarly, *Modernism in the Magazines* relies on Woolf's dating of Modernism to December 1910, but unlike Leonard Woolf, editor of the *Nation & Athenaeum*, Virginia is absent from the volume.[40]

This is an omission that this book cannot rectify: although I hope to further critical engagement with Woolf's journalism (rather than just the essays collected in the *Common Reader*), even a brief cultural history of Woolf and the *Times Literary Supplement* is beyond the scope of this book.

Although Woolf eschewed some forms of advertising, and abhorred the ruthless self-promotion and -commodification she associated with (often female) turn of the century professional authorship, as Corbett shows, she was keenly aware of, and interested in, her financial value and reputation as a writer.[41] This distinctly gendered ambivalence manifests itself on the occasion of her first signed essay in 1905: 'Gerald [ . . . ] tells me my Plague of Essays Article is out in The Academy, with Virginia Stephen signed in full, which seems rather indecent publicity' (*PA* 243). Woolf's unease reminds us of her close temporal proximity to the Victorian period and its preference for female obscurity, and thus offers a useful context for her dislike of late-Victorian professionals. In spite of this, throughout this book, Woolf emerges as a writer who is very conscious of her public persona: she skilfully and subtly positions herself to her own advantage, and in keeping with her Victorian 'tea-table training', implies her difference rather than stating it outright. Woolf's early journalism in particular emerges as a perfect medium for situating herself in relation to nineteenth-century women of letters: writing for a mainstream publication like the *TLS*, her essays impact the public perception of her predecessors even when published anonymously; while the two *Common Readers* as well as *A Room of One's Own* solidify their reputations in relation to Woolf's own at the height of her fame.

In *The Field of Cultural Production*, Bourdieu notes that newly emerging writers 'must assert their difference, get it known and recognized' to successfully signal their occupancy of a unique and legitimate position as a writer; and Woolf unquestionably excelled at this.[42] As a literary critic, Woolf was well positioned to 'consecrate producers or products', i.e. confer legitimacy to other writers even before making a name for herself: her shift away from reviews in a narrow sense and towards essays that combine literary biography and criticism thus allowed her to 'impose the legitimate definition of the writer' on her predecessors as well as contemporaries, or not.[43] In her 'feminist appropriation' of Bourdieu, Toril Moi emphasises the importance of taste as a mechanism that serves to 'condemn to ridicule, indignity, shame, silence . . . men and women who simply fall short, in the eyes of their judges, of the right way of being and doing'.[44] Woolf was not only an arbiter of taste, but also found herself in a position of power over others in the literary field: she was conscientiously aware of this when she 'refused to do Dorothy Richardson for the Supt. The truth is that when I looked at it, I felt myself looking for faults; hoping for them. And they would have bent my pen' (D 1.315). However, she was less scrupulous when mocking the bad biographical writing of Constance Hill, as Chapter 3 will show, or in her attacks on nineteenth-century women writers, as is particularly evident in the cases of Charlotte Brontë (Chapter 4) and Margaret Oliphant (Chapter 5).

Although Bourdieu's theory, like much of Woolf's feminist criticism, emphasises the social and historical contexts of cultural production, it is unsurprisingly silent on issues of gender: however, as Moi persuasively argues, his definition of class is loose enough to allow gender as similarly fundamental. As a relational category, gender has the 'capacity for change in value and importance in its specific social context', making it possible to account for its impact at different stages of Woolf's career with some nuance.[45] Thus, Brosnan notes that in the early twentieth century, Woolf

> occupied a precarious yet enabling borderline position in the world of journalism: her age, gender and inexperience put her on the outside contributor list, but her connections [i.e., her social capital; my addition] established her securely on the roll of insiders.[46]

However, once she was established as a novelist and critic, Woolf's gender works more ambivalently: on the one hand, her writing on women asserts her difference from a predominantly male and frequently misogynist literary establishment, and ensured her a measure of popularity particularly with a female and feminist readership. On the other hand, because Woolf was a woman writing, her judgements on female literary traditions always also reflected back on herself: as Anne Fernald observes, '[f]or Woolf, literary tradition was at once a source of pleasure and a constant reminder of her culture's low estimation of women's intelligence'.[47] Her success as a critic and writer was dependent on her ability to demonstrate the ways in which she (unlike her predecessors) was not limited by her gender. Mary Jean Corbett similarly concludes that 'Woolf achieved "exceptional" status by understanding and even enforcing the rules of a game that otherwise might well have excluded her'.[48] Woolf's journalism and essays on nineteenth-century women writers therefore create a narrative of her own literary exceptionalism by distancing herself from the flaws of her predecessors.

Woolf's ability to define and defend herself against her competitors emerges clearly even in 'The Decay of Essay-writing', her first signed article. There, she skilfully deploys cultural anxieties about mass literature and the reading public to position herself as a literary gatekeeper in a very effective entrance into the literary market. She paints a bleak picture of readers under assault of a constantly increasing flood of '[t]racts, pamphlets, advertisements, gratuitous copies of magazines, and the literary productions of friends' which necessitate '[o]ne member of the household [ . . . ] to stand at the hall door with flaming sword and do battle with the invading armies' (*E* 1.24). Woolf confidently broadcasts her membership of a London elite of literary producers (her social and cultural capital) and establishes herself as a judge of the masses of inferior productions required by 'a monster like the British public' (*E* 1.25), thus laying claim to the role of arbiter of taste. However, her proposed solution is more idiosyncratic and points to the central position that life writing would come to hold in her works: 'if they would write of themselves – such writing would have its own permanent value' (*E* 1.26). This advocacy for biography as a record of lasting historical value also underlies Woolf's fictional experiments of the period, and resurfaces in her writing at various points of her career. This parallel development further emphasises that Woolf's journalism is not a competitor to her fiction. Rather, it complements and enables it: it allowed her to hone her skills as a writer and provided her with an income, but her articles also frequently serve as a testing ground for literary methods and theories of fiction. When *A Room of One's Own* and *Three Guineas* are published, the arguments and analysis underlying both have been germinating in Woolf's journalism since at least the early 1920s.

## 'Those many women who cluster in the shade': Woolf's Feminist Historiography

Max Saunders notes that '[o]f all modernist engagements with life-writing, Virginia Woolf's is the most visible, and her work represents the most sustained and diverse exploration of the relation between fiction and auto/biography'.[49] Woolf's reputation as a biographer rests largely on her experimental New Biography. However, her interest in life writing predates these Modernist experiments by two decades and developed in direct response to late-Victorian theories of historiography and biography.

Biography emerges as a central topic in Woolf's private and professional life from 1904 onwards. While her work as a reviewer offered ample opportunity to reflect on the purpose and value of biography as a popular genre, the death of her father Sir Leslie Stephen, former editor of the *Dictionary of National Biography*, left her in the conventional feminine role of posthumous guardian of his public image. Offering editorial assistance to Frederic Maitland, a prominent legal historian and long-time family friend as well as Stephen's choice of biographer, in writing the *Life and Letters of Leslie Stephen* (1906), Woolf found herself in a position of control over her father's public image: her work consisted in tracking down dates, but also reading, extracting and selecting letters for inclusion in the biography. Her deletions include 'the most tragic thing in his life', 'the history of Laura', her institutionalised half-sister from Stephen's first marriage to Minnie Thackeray (*L* 1.164), but also the private dynamics of 22 Hyde Park Gate. Woolf's brief note, 'Impressions of Sir Leslie Stephen', commemorates a caring and literature-loving father and omits the 'violent temper' that Stephen directed towards the female members of his family (*MoB* 117). In this, she was compelled not only by grief and recent loss, but also concern about misconceptions of her father's personality, writing to Violet Dickinson that

> I see she [Caroline Stephen] is rather nervous of giving her own recollections, which weren't altogether happy or characteristic . . . It is a good deal to dispose of her theories that I want to write something for Fred, who must naturally be guided a good deal by her. (*L* 1.146)

Woolf's anxious account complements Maitland's fundamentally commemorative biography in an act of collusion which she evaluated more critically at the end of her life: recalling that 'Fred Maitland thus refused to believe, though tactfully instructed by Carry, that Leslie's tempers were more than what he called (in his biography) coloured showers of sparks' (*MoB* 148), she retrospectively identified the gendered dynamics which allowed Maitland to dismiss these accounts while asserting that 'not only have I nothing to conceal about Leslie Stephen, but that he had nothing to conceal about himself'.[50]

This ambivalent sense of admiration for these great men and mentors leaves its traces on her early short stories. Following the broader historical and biographical interests of Stephen and Maitland, Woolf positions her first surviving short stories as historical documents rather than experimental fiction (or biografiction, in Saunders' term).[51] 'Phyllis and Rosamond' and 'The Journal of Mistress Joan Martyn' (both 1906) deliberately turn to the ordinary lives of 'those many women who cluster in the shade' that are usually omitted from historical records (*CSF* 17). The choice of 'a faithful outline, drawn with no skill but veracity' recalls her solution to literary overproduction in 'A Plague of Essays', but a view of history as an accumulation of individual and ordinary lives also marked her teaching at Morley College in 1905, with lectures structured around representative historical moments suggesting a similar reliance on a close association between individual lives and national history.[52]

Woolf's understanding of history as an accumulation of ordinary lives, and consequently of historiography and biography as closely related disciplines, is strongly influenced by that of Leslie Stephen. Under his editorship (1882–91), the *Dictionary of National Biography* pursued an inclusive approach that saw it transformed into 'a homage to mediocre, second-rate and neglected lives', as Juliette Atkinson argues.[53] In the essay 'National Biography' (1898), Stephen argues for the historical significance of these lives:

> It is the second-rate people – the people whose lives have to be reconstructed from obituary notices, or from references in memoirs and collections of letters; or sought in prefaces to posthumous works; or sometimes painfully dug out of collections of manuscripts, and who really become generally accessible through the dictionary alone – that provide the really useful reading.[54]

However, Stephen does not see a political dimension to such biographical recovery. In 'Forgotten Benefactors' (1896), a thinly veiled tribute to his recently deceased wife Julia (herself a signatory of Augusta Ward's 1889 'Appeal Against Female Suffrage'), he celebrates the 'enormous value of the services, whether of man or woman, done in the shade, and confined within a very limited area'.[55] He extols the moral value of the domestic sacrifices of 'people condemned, or perhaps I should say privileged, to live in obscurity, whose very names shall soon be forgotten, and who are entirely eclipsed by people whose services, though not equally valuable, are by their nature more public'. Stephen readily distances himself from 'any of the political theories of women's rights' in celebrating the value of a domestic, hidden existence: as Atkinson notes, '[t]here is no sense that drawing attention to the obscure might destabilize social boundaries, just as there is no conception that in having attention paid to them, the obscure will transcend their condition'.[56] In contrast, his daughter subversively re-appropriates Victorian anti-suffragist rhetoric to argue for women's central historical relevance: 'a study of history and biography convinces any right minded person that these obscure figures occupy a place not unlike that of the showman's hand in the dance of the marionettes' (*CSF* 17).[57]

In Woolf's hands, obscurity therefore becomes politically significant, and biography an important tool for a feminist recovery. Drawing on her own experience, 'Phyllis and Rosamond' chronicles the tedious existence of two Edwardian 'daughters at home' and their brief escape to a Bloomsbury party. Written two years after Woolf moved from the Victorian household of 22 Hyde Park Gate to 46 Gordon Square, the story pits the two incarnations of Woolf's life against each other, and is therefore situated 'at the intersection of autobiography, biography and history and sociology', as Snaith observes.⁵⁸ Woolf traces the wide gulf that separates the two phases of her life through the mutual incomprehension of Phyllis and Rosamond and their hostess: although she is a writer with 'a literary delight in seeing herself reflected in strange looking-glasses, and of holding up her own mirror to the lives of others [ . . . ] she had never considered the Hibberts as human beings before; but had called them "young ladies"' (*CSF* 26). Likewise, Phyllis's honest self-examination only results in a resigned acceptance of her inability to change her situation: 'what did she really want, she asked herself? What was she fit for? to criticise both worlds and feel that neither gave her what she needed' (*CSF* 28). This commitment to capturing the specific frustrations of such a domestic existence even leads Woolf to reject a closer analysis of two 'professional' daughters: 'their careers have so much likeness to those of men themselves that it is scarcely worth while to make them the subject of special enquiry' (*CSF* 18).

This vision of biographical fiction as a means of understanding parallel existences also drives 'The Journal of Mistress Joan Martyn'. Here, it is the gap between medieval and modern life that her fiction seeks to bridge. Woolf distances the story from her immediate experience by historicising women's domestic life through the fictive medieval diary of Joan, while modelling a modern professional life through the inclusion of the historian Rosamond Merridew. Nevertheless, in envisioning the life of a professional historian, Woolf appears to be playing through another possible iteration of her life: Leslie Stephen had envisioned a historical career for his daughter, a familial expectation which recurs in her complaint that 'I got sat upon as usual by the Quaker – [ . . . ] for 'journalism' – She thinks I am going to sell my soul for gold, which I should willingly do for gold enough, and wants me to write a solid historical work!!' (*L* 1.166).⁵⁹ Woolf explores and ultimately dismisses an imagined future in Rosamond Merridew's professional struggles in a male-dominated discipline, but also showcases her extensive research skills in fictionalising the history of her Norfolk holiday accommodation Blo' Norton Hall and its tenants: however tentative, this is an early instance of the New Biography's interplay of fact and fiction.⁶⁰ However, 'The Journal of Mistress Joan Martyn' also offers a pointed feminist revision of the figure of the historian. Leena Kore-Schröder convincingly argues that Frederic Maitland served as 'a historiographical model which strongly inspired and supported' Woolf in devising her medieval historian. However, Kore-Schröder sees the story as an affectionate '[h]alf-tribute, half-joke in the same way that the contemporaneous "Friendship's Gallery" is written for Violet Dickinson, and much later, *Orlando* for Vita Sackville-West'.⁶¹ However, Woolf deviates from

Maitland's example in some crucial aspects: most importantly, she imagines a female historian and uses her to draw attention to the customary exclusion of women from historical narratives. Woolf's choice of document further supports this reading: focusing on a private diary instead of the medieval court roll, which was Maitland's speciality, she privileges women's domestic lives over male, more public forms of writing and deliberately writes Maitland out of his own specialty. In both stories, Woolf therefore revises male late-Victorian historiography to discover more congenial ways of exploring women's lives. Fusing autobiography, history and fiction into a generically ambiguous whole like Merridew, who exclaims 'Let me draw a line here then so — and put the whole of this question of right and wrong, truth and fiction behind me' (*CSF* 35), Woolf offers an implicit argument for an authenticity that exists independent of factuality.

While 'Phyllis and Rosamond' and 'The Journal of Mistress Joan Martyn' offer a theoretical foundation of sorts for Woolf's feminist historiography, 'Friendship's Gallery' (1907), the sole survivor of a series of comical lives of friends and family, interrogates its formal constraints.[62] Woolf's sustained interest in these biographical experiments confirms that the New Biography was the result of a long period of experimentation with nineteenth-century roots and not solely a Modernist breakthrough, but also shows that programmatic feminist historical biography coexisted with more creative explorations of personality and narrative structures throughout her writing life (as this book will trace in subsequent chapters). A comic life in three chapters, 'Friendship's Gallery' is a clear precursor to *Orlando*. Woolf playfully incorporates different styles of literary discourse from romance novel to conventional biography, and critiques conventional narrative approaches to women's lives by balancing the account of Violet Dickinson's first season (a failure, she never married), with her purchase of a house and her travels to Japan. However, the narrator's complaint that

> Often [my heroine] has whisked behind a paragraph and it was only when I had done it and set it proudly in its place in the pile raised to her honour that I discovered that she was behind and not in front; that I had made a screen and no pane of glass. (*E* 6.534)

introduces the first of many sceptical notes in Woolf's engagement with life writing. While 'Friendship's Gallery', however humorously, presumes the fault to lie with the inept biographer, in time, this uncertainty grows to encompass the inherent impossibility of capturing Orlando's 'many thousand' selves (*O* 213) and the 'fifty pairs of eyes' required to properly see Mrs Ramsay (*TL* 214). These early experiments offer a view of Virginia Woolf practising: although her writing is frequently stilted and formal, the themes these stories introduce – a feminist historiography, the belief in the transformative power of an authentic (if fictional) historical moment for our understanding of larger social problems, a desire to expand the conventional forms of biography to better represent life and personality in all their complexity alongside some doubts about the possibility of doing so – continue to underlie and shape the majority of Woolf's future biographical writing. She therefore proves to be an amazingly consistent biographer: although her position frequently grows more nuanced, once having set out the scope of her interest, she maintains it for the rest of her career.

In these private experiments, the political significance of the representation of women's lives is a dominant concern, but Woolf's first attempt at a publishable work offers a more complex assessment of biography's power to remedy female obscurity, raising questions like 'What right has the world to know about men and women? What can a biographer tell it?' but most importantly, 'In what sense can it be said that the world profits?' (*CSF* 69). Like her previous stories, 'Memoirs of a Novelist' (1909) occupies a fundamentally ambiguous generic position: it is a review of a fictional biography of an invented Victorian novelist, unsuccessfully written for publication in the *Cornhill Magazine*. The story draws on Woolf's by now substantial experience as a reviewer of memoirs and biographies: Rachel Crossland makes a compelling case for Woolf's use of the Cornhill-reviewed biography of suffragist and founder of St Hilda's College (Oxford), *Dorothea Beale of Cheltenham*, as an inspiration for some of her biographical criticisms.[63] Woolf's subject Miss Willatt, however, is a minor popular novelist of the 1860s and 1870s, whose biography is badly but admiringly written by her faithful friend of fourteen years, Miss Linsett. There is some scope for reading 'Memoirs of a Novelist' as partially a literary satire of George Eliot: Miss Willatt's early life, dominated by her lack of beauty as well as excessive learning, a youthful period of strong religiosity, and the decision to move to London after her father's death, match key points of Eliot's life; and Woolf's malicious satire of Willatt's eminence in a circle of misguided female admirers anticipates her critical examination of Eliot as 'a deluded woman who held phantom sway over subjects even more deluded than herself' (*E* 4.171), as I will discuss in Chapter 5. Even more tantalisingly, it is possible to wonder if Miss Linsett is based on Eliot's friend and admirer Edith Simcox: although Simcox's passionate *Autobiography of a Shirtmaker* with its detailed chronicle of her love for Eliot would not have been known to Woolf, her speculation on Miss Linsett's motives – 'It seemed to her that if she did not speak at once something would be lost' (*CSF* 69) – allows a certain ambiguity about the exact nature of Miss Linsett's feelings for her friend.[64]

In making her subject a minor Victorian novelist rather than one of the ordinary women that populated her earlier stories, Woolf signals a shift in her focus: the review functions as a first tentative thinking through her own literary lineage, but also significantly complicates the notions of obscurity and recovery that appeared straightforward in her earlier work. The review targets conventionalism and superficial respectability as forces which stand between the reader and a proper knowledge of the biographical subject. Woolf laments Miss Linsett's careful concealment of Miss Willatt's disappointments in love, noting that '[t]he most interesting event in Miss Willatt's life, owing to the nervous prudery and the dreary literary conventions of her friend, is thus a blank' (*CSF* 73). Woolf argues that concealment also operates on the level of language, where conventional clichés replace interiority:

> 'Although she felt his (her father's) death with the tenderness of a devoted daughter, she did not give way to useless and therefore selfish repining . . . The poor, it might be said, took the place to her of her own children.' To pick out such phrases is an easy way of satirising them, but the steady drone of the book in which they are embedded makes satire an afterthought; it is the fact that Miss Linsett believed these things and not the absurdity of them that dismays one. (*CSF* 74)

Read against her own retrospective ambivalence towards Leslie Stephen – 'His life would have entirely ended mine', she noted on his ninety-sixth birthday (*D* 3.208) – as well as George Eliot's liberation by her father's death, Woolf offers a subtle commentary on the way biography suppresses the inconvenient truths of female lives. Miss Willatt's lack of repining may be selflessness, or be an outward sign of her secret relief at her release from domestic servitude. As in much of Woolf's early biographical writing, non-verbal clues therefore appear superior to and more truthful than the written word: the silences, gaps and internal contradictions of Miss Linsett's narrative prove more revealing than her writing, and offer a tantalising glimpse at the woman behind the narrative. Additionally, however, the impact of Woolf's strong interest in painting and painterly language shows in her focus on a portrait as the only reliable clue for Miss Willatt's personality: 'The sight of that large, selfish face, with the capable forehead and the surly but intelligent eyes discredits all the platitudes on the opposite page; she looks quite capable of having deceived Miss Linsett' (*CSF* 74). A similar moment of connection later occurs in *Night and Day* (1919), where the portrait of her great ancestor Richard Alardyce affords Katharine Hilbery a moment of real understanding amid the censorship and hero worship by her parents. Throughout the 1910s, Woolf's *TLS* leaders will attempt to offer the written equivalent to such a portrait: a brief but truthful insight into a novelist's character, gathered from the clues left in their works and biography.

Although Miss Willatt's life has been recorded, Woolf cynically concludes that '[i]t does not seem, to judge by appearances, that the world has so far made use of its right to know about Miss Willatt' (*CSF* 70). 'Memoirs of a Novelist' therefore tentatively questions whether all lives are equally worthy of being recorded, and whether such a record will result in political or social change. Although Miss Willatt's recent Victorian past is easily accessible to common reader and critic alike (particularly compared to Joan Martyn's private medieval diary), Woolf is beginning to develop a more nuanced policy of conservation, one which distinguishes between desirable and undesirable obscurity. While the impenetrable obscurity of Miss Willatt's character works in her favour and makes her a tantalisingly inaccessible subject, Chapter 5 will show that Woolf undermines well-documented mid-Victorian novelists like Mary Augusta Ward, Margaret Oliphant and even George Eliot, and dismisses them into obscurity. At the same time, 'Memoirs of a Novelist' also suggests a genesis for women's writing in the second half of the nineteenth century:

> After all, merely to sit with your eyes open fills the brain, and perhaps in emptying it, one may come across something illuminating. George Eliot and Charlotte Brontë between them must share the parentage of many novels at this period, for they disclose the secret that the precious stuff of which books are made lies all about one, in drawing-rooms and kitchens where women live, and accumulates with every tick of the clock. (*CSF* 75)

Pointing to Eliot and Brontë as important figures who transformed literary history by valuing women's lived experiences, Woolf nevertheless inserts a subtle barb against the likes of Miss Willatt: filling and emptying their brains without much conscious reflection on the writing process, they deservedly fall into oblivion. This turn towards literary traditions and forgotten (rightfully or not) female predecessors occurs contemporaneously to Woolf's first drafting of *Melymbrosia*, which would eventually become *The Voyage Out* (1915). It is a clear signal that she was beginning to search for her literary origins and her exact relationship to literary tradition which would intensify during the 1910s and 1920s and reach its peak with *A Room of One's Own*. As the following chapters will trace in relation to a variety of nineteenth-century authors, this process involved finding a position for herself in the literary field, and establishing herself as different from, and yet a descendant of, canonical writers like Jane Austen and Charlotte Brontë, but also exploring the lives of comparatively obscure writers like Mary Russell Mitford and Elizabeth Barrett Browning to assess whether they merited a return to public awareness or not.

## 'Rainbow and granite': The New Biography and Women's Lives

Virginia Woolf's career coincided with a particularly fruitful time for biographical writing. Claire Battershill records that '[i]n the interwar period, biographies were being published in greater and greater numbers', a trend in which Woolf, both as a writer and as a publisher for the Hogarth Press, was directly involved.[65] The press published both popular and Modernist biographies, and Woolf's most frequently discussed biografictions, *Orlando* (1928), *Flush* (1933) and the programmatic essay 'The New Biography' (1927) were all written during this period. However, this critically recognised movement does not capture all of Woolf's engagement with life writing during the 1920s and 1930s: her attention is split between these Modernist experiments and her feminist biography, which continued to use more traditional life narratives as a supplement to male historiography, as discussed in the previous section. Both of these continue Woolf's enduring engagement with the Victorian period: while much of her feminist analysis examines exemplary case studies from the nineteenth century, her New Biography attempts to establish itself as its antithesis.

Published in *The New York Herald Tribune* in 1927, 'The New Biography' continues Woolf's dialogue with late-Victorian life writing begun in her earliest fiction. The essay opens programmatically, with a citation from Stephen's *Dictionary of National Biography* co-editor (and eventual successor) Sidney Lee: 'The aim of biography [ . . . ] is the truthful transmission of personality' (*E* 4.473), a quotation taken from Lee's 1911 Leslie Stephen Lecture at Cambridge, 'Principles of Biography'. However, Woolf argues, Lee's superficially simple statement really reveals the fundamental problem of biographical writing:

> if we think of truth as something of granite-like solidity and of personality as something of rainbow-like intangibility and reflect that the aim of biography is to weld these two into one seamless whole, we shall admit that the problem is a stiff one and that we need not wonder if biographers have for the most part failed to solve it. (*E* 4.473)

These problems of characterisation and the representation of consciousness are characteristic of Woolf's fiction: while her *TLS* leaders of the previous decade offer skilful and insightful character studies of individual authors, the central mystery of Jacob's inner life in *Jacob's Room* (1922), the 'tunnelling' structure that fuses past and present in Clarissa Dalloway's experience of daily life, and the delicate balance between autobiographical commemoration and literary innovation in *To the Lighthouse* (1927) all attempt to find an authentic expression of human experience. Deftly positioning herself as a Modernist innovator, Woolf uses the essay to sever all ties to the past: 'Victorian biography was a parti-coloured, hybrid, monstrous, birth', bent on presenting 'truth in its hardest, most obdurate form', all traces of personality fossilised by its 'amorphous mass' of facts (*E* 4.474, 473, 475). Painting a gloomy image of a genre dedicated to producing superficial portraits of great men 'above life size in top hat and frock coat' for public veneration (*E* 4.475), Woolf's criticism recalls her own 'Impressions of Sir Leslie Stephen' as well as Miss Linsett's ineptitude in 'Memoirs of a Novelist'.

The New Biography, Woolf claims, is everything that this 'artistic wrongheadedness' is not: the biographer 'preserves his freedom and his right to independent judgement', uses artistically challenging novelistic strategies and synthesises meaningful scenes into a representative whole, the 'queer amalgamation of dream and reality, that perpetual marriage of granite and rainbow' (*E* 4.475, 478). Although there are occasional instances of fictionalised biography in Woolf's writing on Jane Austen and Mary Russell Mitford, which I will explore in Chapters 2 and 3 respectively, her New Biography is a tantalising theory that is perhaps best suited to explaining her method in *Orlando*. '[A] biography beginning in the year 1500 & continuing to the present day, called Orlando: Vita [Sackville-West]; only with a change about from one sex to another' (*D* 3.161), *Orlando* questions fundamental concepts such as time, sex and the human lifespan, and prioritises atmosphere and character over factual veracity. While Orlando shares important personality traits with Sackville-West, (s)he also lives through defining moments in her ancestral as well as British literary history. Additionally, *Orlando*'s illustrations complicate Woolf's previous reliance on visual clues by including portraits and photographs not only of Sackville-West and her ancestors, but also Woolf's niece Angelica Bell, that playfully question the reliability of such evidence. However, even the New Biography has its limits: cultural and social constraints as well as a consideration for privacy mean that Sackville-West's extra-marital lesbian affairs are merely hinted at. Likewise, it is questionable how widely applicable Woolf's new method really is, as the essay finds the biography under review,

Harold Nicolson's semi-fictional *Some People* (1927), ultimately unsatisfactory, leaving *Orlando* as the genre's only true representative.

Woolf's essay is polemical: it subsumes all Victorian life writing into a monolith. Although she had criticised bad biographical writing in 'Memoirs of a Novelist', she did so without ever identifying Miss Willatt's life as Victorian or Edwardian: the deployment of such period 'shorthand' is 'more often than not, [ . . . ] highly self-conscious, even strategic', as Corbett observes.[66] Her retrospective label ignores the actual breath and diversity of Victorian biography, which included domestic biography written by mourning family members (Chapter 5 will touch upon the Stephen family tradition of life writing), lives of working-class 'hidden' figures, failed men of great promise, minor women writers and obscure Romantic poets, as Juliette Atkinson maps out in *Victorian Biography Reconsidered*. These lives often valorised the 'hidden, private, sphere' as a respite from a corrupting public life, and celebrated hidden contributions to the nation's history, as set out in the previous section.[67] This immense Victorian interest in biography is also reflected in the vast amounts of critical debate on its nature, limitations and purpose in literary journals, with a resulting diversity of opinions on a biographer's duties.[68] Likewise, Woolf's own reading belies the construct she offers here: not only is much of her cultural criticism of the 1930s based on sociological analysis of nineteenth-century life writing, as a reviewer, she was also intimately familiar with the shortcomings of much contemporary biography, such as Mary Augusta Austen-Leigh's *Personal Aspects of Jane Austen* (1920), discussed in Chapter 2, or Constance Hill's *Mary Russell Mitford and Her Surroundings* (1920), discussed in Chapter 3. 'The Wrong Way of Reading', written about the latter, even celebrates such bad biography for the creative licence it gives its readers (and reviewers); a sentiment which is repeated in 'On Being Ill' (1926, *New Criterion*) with its self-indulgent immersion in Augustus Hare's *The Story of Two Noble Lives* (1893), a three-volume biography of Victorian artists and sisters Charlotte Canning and Louisa Beresford: 'short of the best in literature we like the worst – it is mediocrity that is hateful' (*E* 4.325). Likewise, the lecture-turned-essay 'How Should One Read a Book?' celebrates the ability of biographies and memoirs to 'light up innumerable houses: they show us people going about their daily affairs, toiling, failing, succeeding, eating, hating, loving, until they die': 'how absorbing it is now and again to go through the rubbish-heaps and find rings and scissors and broken noses buried in the huge past and try to pierce them together' (*E* 5.575, 577). Much as in 'The Wrong Way of Reading', Woolf praises such 'rubbish-reading' for its ability to 'refresh and exercise our creative powers' (*E* 5.577, 576): 'Woolf advocated reading anything and everything one wants', as Cuddy-Keane summarises.⁶⁹

Although Woolf's deployment of period shorthand denies all links between the New Biography and the nineteenth century, it represents a development, not a complete departure from earlier biographical methods. In the later essay 'The Art of Biography' (1939), she traces a more coherent line of development from the unprecedented frankness of Froude's *Life of Thomas Carlyle* (1882–4) to the deliberate iconoclasm of Edwardian works like Edmund Gosse's *Father and Son* (1907) and finally Lytton Strachey's *Eminent Victorians* (1918). In contrast, in 'The New Biography' she manipulates her material to obscure how late-Victorian biography sought to distance itself from earlier, more didactic modes of writing lives. Ray Monk points to Woolf's omission of the beginning of Lee's sentence, 'The aim of biography is not the moral edification which may flow from the survey of either vice or virtue' as a misrepresentation of his argument that creates an artificial distance between their positions: in fact, Lee's overarching aim is to argue for 'the *autonomy* of biography' from 'moral instruction, history, or science'.⁷⁰ Laura Marcus similarly finds much cohesion between the editorial policy of the *Dictionary of National Biography*, which specified 'No flowers by request' (i.e. no eulogies) as well as 'concision, candour, and analysis and synthesis rather than the accumulation of facts' and the qualities that Woolf endorses in 'The New Biography'.⁷¹ Paradoxically, Woolf's decision to erase the late-Victorian influences on her writing also extends to her feminist revisions of Stephen and Maitland's historiography. Women are consequently conspicuously absent from 'The New Biography': the essay traces an exclusively male tradition of biography, omitting even Elizabeth Gaskell's *Life of Charlotte Brontë* (1857), and fails to mention the challenges of writing women's lives outside of traditional narratives of courtship and marriage, which 'Friendship's Gallery' had flagged as early as 1907. This signals a deep division between Woolf's Modernist theorising of biography, strongly attuned to character and individuality, and her feminism, which tends to read women's lives collectively to gain insight into social hierarchies and prejudices.

This use of biography as a substitute for missing historical records is at its most pronounced in her feminist polemics *A Room of One's Own* (1929) and *Three Guineas* (1938). Wood situates Woolf's cultural criticism of the 1930s with its 'emphasis on personal testimony' and factual veracity as part of a documentary turn within literature, and it is possible to see early traces of this even in *A Room of One's Own*: as Woolf's most political works, both texts offer a sustained analysis of how women's marginalised positions in society affect their lives, using biography systematically to establish an argument that moves beyond the individual life.[72] As before, these contemporary influences combine with Victorian legacies. Thus, Alison Booth sees both works as evidence that 'Woolf seems oblivious to her own immersion in a collective biographical tradition'.[73] Most obviously, Woolf offers a corrective to the *Dictionary of National Biography*'s most glaring oversight by providing an alternative history of women's contributions to national, literary and social history, exploring what it means to be English and female and moving women writers, feminist activists and social reformers out of obscurity.[74] *A Room of One's Own* sketches out this project:

> It would be ambitious beyond my daring, I thought, looking about the shelves for books that were not there, to suggest to the students of those famous colleges that they should rewrite history, though I own that it often seems a little queer as it is, unreal, lop-sided; but why should they not add a supplement to history? calling it, of course, by some inconspicuous name so that women might figure there without impropriety? For one often catches a glimpse of them in the lives of the great, whisking away into the background, concealing, I sometimes think, a wink, a laugh, perhaps a tear. (*AROO* 41–2)

This commitment to biography as historiography informs *A Room of One's Own*: the fusion of fiction, autobiography and historical analysis signals a return to the methods of Woolf's earlier stories, which is also reflected in the central position of her fictional life of Judith Shakespeare. Again, Woolf is drawn to an idealised version of the obscure and unknown woman writer of the past. Judith possesses a fascination that existing writers like Aphra Behn can never match: without any documented biographical and literary history, she can be reshaped and adapted to Woolf's purpose. The narrator's complaint that 'we have lives enough of Jane Austen; [ . . . and] as for myself, I should not mind if the homes and haunts of Mary Russell Mitford were closed to the public for a century at least' (*AROO* 42) suggests a weariness with a well-established female literary tradition: Booth therefore notes that

> [t]he ample supply that was at Woolf's fingertips appeared too substantially personal (like woman writers who expose their anger) or too domesticated by common recognition. The desired history of women consists of elusive traces, departed beings to whom one attributes bodies and passions but not, in Woolf's imagining, registered names.[75]

Yet paradoxically, much of Woolf's discussion is framed by the lives of Jane Austen, Charlotte Brontë and George Eliot, all writers with well-established literary afterlives. As in the earlier fiction, these sources are used as a corrective to the biases of male-dominated historical narratives: researching in the British Museum, Woolf's narrator notes that many of her sources are written 'in the red light of emotion, and not in the white light of truth' (*AROO* 30). *Three Guineas*, consisting of another semi-autobiographical three-part epistolary response, similarly bases its argument on biographical facts: after 'observing & collecting these 20 years' (*D* 4.133), Woolf was 'quivering & itching to write my – whats it to be called? – "Men are like that"? – no thats too patently feminist: the sequel then, for which I have collected enough powder to blow up St. Pauls' (*D* 4.77). While *The Pargiters* had attempted to blend the history of yet another semi-autobiographical Victorian family with essays on politics, society and gender, its division into *The Years* (1937) and *Three Guineas* resulted in a text that in some ways takes its non-fictionality more seriously than *A Room of One's Own*. Woolf scrupulously documented her sources in extensive footnotes despite feeling 'suspicious of the vulgarity of the notes: of a certain insistence' (*D* 5.134): 'I feel now & then the tug to vision, but resist it' (*D* 4.129). However, *Three Guineas* is also more suspicious of biography itself: Woolf embeds individual experiences in statistics and social trends, supplementing 'the coloured light of biography' with 'the white light of facts' collected in her three scrapbooks of newspaper articles (*3G* 167).

This scepticism is characteristic of Woolf's late biography: her final work on the genre, 'The Art of Biography' (*Atlantic Monthly*, 1939), is in many ways the antithesis of 'The New Biography'. The essay is informed by the experience of writing *Roger Fry* (1940), Woolf's only conventional biography, which required a delicate negotiation between her own desire for a truthful depiction of Fry's love life in particular, and his family's wish to sanitise it.[76] Forced to partially relinquish her creative control over the narrative, Woolf also struggled with the mass of information available in the form of letters and lectures, complaining that her writing was 'too minute & tied down' (*D* 5.155), 'too detailed & flat' (*D* 5.165): without the creative release provided by fictionality, the commitment to factuality was limiting and caused her to see the biography as 'a failure – & what a grind . . . ' (*D* 5.248). A similar problem is evident in Woolf's writing on mid- and late-Victorian women writers: as she notes in the essay 'Personalities', we know too much of the Victorians to imagine 'George Eliot gathering her skirts about her and leaping from a cliff' the way Sappho did (*E* 6.438). In the lifelong interplay of biography and fiction that shapes Woolf's writing life, 'The Art of Biography' ultimately declares the superiority of fiction: 'For the invented character lives in a free world where the facts are verified by one person only – the artist himself. Their authenticity lies in the truth of his own vision' (*E* 6.185). Although she was working on 'A Sketch of the Past', her own memoir, by this point, there is a noticeable dropping-off of Woolf's literary biography after the early 1930s: the publications of the *Common Reader: Second Series* (1932) and *Flush* (1933) mark the informal end of a period of an intense engagement with life writing and female literary traditions, and the few brief references in *Three Guineas* consider women writers as women first and foremost.

Informed by a lifetime of writing, 'The Art of Biography' meditates extensively on the malleability of human life. Woolf notes the changing attitudes to gender and homosexuality – facts of a life that are yet 'not like the facts of science – once they are discovered, always the same', as well as the multiplicity of competing points of view modernity can offer:

> Then again, since we live in an age when a thousand cameras are pointed, by newspapers, letters, and diaries, at every character from every angle, he [the biographer] must be prepared to admit contradictory versions of the same face. Biography will enlarge its scope by hanging up looking glasses at odd corners. (E 6.186)

## Outline of the Book

With its considerable scepticism towards the way biographical narratives are produced, 'The Art of Biography' reflects some of the larger themes that emerge in this study of Woolf's literary biography. Woolf's unique perspective, and the changing angles from which she approaches individual writers' lives, as well as the provenance of the facts that shape her narratives will be my focus in the following chapters. I will trace Woolf's representations of women's writing and the changing modes of female authorship across her reviews and essays, arguably her largest work of collective biography, from her first published article, 'Haworth, November 1904' to *A Room of One's Own*, and finally *Three Guineas* (1938), her last significant engagement with biography. Although this is not a genetic study as such, my diachronic approach will show how Woolf's perspective on women writers changes through new biographical discoveries and in response to her own development as writer.

Virginia Woolf was a prolific journalist, and the nineteenth century a period of rapid expansion of female authorship. This study therefore does not attempt to offer a comprehensive overview of all nineteenth-century women writers that Woolf ever reviewed, or wrote about. Rather, I have selected those that elicit a strong biographical response, and receive a disproportionate amount of her attention. Unsurprisingly, this means my selection skews canonical: both because by and large, Woolf's own does, but also because canonicity and a particularly rich afterlife tend to go hand in hand. Elizabeth Gaskell (examined in more detail by Emily Blair), Christina Rossetti and Harriet Martineau are just some of the writers whom Woolf reviews in her articles, but who do not suit my biographical focus; as is Anny Thackeray Ritchie, whose influence on Woolf has been explored extensively by Marion Dell.[77]

Virginia Woolf's female literary canon begins in earnest with Jane Austen, as does Chapter 2 of this book. Although Austen's novels predate the Victorian period, her persona is fundamentally a product of the 1870s. The Austen family's construction of a saintly maiden aunt perfectly complements Victorian critics' praise for Austen's feminine awareness of her own limitations and small-scale perfection, but caused considerable unease for her literary successors. I therefore argue that Woolf's unease with Austen's status as an example of specifically female perfection is a reaction to Austen's biographical afterlife, demonstrating the fundamental importance of biographies like Austen-Leigh's *A Memoir of Jane Austen* and other hagiographic family biographies to Woolf's literary criticism. Biography not only creates, but also resolves this tension: with the publication of Austen's juvenilia and letters in 1922 begins a process of recovery that leads Woolf to rewrite her as a satirical and irreverent commentator on patriarchal culture as well as a proto-Modernist foremother of her own, and ultimately all women's writing.

Chapter 3 focuses on Mary Russell Mitford and Elizabeth Barrett Browning, usually found as background figures in discussions of Woolf's *Flush*, the biography of Mitford's canine gift to Barrett Browning. Like Austen, Mitford's career largely predates the Victorian period, yet Woolf approaches her through the prism of a Victorian cult of literary tourism. Woolf challenges nostalgic accounts of a rural Victorian idyll by exploring Dr Mitford's emotional and financial abuse of his daughter, while cautiously testing core ideas of her New Biography in a series of increasingly fictionalising reviews of *Mary Russell Mitford and Her Surroundings* (1920). Woolf's writing on Barrett Browning responds similarly to contemporary sensationalist representations of domestic tyranny such as *The Barretts of Wimpole Street* (1930) to reframe her life as wide-reaching critique of patriarchal society's worst excesses. The chapter therefore offers an example of biographical experimentation and feminist historiography in Woolf's engagement with minor Victorian women writers, as she is drawn to their lives as a testimony to the complex interrelation of money, authorship and domestic tyranny that underpins her analysis in *A Room of One's Own* and *Three Guineas*. However, their ultimate eclipse by Flush the dog also shows how Woolf marginalises their literary achievements to foreground her own creativity and prowess as a writer.

Chapter 4 offers a counterpoint to Woolf's engagement with Austen by examining her ambivalent response to Charlotte Brontë's rebellious femininity. Although Woolf's early reviews convey a palpable fascination with Brontë's strength of character, she is quickly transformed into a symbol of the inherently flawed Victorian women writer: I argue that Woolf's depiction of Brontë weaponises her life against her artistic achievements. Drawing on Gaskell's *Life of Charlotte Brontë* to justify her portrait of a writer in social and cultural isolation, Woolf also utilises the revelation of the Heger letters to question Brontë's creativity as a writer, and perpetuates Victorian tropes of unfeminine passion found in Leslie Stephen's literary criticism. Woolf contextualises Brontë's anger at women's oppression in a wider feminist argument and frequently uses it in an act of ventriloquism that is reminiscent of her earlier admiration, but her lasting legacy is *A Room of One's Own* condemnation of the artistic damage it caused: this chapter therefore demonstrates that Woolf's feminist aims often operate at the expense of individual writers.

Chapter 5 explores the gaps in Woolf's canon, as I argue that Woolf ignores changing modes of female authorship and systematically silences and misrepresents mid- and late-Victorian novelists to maintain the illusion that Victorian women's writing was solely carried out by domestic amateurs (thus complementing Mary Jean Corbett's work on Woolf and the fin-de-siècle).[78] I study Woolf's engagement with George Eliot as well as popular writers Mary Augusta Ward and Margaret Oliphant to demonstrate that Woolf excludes the high-art woman of letters alongside bestselling popular writers to create a narrative of artistic exceptionalism.

In Chapter 6, I turn to Virginia Woolf herself. Strikingly, for a writer so attuned to the importance of female biography, and in spite of a wealth of materials – letters, diaries and memoir fragments, Woolf has not left us with an account of her life as a writer. Although *A Room of One's Own* and 'Professions for Women' can be read as semi-autobiographical accounts of her own experience, Woolf's autobiographical fragments, largely written for a more private audience, don't offer a sustained account of her life past 1910 and thus reflect an ongoing struggle to leave the Victorian period behind entirely. 'Reminiscences' (1907) grapples with exactly those clichéd and euphemistic descriptions of character and family dismissed as the worst excesses of Victorian biography in 'Memoirs of a Novelist'; while the artistic ambitions and achievements of Vanessa and Virginia remain unspeakable for narrator and subject alike. 'A Sketch of the Past' in contrast ignores all outward signifiers of professional success but weaves Woolf's writerly identity into the narrative to assert that writing was her social and biological destiny.

However, Woolf also enacts the ways in which her genetic legacies continue to shape her world socially by encoding her Victorian upbringing as an inheritance of femaleness: positing her identity as a woman and a writer as equally fundamental, they ultimately remain hard to reconcile.

## Notes

1. Mark Goldman, *The Reader's Art: Virginia Woolf as Literary Critic* (The Hague: Mouton, 1976), p. 1.
2. Alice Wood, *Virginia Woolf's Late Cultural Criticism: The Genesis of 'The Years', 'Three Guineas' and 'Between the Acts'*, Historicizing Modernism series (London: Bloomsbury, 2013), p. 14; Leila Brosnan, *Reading Virginia Woolf's Essays and Journalism: Breaking the Surface of Silence* (Edinburgh: Edinburgh University Press, 1999), p. 4.
3. Humble contextualises her discussion of the reading body and its positioning against the emergence of English Literature as a 'serious' academic discipline that seeks to distinguish itself from the leisure reader who reads sitting back, 'relaxing into his book and chair, spine curled, virtually foetal, fleeing into the body with the comfort of sleep or womb rather than in monastic disavowal of its needs' (p. 48).

    My usage of Middlebrow draws on its current meaning in Middlebrow scholarship; very broadly encompassing non-canonical novels often written by women for women, or, as quoted above, fiction of any kind read for entertainment purposes. For a discussion of Woolf's decidedly more pejorative use and construction of this term, see Cuddy-Keane.

    Nicola Humble, 'Sitting Forward or Sitting Back: Highbrow v. Middlebrow Reading', *Modernist Cultures*, 6.1 (2011), 41–59 (p. 46); Melba Cuddy-Keane, *Virginia Woolf, the Intellectual and the Public Sphere*, p. 51.
4. Middlebrow heroines are frequently defined by their love of reading. While they often reject highbrow (or Modernist) works of literature for their intellectual pretensions, the works (and lives) of the Brontës, as well as Charles Dickens and Charlotte Yonge enjoy a lasting popularity.

    For a discussion of Woolf and pleasurable reading see Humble, 'Sitting Forward or Sitting Back', p. 51; for Middlebrow heroines' reading practices, Faye Hammill, *Women, Celebrity, and Literary Culture between the Wars* (Austin: University of Texas Press, 2007), pp. 194–200; Nicola Humble, 'The Feminine Middlebrow Novel', in *The History of British Women's Writing, 1920–1945: Volume Eight*, ed. by Maroula Joannou (London: Palgrave Macmillan, 2013), pp. 97–111 (pp. 101–4) <https://doi.org/10.1057/9781137292179_6>; Nicola Humble, *The Feminine Middlebrow Novel, 1920s to 1950s: Class, Domesticity, and Bohemianism* (Oxford and New York: Oxford University Press, 2001), pp. 9, 53–5.
5. Elena Gualtieri, *Virginia Woolf's Essays: Sketching the Past* (Basingstoke: Palgrave Macmillan, 2000), p. 59.
6. Melba Cuddy-Keane, *Virginia Woolf, the Intellectual and the Public Sphere* (Cambridge: Cambridge University Press, 2003), pp. 13, 8.

7. Alison Booth, *How to Make It as a Woman: Collective Biographical History from Victoria to the Present* (Chicago: University of Chicago Press, 2004), pp. 227, 225.
8. Andrew McNeillie, 'Introduction', in *The Essays of Virginia Woolf: Volume 4 (1925–1928)* (London: Harcourt, 1994), pp. xi–xxiii (p. xii).
9. Steve Ellis, *Virginia Woolf and the Victorians* (Cambridge: Cambridge University Press, 2007), p. 1.
10. The same can of course be said of most of the essays discussed here. Mark Goldman makes a similar point, noting that 'Many of Mrs. Woolf's essays on women are expanded studies of the writers mentioned in *A Room Of One's Own* and are naturally concerned with the feminist questions raised in that essay. The individual portraits are also part of the capsule history of feminine literature which Mrs. Woolf traces in *A Room Of One's Own*'. Mark Goldman, p. 68.
11. Although I disagree with the extremely Freudian reading on which Bloom's anxiety of influence and consequently the anxiety of authorship are based, the fundamental problem of women's lack of clear role models within a patriarchal literary tradition still applies. See Sandra M. Gilbert and Susan Gubar, *The Madwoman in the Attic: The Woman Writer and the Nineteenth-Century Literary Imagination*, 2nd edn (New Haven, CT and London: Yale University Press, 2000), pp. 48–9.
12. Woolf, Leonard, *Downhill All the Way: An Autobiography of the Years 1919–1939* (London: The Hogarth Press, 1967), p. 204; See also Alice Wood, pp. 14–17 for a more detailed overview of Woolf's critical transformation from apolitical aesthete to a highly political feminist thinker.
13. Brenda R. Silver, 'What's Woolf Got to Do with It?: Or, the Perils of Popularity', *MFS Modern Fiction Studies*, 38.1 (2009), 20–60 (p. 23).
14. Gualtieri, p. 12.
15. Jane Marcus, 'Daughters of Anger/Material Girls: Con/Textualizing Feminist Criticism', *Women's Studies: An Interdisciplinary Journal*, 15 (1988), 281–308 (p. 282).
16. Anne Fernald, *Virginia Woolf: Feminism and the Reader* (Basingstoke: Palgrave Macmillan, 2006), p. 5.
17. Fernald, p. 2.
18. Jane Marcus, *Art and Anger: Reading Like A Woman* (Columbus: Ohio State University Press, 1988), p. 79.
19. Italics in original. Jane Marcus, 'Daughters of Anger/Material Girls: Con/Textualizing Feminist Criticism', p. 291.
20 Corbett notes that Woolf's relationship to this earlier generation is by no means uncritical, however, 'their greatness is seldom called into question' – possibly also, as she notes, because to Woolf, greatness is a heavily gendered concept and most representatives of this generation are (in Corbett's reading) male. Mary Jean Corbett, *Behind the Times: Virginia Woolf in Late-Victorian Contexts* (Ithaca, NY and London: Cornell University Press, 2020), p. 36; Marion Dell. *Virginia Woolf's Influential Forebears: Julia Margaret Cameron, Anny Thackeray Ritchie and Julia Prinsep Stephen* (Basingstoke: Palgrave Macmillan, 2015).

21. Janet Todd, 'Who's Afraid of Jane Austen?', in *Jane Austen: New Perspectives*, Women & Literature (New York; London: Holmes & Meier, 1983), pp. 107–27 (pp. 108–9).
22. Naomi Black, *Virginia Woolf as Feminist* (Ithaca, NY: Cornell University Press, 2018), pp. 2–5; quotation on p. 5.
23. Emily Blair, *Virginia Woolf and the Nineteenth-Century Domestic Novel* (Albany, NY: State University of New York Press, 2007), p. 22.
24. Fernald, p. 15.
25. Elaine Showalter, *A Literature of Their Own: British Women Novelists from Bronte to Lessing* (Princeton, NJ: Princeton University Press, 1977), p. 285; Anna Snaith, *Virginia Woolf: Public and Private Negotiations* (New York: St Martin's Press, 2000), p. 2.
26. Koutsantoni's article also offers a detailed overview over feminist criticism (positive and negative) of *A Room of One's Own*. Katerina Koutsantoni, 'The Impersonal Strategy: Re-Visiting Virginia Woolf's Position in The Common Reader Essays', *Women: A Cultural Review*, 20.2 (2009), 157–71 (p. 169) <https://doi.org/10.1080/09574040903000829>.
27. Victoria Rosner, *Modernism and the Architecture of Private Life*, Gender and Culture (GandC) series (New York: Columbia University Press, 2005), p. 122.
28. See also Corbett, *Behind the Times: Virginia Woolf in Late-Victorian Contexts*, pp. 109–45; as well as '"Ashamed of the inkpot": Virginia Woolf, Lucy Clifford, and the Literary Marketplace', *Nineteenth Century Gender Studies*, 11.3 (2015) <http://www.ncgsjournal.com/issue113/corbett.html> (accessed 6 April 2017).
29. See Brosnan, pp. 38–69 for a detailed overview of Woolf's working relationships and feelings about her various editors.
30. Koutsantoni argues that Woolf's frequent use of an authorial 'we' in the *Common Reader* acts as a gender-neutral pronoun that brings together author and readers irrespective of gender: 'She thus managed to hold on both to her outsider status and to her establishment credentials. [ . . . ] She tried to dissolve rigid distinctions between male and female, pursuing a more fluid domain in which the common reader could function'. I like this reading as an act of feminist reclamation, but slippages such as the use of male pronouns in 'Professions for Women' to me suggest that patriarchal thinking is so firmly linguistically embedded that anything less that explicitly female pronouns will be read as male by the majority of readers. Katerina Koutsantoni, *Virginia Woolf's Common Reader* (Farnham: Ashgate, 2009), p. 138; 'The Impersonal Strategy', p. 169.
31. Q. D. Leavis, *Fiction and the Reading Public* (London: Chatto & Windus, 1939), p. 20; Fernald, p. 89.
32. Andrew McNeillie, 'Introduction', in *The Essays of Virginia Woolf: Volume 1 (1904–1912)* (London: Harcourt, 1994), pp. xi–xxiii (p. xv).
33. Leavis, p. 20.
34. McNeillie, 'Introduction', p. xvii. E 6.673.
35. Stuart Clarke gives an estimated payment between £25 and £28 for each article in the 1930s: a general fee according to length and an individual £15 bonus. (*E* 6.673)

36. Wood counts fifty journalistic articles in the decade preceding Woolf's death compared to 117 in 1925–30. Alice Wood, p. 11.
37. See Stuart N. Clarke, 'Introduction', in *The Essays of Virginia Woolf, 1929–32* (London: The Hogarth Press, 2009), pp. ix–xxi (pp. xi–xv) for some examples of its reception across the British and American Press.
38. Gualtieri; Koutsantoni, *Virginia Woolf's Common Reader*; Brosnan, p. 5; Cuddy-Keane, p. 8; Claire Battershill, *Modernist Lives: Biography and Autobiography at Leonard and Virginia Woolf's Hogarth Press* (London: Bloomsbury Academic, 2018), pp. 9–11, 29–30.
39. Jane Garrity, 'Selling culture to the "civilized": Bloomsbury, British Vogue, and the Marketing of National Identity', *Modernism/Modernity*, 6.2 (1999), 29–58 <https://doi.org/10.1353/mod.1999.0016>; Jane Garrity, 'Virginia Woolf, Intellectual Harlotry, and 1920s British Vogue', in *Virginia Woolf in the Age of Mechanical Reproduction*, ed. by Pamela L. Caughie (New York and London: Garland, 2000), pp. 185–218; Alice Wood, 'Modernism and the Middlebrow in British Women's Magazines, 1916-1930', in *Middlebrow and Gender, 1890–1945*, ed. by Christoph Ehland and Cornelia Wächter (Leiden: Brill Rodopi, 2016), pp. 39–59; Lise Jaillant, *Cheap Modernism: Expanding Markets, Publishers' Series and the Avant-Garde* (Edinburgh University Press, 2017), pp. 120–49.
40. Robert Scholes and Clifford Wulfman, *Modernism in the Magazines: An Introduction* (New Haven, CT: Yale University Press, 2010); *Women, Periodicals and Print Culture in Britain, 1890s-1920s: The Modernist Period*, ed. by Faith Binckes and Carey Snyder (Edinburg: Edinburgh University Press, 2019).
41. Corbett, *Behind the Times: Virginia Woolf in Late-Victorian Contexts*, pp. 128–31.
42. Pierre Bourdieu, *The Field of Cultural Production: Essays on Art and Literature*, ed. by Randal Johnson (New York: Columbia University Press, 1993), p. 58.
43. Pierre Bourdieu, p. 42.
44. Toril Moi, 'Appropriating Bourdieu: Feminist Theory and Pierre Bourdieu's Sociology of Culture', *New Literary History*, 22.4 (1991), 1017–49 (p. 1026) <https://doi.org/10.2307/469077>.
45. Moi, pp. 1034–6, quotation on p. 1035.
46. Brosnan, p. 47.
47. Fernald, p. 3.
48. Corbett, '"Ashamed of the inkpot"', para. 6.
49. Max Saunders, *Self-Impression: Life-Writing, Autobiografiction, and the Forms of Modern Literature* (Oxford: Oxford University Press, 2010), p. 438.
50. Frederic Maitland, *The Life and Letters of Leslie Stephen* (London: Duckworth & Co., 1908), p. 3. Maitland's optimism about Stephen's honesty is misplaced, as Chapter 6 will show.
51. Saunders, p. 7. I'm drawing on Saunders's usage of the term here to connote the literary relationship between fiction and a person's biography.
52. Clara Jones, *Virginia Woolf: Ambivalent Activist* (Edinburgh: Edinburgh University Press, 2015), pp. 33–7.

53. Juliette Atkinson, *Victorian Biography Reconsidered: A Study of Nineteenth-Century 'Hidden' Lives* (Oxford, England: Oxford University Press, 2010), p. 222.
54. Leslie Stephen, 'National Biography', in *Studies of a Biographer, Volume I* (London: Duckworth & Co., 1898), pp. 1–36 (p. 21).
55. Leslie Stephen, 'Forgotten Benefactors', in *Social Rights and Duties, Volume II* (London: Swan, Sonnenschein & Co., 1896), pp. 225–67 (p. 251).
56. Atkinson, p. 239.
57. Valerie Sanders, *Eve's Renegades: Victorian Anti-Feminist Women Novelists* (Basingstoke: Macmillan, 1996), pp. 17–19.
58. Anna Snaith, '"My poor private voice": Virginia Woolf and Auto/Biography', in *Representing Lives: Women and Autobiography*, ed. by Alison Donnell and Pauline Polkey (Basingstoke: Macmillan, 2000), pp. 96–104 (p. 98).
59. See Katherine C. Hill, 'Virginia Woolf and Leslie Stephen: History and Literary Revolution', *PMLA*, 96.3 (1981), 351–62 (pp. 351–5).
60. Heidi Stalla, 'The Play of Fact and Fiction in Virginia Stephen's "The Journal of Mistress Joan Martyn"', in *Virginia Woolf and Heritage: Selected Papers from the Twenty-Sixth Annual International Conference on Virginia Woolf*, ed. by Jane de Gay, Tom Breckin and Anne Reus (Clemson, SC: Clemson University Press/Liverpool University Press, 2017), pp. 190–95; Catherine F. Smith, 'Histories of a House', *Virginia Woolf Miscellany*, 18 (1982), 2.
61. Lena Kore-Schröder, 'Who's Afraid of Rosamond Merridew?: Reading Medieval History in "The Journal of Mistress Joan Martyn"', *Journal of the Short Story in English*, 50 (2008), paras 8, 12 <http://jsse.revues.org/719> ((accessed 12 January 2015).
62. Others are the lost lives of her aunts Caroline Stephen and Mary Fisher (both 1904; *L* 1.163–4) and 'On a Faithful Friend', the life of Shag, the family dog (1905, *E* 1.12), as well as a provisional sketch of Clive Bell (*PA* 383–4).
63. Rachel Crossland, 'Virginia Stephen's Books on the Table: The Cornhill Magazine Reviews'. Paper presented at 'Virginia Woolf and the World of Books', 27th Annual International Conference on Virginia Woolf, University of Reading, 29 June–2 July 2017.
64. Like Miss Linsett, Simcox wrote a posthumous 'appreciation in a thousand words' (*CSF* 70) of her friend, which could have been familiar to Woolf from Leslie Stephen's research for his 1902 volume for Macmillan's English Men of Letters series. Edith Simcox, 'George Eliot', *The Nineteenth Century: A Monthly Review*, May (1881), 778–801.
65. Battershill, p. 4.
66. Corbett, *Behind the Times: Virginia Woolf in Late-Victorian Contexts*, p. 32.
67. Atkinson, p. 13.
68. Ray Monk, 'Life without Theory: Biography as an Exemplar of Philosophical Understanding', *Poetics Today*, 28.3 (2007), 527–70 (pp. 533–5).
69. Cuddy-Keane, p. 172.
70. Ray Monk, 'This Fictitious Life: Virginia Woolf on Biography, Reality, and Character', *Philosophy and Literature*, 31.1 (2007), 1–40 (p. 30) <https://doi.org/10.1353/phl.2007.0015>; 'Life without Theory', p. 535.

71. Laura Marcus, 'The Newness of the "New Biography": Biographical Theory and Practice in the Early Twentieth Century', in *Mapping Lives: The Uses of Biography*, ed. by William St Clair and Peter France, British Academy Centenary Monographs series (Oxford: Oxford University Press, 2004), pp. 193–218 (p. 196); Atkinson similarly argues that Woolf's attention to obscure lives draws on established Victorian practices as well as Leslie Stephen in particular. Atkinson, pp. 252–64.
72. Alice Wood, pp. 11–13.
73. Booth, *How to Make It as a Woman*, p. 229.
74. Women accounted for only 5 per cent of the original *DNB* entries (as opposed to 10 per cent of the *ODNB*). James Raven, 'The Oxford Dictionary of National Biography: Dictionary or Encyclopaedia?', *The Historical Journal*, 50.4 (2007), 991–1006 (p. 995).
75. Booth, *How to Make It as a Woman*, p. 232.
76. Hermione Lee, *Virginia Woolf* (London: Vintage, 1997), p. 709.
77. Gaskell is central to *Virginia Woolf and the Nineteenth-Century Domestic Novel*. Blair, chap. 3; Dell.
78. Mary Jean Corbett has written extensively about Woolf's troubled relationship with late-Victorian women writers and activists. Corbett, *Behind the Times: Virginia Woolf in Late-Victorian Contexts*; 'Behind the Times? Virginia Woolf and the Third Generation', *Twentieth Century Literature*, 60.1 (2014), 27–58; '"Ashamed of the inkpot"'.

# Chapter 2

# 'Vain are these speculations': Jane Austen and Female Perfection

In 'Impressions of Sir Leslie Stephen', Virginia Woolf recalls that her father 'read Miss Austen through' as part of his nightly reading aloud to his children. Unlike Thackeray's 'too terrible' *Vanity Fair*, Austen passed muster as drawing room entertainment suitable for the entire family:[1] from the first, Woolf's engagement with Jane Austen (1775–1817) is therefore mediated by paternal(istic) approval, making her a model of female writing but also threatening a reductive and outmoded ideal of femininity.

Although few would contest Pam Morris's assertion that '[i]f Woolf has a literary mother it must surely be Jane Austen', most critics also note that Austen occupies an ambivalent position in Woolf's work. Austen's legacies, the courtship narrative and the domestic novel, are prominent but not always uncontested influences on *The Voyage Out* (1915) and *Night and Day* (1919).[2] Thus, Jane de Gay notes that Woolf's textual references to Austen '[raise] concerns about the patriarchal custodianship of literature', and seek to move beyond the didactic constraints of Austen's novels, while Kathryn Simpson traces how Woolf's revised Austenian romance narrative explores 'the unsaid and unspecified of women's desire'.[3] Woolf's ambivalence is also evident in *A Room of One's Own* as well as the first *Common Reader* essay, as Janet Todd and Jean Long have noted.[4] However, with the exception of de Gay, who briefly touches upon Austen's biographical baggage, the majority of critical engagements with Woolf's Austen are intertextual studies that focus on her literary legacy. Reading them, one would be forgiven for thinking that Austen, although without a doubt 'thumbed, scored, annotated, magnified' through her novels, persisted in personal anonymity:

> living almost within the memory of man, she flatters and cajoles you with the promise of intimacy and then, at the last moment, there is the same blankness.

Are those Jane Austen's eyes or is it a glass, a mirror, a silver spoon held up in the sun? ('Personalities', E 6.439–40)

Yet Woolf's insistence on Austen's ability to deflect her audience's gaze in 'Personalities' (undated) is evidence of her own persistent search for an authentic persona at the core of the Austen mythology. Todd notes that 'She is said to have written a female sentence, and to have created a universal, perfect prose, but there is no analysis'.[5] If Woolf's engagement with Austen's fiction happens predominantly intertextually in her novels, her essays' persistent focus on the personal can be explained through Austen's exemplary afterlife. '[T]he impulse to make use of Austen's life and writings to address social issues and concerns began shortly after her death and persisted throughout the nineteenth century', so that by its end, 'the domesticated, idealized image that was being marketed as "Jane Austen"' was an obvious corrective to invoke against changing gender roles.[6] Woolf's cautious disavowal of this exemplary woman writer determines the tone of her reviews of the Austen family biographies in the 1910s and early 1920s, but is fundamentally reversed by the publication of Austen's juvenilia and letters, which for the first time offer a seemingly uncensored view on a satirical and irreverent writer. Biography therefore underpins Woolf's understanding of Austen's fiction and supplies a trajectory for her transformation from a writer whose restrictively tight 'plait/plot'[7] needs unravelling to the mythical originator of the woman's sentence in *A Room of One's Own*. Woolf's engagement with Jane Austen crystallises her own wavering commitment to political criticism and a female tradition: fictional biography drives Austen's transformation into a proto-Modernist predecessor, but Woolf's resistance to the political dimensions of Austen's fiction also highlights the shortcomings of a subtle feminine approach.

### 'Dear Aunt Jane'

Originally a Regency writer, Jane Austen became a Victorian in her afterlife. Although her novels remained in print throughout the nineteenth century, Austen's popularity rose steeply with the publication of her nephew's *Memoir of Jane Austen* in 1870. Cheryl Wilson observes that

> [p]rior to the publication of the *Memoir*, writers and critics had only Austen's novels, and a handful of brief biographical sketches [ . . . ] Their Jane Austen was first and foremost a writer, and her popularity was generally greatest in literary circles and stimulated intellectual inquiry from writers such as

George Henry Lewes and Thomas Macaulay. After 1870, she quickly became, in the words of Henry James, 'everybody's dear, Jane,' [ . . . ] Austenmania that would continue to gather momentum through the twentieth and twenty-first centuries.[8]

Austen's popularity required the cooperation of an enthusiastic reading public, yet it is also a family affair: Hermione Lee notes that 'the best-known fact about Jane Austen's posthumous life is that her story was guarded and shaped by her family'.[9] From Cassandra Austen's almost complete destruction of her letters, J. E. Austen-Leigh's sanitisation of his aunt in the *Memoir of Jane Austen* (1870), to her great-nephew Lord Brabourne's promise that only his *Letters of Jane Austen* (1884) allowed an insight into 'the confidential outpourings of Jane Austen's soul',[10] her afterlife was shaped by a series of family interventions that fluctuated between the desire for obscurity and the wish to control her public image, as well as competing gendered and generational perspectives.

Austen's death in 1817 was followed by the posthumous publication of *Persuasion* (1818) which lifted the veil of anonymity with a brief 'Biographical Notice'. Commonly attributed to Henry Austen,[11] this short sketch presents a blandly virtuous portrait of 'a life of usefulness, literature and religion' and took pains to emphasise that 'her opinions accorded strictly with those of our Established Church'.[12] This propriety extends to Austen's authorship:

> Every thing came finished from her pen; for on all subjects she had ideas as clear as her expressions were well chosen. It is not hazarding much to say that she never dispatched a note or letter unworthy of publication.[13]

The Notice blurs the lines between Austen's public authorship and her private correspondence, and draws the former back into domestic routine: a strategy to de-professionalise female authorship that is also evident in the insistence that Austen 'became an authoress entirely from taste and inclination. Neither the hope of fame nor profit mixed with her early motives'.[14]

However, more important than the 'Biographical Notice' and Henry Austen's slightly extended 'Memoir of Miss Austen' (1833) is James Edward Austen-Leigh's *Memoir of Jane Austen* (1870), which transformed his aunt into a model of femininity and gave a new impetus to Austen's Victorian afterlife. With the death of Cassandra Austen in 1845, Jane's surviving manuscripts and letters were distributed among the different branches of the Austen family, intensifying their desire to assert their particular perspective on Jane Austen as the only right one.[15] Nevertheless, Austen-Leigh's account of his aunt's life and character forms the basis of virtually all subsequent biographies: he collected memorabilia and memories from the ageing and dying generation of eye-witnesses to Austen's life – her siblings and their spouses, as well as their children. More cynically, Kathryn Sutherland also notes that it was timed 'to coincide with the reissue of Austen's novels in Bentley's "Favourite Novels" series', and thus succeeded in 'bringing Austen back into periodical culture and the literary marketplace and providing opportunities for readers and reviewers to re-engage with the novels'.[16] Lacking access to the majority of Austen's surviving letters, the *Memoir* focuses instead on a tightly controlled image of a domestic saint, the 'dear Aunt Jane' of her nephews' and nieces' early childhood recollections of Steventon parsonage and Chawton Cottage:

> 'St. Aunt Jane of Steventon-cum-Chawton Canonicorum', as Austen-Leigh's hagiographical portrait has been wittily dubbed, is a comfortable figure, shunning fame and professional status, centred in home, writing only in the intervals permitted from the more important domestic duties of a devoted daughter, sister and aunt.[17]

That the Jane Austen of this memoir is judged against contemporary rather than Regency standards of female education is clear from Austen-Leigh's apologetic admission that 'she was not highly accomplished according to the present standard'. His *Description of Jane Austen's person, character and tastes* lists the gaps in her accomplishments – drawing, German, the finer points of history, contemporary politics – alongside a brief acknowledgement of her extensive knowledge of literature; before finding comfort in her popularity with children: 'It was not, however, what she *knew*, but what she *was*, that distinguished her from others'.[18] Sutherland notes that Austen-Leigh attempts to 'deflect enquiry from anything as intense, familially disruptive, or counter-social as writing and disingenuously disclaims the existence of what he cannot (or will not) know about creative genius'.[19]

This domesticating mission required a careful editing of Austen's juvenilia and letters: Auerbach traces how Austen-Leigh preserved domestic gossip but deleted references to miscarriages, fleas and bad breath as well as Austen's extensive reading. Additionally, his selection from Austen's juvenilia, a brief parodic 'Mystery Play', lacks the transgressiveness of 'his supposedly docile aunt's iconoclastic minor writings, those rowdy spoofs and satiric fragments about young women who toss rivals out the window, raise armies, and get "dead Drunk"'.[20] Austen-Leigh's innocent maiden aunt endures most persistently in her visual impact: the engraved portrait included in the *Memoir* has become the standard portrait of Austen and was used to commemorate her on the British

£10 notes.²¹ Based on a watercolour sketch by Cassandra Austen, the engraving improves upon a tired-looking Austen, her face dominated by 'dark, staring eyes and the unsmiling, unpretty mouth' with 'the faintest suggestion that a sardonic smile might be about to break', to present a serenely smiling, younger, prettier woman with a decorative lace cap.²² As neither portrait was considered a great likeness by eyewitnesses,²³ this beautification is symptomatic of Austen-Leigh's feminising mission.

Woolf's first article on Austen, a 1913 lead article reviewing William and Richard Arthur Austen-Leigh's *Jane Austen. Her Life and Letters. A Family Record. With a Portrait* for the *Times Literary Supplement* tackles this family legacy from its first sentence: ²⁴

> In many ways Jane Austen must be considered singularly blessed. The manner in which from generation to generation her descendants respect her memory is, we imagine, precisely that which she would have chosen for herself – and she would have been hard to please. (E 2.9)

The singular blessing of the Austen 'family taste and modesty' is of course double-edged. The review reveals Woolf's understanding of Austen as a carefully curated family construct, created to conceal and reveal specific aspects of her life and personality, and cuts through these myths in search for a more authentic Jane Austen. Likewise, the phrasing is stilted but revealing: the Austen family's choice to 'respect her memory' recalls Woolf's attack on such superficial and deferential forms of biographical commemoration in 'Memoirs of a Novelist'. The review thus politely undercuts the Austen family's biographical project from the beginning. Tracing Austen's afterlife from her nephew's *Memoir*, which 'reproduced the atmosphere in which [her] life was lived so instinctively that his book can never be superseded' to 'this final biography, for surely no other will be possible', Woolf casts doubt upon the necessity for further commemorations. Noting that *Jane Austen. Her Life and Letters. A Family Record. With a Portrait* has 'brought together all that is known about Jane Austen', she judges that the biography nevertheless fails to shed new light on her (E 2.9).²⁵

Against this family project, Woolf pits Austen herself as well as her own knowledge of her character gained from her fiction. The review recentres the biographical discourse around Jane Austen as a biographical subject with agency: in conspiracy with her sister Cassandra, she baffles her male biographers and retains her secrets because '[t]o her alone did Jane Austen write freely and impulsively' (E 2.9). Woolf's account of Austen's biographical afterlife prioritises the unmediated access of Jane's letters over the recollections of later, temporally and socially further removed generations: arguing that Cassandra Austen 'put [the ability to say anything fresh about her] effectively beyond their power', she makes Cassandra's destruction of her sister's letters the decisive event in Jane's afterlife. Woolf thus prioritises an affective interiority that more closely resembles that of the characters in Austen's fiction, but also aligns her with her own literary experiments: by positing Austen as a wilfully elusive biographical subject, the review recalls Woolf's 'Memoirs of a Novelist', which ascribes similar motives to its 'lost' protagonist Miss Willatt. As in the short story, Woolf prioritises visual clues where textual evidence fails to offer the desired outcome:

> we cannot grudge Jane and Cassandra the glance of satisfaction which they must cast at each other as after fresh scrutiny of that serene and smiling face we turn away baffled, and they know that their secrets are their own forever. (E 2.10)

Although the 'serene and smiling face' is that of Austen-Leigh's creation, Woolf's discovery of hidden depths behind the perfectly smooth surface of the family biographies reveals the potential of an entirely blank slate: lacking definite evidence of Austen's character, Woolf can confidently assert her collusion in her own disappearance, and thereby invalidates the biographical labour of generations of male Austens by redirecting the readers' attention to the sisters' relationship with each other, and a female perspective on Austen that has been lost.

Although she nominally reviewed the Austen-Leighs' biography alongside Sybil Brinton's *Old Friends and New Faces: An Imaginary Sequel to the Novels of Jane Austen* (1913), Woolf deals rather cursorily with these texts: Brinton's book, ostensibly the first Austen fan fiction and evidence that Austen was increasingly and overtly commodified, is dismissed as 'a work of great love and ingenuity which, if taken not as fiction but as talk about Jane Austen's characters, will please the select public which is never tired of discussing them' (E 2.11).[26] Instead, Woolf draws extensively on Austen's novels to offer a counter-narrative to these non-literary contexts. She quotes a series of anecdotes from outside the family circle that complicate the image of a domesticated 'Aunt Jane': Philadelphia Austen remembers her 'whimsical and affected' teen-aged cousin, Mrs Mitford recalls the 'prettiest, silliest, most affected, husband-hunting butterfly', and an acquaintance of her daughter Mary remembers the 'most perpendicular, precise, taciturn piece of "single blessedness" that ever existed' (E 2.10). Although Woolf confidently dismisses these critics, noting that 'it is amusing to see as clearly as we do why they went wrong' she does not let her readers into her secret. Yet she is 'ready to bless Marianne Knight perpetually' for her account of how 'Aunt Jane would sit very quietly at work beside the fire at Godmersham library, then suddenly burst out laughing, jump up, cross the room to a distant table with paper lying on it, write something down' (*E* 2.10). This insight into Austen's composition habits allows Woolf to reconstruct a writer who seamlessly integrated her craft into her domestic routine: 'it is by the means of such trifles that we draw a little closer to the charm, the brilliance, the strength and sincerity of character that lay behind the novels' (*E* 2.10).

While Woolf is critical in her engagement with the family biographies and sceptical of their domesticating project, her evaluation of Austen's literary qualities is more firmly influenced by Victorian criticism. The larger part of the article is devoted to a discussion of Austen's merits and flaws as a writer, both compensating for the biography's shortcomings and offering Woolf an opportunity to assess Austen's literary afterlife alongside her biographical legacy. The problem of women and fiction haunts every step of Woolf's discussion, yet is never made explicit: this grappling with Austen's anomalous status as the canonical woman writer par excellence goes some way in explaining the enduring Victorian echoes in Woolf's analysis. Observing that Austen is '[u]nlike other great writers in almost every way', Woolf suggestively but vaguely hints at her difference by virtue of her gender: as ever, literary greatness is male (*E* 2.11). Woolf notes Austen's slow rise to popularity – 'she has limitations of a kind particularly likely to cramp a writer's popularity' – with another obliquely gendered reference:

> The mere sight of her six neat volumes suggests something of the reason, for when we look at them we do not remember any page or passage which so burnt itself into our minds that from time to time we take the book down, read that sentence again and exalt. [ . . . ] She was never a revelation to the young, a stern comrade, a brilliant and extravagantly admired friend, a writer whose sentences sang in one's brain and were absorbed into one's blood. (*E* 2.11)

Continuing the play between surface and depth which characterised her approach to the biographies, Woolf's 'six neat volumes' continue the metonymical slippage between author and work and recall the family biography's bland image of feminine perfection in their faultless propriety.

However, Victorian critical legacies are most prominent in Woolf's contextualisation of Austen's exemplary femininity. Suggesting that Austen 'has too little of the rebel in her composition, too little discontent, and of the vision which is the cause and reward of discontent' (*E* 2.11), Woolf obliquely pits her against another clergyman's daughter, Charlotte Brontë. This is a return to familiar territory:

Elizabeth Gaskell's *The Life of Charlotte Brontë* (1857) had publicised Brontë's side of an epistolary debate with George Henry Lewes about Austen's merits as a model of women's writing. Although Brontë received Lewes's criticism of *Jane Eyre* politely, she was evidently not inclined to follow his recommendation of modelling her own writing after Austen's: 'I *think*, too, I will endeavour to follow the counsel which shines out of Miss Austen's "mild eyes," "to finish more and be more subdued;" but neither am I sure of that'. Brontë's defence of her own mode of writing notes the gulf that separates Austen's 'carefully-fenced, highly cultivated garden, with neat borders and delicate flowers' (all carefully curated femininity und pleasantly neat) from her own style of writing: 'Can there be a great artist without poetry? [ . . . ] Miss Austen being, as you say, without "sentiment," without *poetry*, maybe is *sensible*, real (more *real* than *true*), but she cannot be great'.[27] Although Wilson cautions that 'Brontë and Austen have both been poorly served by the ways in which a few critical comments, taken out of context, have often come to overshadow a more complex relationship', Brontë's resistance to Austen here clearly offers Woolf a model for refusing to be judged on this very narrow definition of literary merit: as Jane de Gay observes, 'Patriarchal approval marginalised Austen as much as it valued her'.[28] Woolf's references to a more passionate and lyrical mode of writing than Austen's tightly controlled sentences echo her engagement with Brontë during the 1910s, as Chapter 3 will show: during this period, Woolf praises Brontë's passion and discontent and she functioned as the 'brilliant and extravagantly admired friend' Austen cannot be: 'one is conscious of irony with which she would have disclaimed any such wish or intention' (*E* 2.11).

Austen's very awareness of her limitations as well as her calm acceptance of them reveals another Victorian influence on Woolf. Her ideological critique of Austen's 'conservative spirit' (*E* 2.12) draws heavily on Leslie Stephen's criticism and scepticism towards Austen. Stephen's *Dictionary of National Biography* entry follows the Austen family tradition and almost exceeds Austen-Leigh's editorial stance in celebrating Austen's exemplary domesticity: 'Her domestic relations were delightful, and she was especially attractive to children'.[29] Stephen's engagement with Austen is fundamentally determined by her femininity: he praises her awareness of 'the precise limits of her own powers', the 'unequalled finesse of her literary tact' and her novels' 'unconscious charm', applying highly gendered behavioural expectations to literary texts and assuming female (literary) inferiority. As he frames this criticism of Austen's work with several disparaging quotes from Brontë's letters, Stephen's *DNB* entry even supplies a structural model for the first part of Woolf's *TLS* review; while its second part draws on his *Cornhill* article 'Humour'. Writing as the magazine's editor and without the objectivity that the *DNB* required, Stephen responds less than enthusiastically to the newly established celebrity writer: 'Austenolatry is perhaps the most intolerant and dogmatic of literary creeds'.[30] A champion of eighteenth-century satirists like Swift or Fielding, Stephen forcefully undercuts Austen's powers as a satirist by associating her with a prudish Victorian middle class who enjoy novels only because they are proper and respectable:

> There is not only nothing improper in her books [ . . . ] She is absolutely at peace with her most comfortable world. She never even hints at a suspicion that squires and parsons of the English type are not an essential part of the order of things; if she touches upon poverty, the only reflection suggested is one of gentle scorn for people who can't keep a butler to themselves or take tea with people who do so. When the amiable Fanny Price in *Mansfield Park* finds that her mother has to eat cold mutton and mend the children's clothes, her only thought is to return to her rich uncle.[31]

Stephen's reading of *Mansfield Park* is uncharitable if not outright wrong: had Austen scorned poverty in all its forms, Fanny Price's only thought upon witnessing her family's poverty would have been to bow to her uncle's will and accept Henry Crawford. Instead, the Price parents' 'negligence and error' (Chapter XL) are mirrored (and arguably even surpassed, considering that a lack of resources isn't an issue) by that of the Bertrams; and her return 'home' prompts Fanny to develop a sense of agency in resolving domestic quarrels, subscribing to a library, and educating her sister Susan. Stephen's condemnation of Austen's disregard of the 'harsh hideous facts with which ninety-nine out of a hundred of our fellow-creatures are constantly struggling' suggests her falling short of his ideals of female philanthropy: Fanny's experience of 'confer[ring] favours [ . . . ] on the very poor' (Chapter XL) clearly doesn't meet Stephen's more exalted standards. Although passive and compliant Fanny Price is undoubtedly Austen's least popular heroine, recent readings of the novel nevertheless emphasise Fanny's efforts to promote her family's, and particularly her sister's, welfare from her own relative position of privilege: her marriage to Edmund Bertram goes some way towards healing the rift that unequal marriages had caused between the Ward sisters.[32]

Indeed, considering that one central tenet of *Mansfield Park* is 'to think that where nature had made so little difference, circumstances should have made so much' (Chapter XLII), Stephen's accusation that

Austen is 'too much at peace in her comfortable world' seems particularly short-sighted. Austen's novels mercilessly expose how inextricably marriage and financial security are linked for Regency women, from the Dashwoods' loss of their home at the beginning of *Sense and Sensibility*, and Mrs Bennet's overwhelming anxiety for her daughters' future in *Pride and Prejudice*, to Emma's lack of incentive for swapping her fortune and independence for matrimony. Morris points to the pervasiveness of broad generalisations in debates of Austen's (lack of) radicalism, noting that '[t]he deployment of terms like 'gentry', 'middle class', or 'landowners' in discussions of Austen's novels are at times too static and homogeneous in implication to comprehend the complex dynamics of the social world that the fiction represents'.[33] Stephen's 'comfortable world' of 'squires and parsons' therefore ignores that 'Austen's novels persistently enact the inevitability of change and dramatise this process in the narrative experience of her female protagonists, encompassing a transition from stability to mobility, from social homogeneity to social heterogeneity'.[34]

Amid all this, Stephen does concede that

> [t]o deny Miss Austen's marvellous literary skill would be simply to convince oneself of the grossest stupidity. It is probable, however, that as much skill may have been employed in the painting of a bit of old china as in one of Raphael's masterpieces. We do not therefore say it possesses equal merit. And, on the same principle, allowing all possible praise to Miss Austen within in her own sphere, I should dispute the conclusion that she was therefore entitled to be ranked with the greatest authors.[35]

Stephen's firm dismissal of Austen from the ranks of great authors thus provides the background for Woolf's unease in asserting that Austen is 'unlike other great writers in almost every way'. Although she partially revises his judgement, elements of his preference for a wider sphere and openly political satire influence her analysis. Woolf frames Austen's understanding of her own sphere through the famous 'little bit (two inches wide) of ivory' alongside the first sentence of the final chapter of *Mansfield Park*, 'Let other pens dwell on guilt and misery. I quit such odious subjects as soon as I can', thus picking up Stephen's train of thought alongside direct verbal echoes of his review. Austen 'accepted life too calmly as she found it', her 'world made up of big houses and little houses, of gentry inhabiting them who were keenly conscious of their grades of gentility', and was 'debarred from the most profound insight into human nature by the respect which she pays to some unnatural convention': 'these defects are due to the fact that she is content to take it for granted that such characters [Elinor Dashwood and Fanny Price] and conduct are good without trying to see them in a fresh light for herself' (*E* 2.12). However, where Stephen judges Austen for performing the very femininity he also expects from her, Woolf is already invested in tracing its impact on women writers' development. To her, the problem lies with patriarchal culture, not women themselves. 'A clergyman's daughter in those days was, no doubt, very carefully brought up', and 'the chief damage which this conservative spirit has inflicted on her art is that it tied her hands together when she dealt with men'. In one of the less tightly controlled moments of the essay, Woolf's frustration bursts forth spontaneously: 'This is the more annoying because we are inclined to think that she could have run almost all the risks and triumphed' (*E* 2.12).

This enthusiasm for Jane Austen the writer that transcends the biographical tradition resurfaces at the end of Woolf's review: her sketch of Austen constructs her as a model of artistic contentment that is far from the smug conservatism of the previous section. Noting that in spite of her social satire, Austen lacked bitterness, Woolf offers a more positive interpretation of Austen's contentment: 'Life itself – that was the object of love, of her absorbed study; that was the pursuit which filled those unrecorded years [ . . . ] More than any other novelist she fills every inch of her canvas with observation' (*E* 2.14). This portrait, like Marianne Knight's recollection of her aunt's writing habits, corrects the image of virtuously unobtrusive literary activity by positing writing as the centre of Austen's existence and expands the scope of her little bit of ivory considerably. Woolf also begins to chip away at the myth of effortless literary perfection:

> Only those who have realised for themselves the inadequacy of a straight stick dipped in ink when brought into contact with the rich and tumultuous glow of life can appreciate the full wonder of her achievement, the imagination, the penetration, the insight, the courage, the sincerity which are required to bring before us one of those perfectly normal and simple incidents of an average human life. (*E* 2.14)

The publication of Woolf's review coincided with Gerald Duckworth's acceptance for publication of *The Voyage Out* (*E* 2.15n). This final emphasis on their shared experience as writers therefore suggests a new understanding of Austen based on Woolf's search for her own method: as the next section will show, her legacy of form and genre as well as the difficulties of capturing ordinary life dominate Woolf's thinking on writing for years to come.

## 'Jane Austen Over Again'

The question of Austen's relevance to modern(ist) literature haunts Woolf's thinking over the next decade. She invokes her in a variety of contexts, ranging from intertextual engagement in *The Voyage Out* (1915), brief comments in the *TLS* reviews 'A Scribbling Dame' (1916) and 'Mr Howells on Form' (1918), and a diary entry concerning Katherine Mansfield's verdict on *Night and Day* ('Miss Austen up to date') to 'Jane Austen and the Geese' (*TLS*, 1920), a review of yet another Austen family biography. In all of these texts, Austen's persona and her works continue to be intertwined, causing contradictory responses: on the one hand, she emerges as a fictional model, on the other, her biographical baggage makes her an easy target for a performative rejection of outdated models of women's writing. Woolf's responses thus follow a well-established tradition: Wilson notes that 'one of the reasons that Austen may have been so useful for the Victorians was that her works offered opportunities for broader discussions about genre and continued to influence the production of new fiction' long after their original publication.[36]

All of Woolf's novels are densely intertextual; and critics such as Jane de Gay, Nick Smart, Kathryn Simpson and Susan Hudson Fox have read *The Voyage Out* and *Night and Day* in the context of Jane Austen and the tradition of domestic writing she represents. However, Woolf's engagement with Austen in *The Voyage Out* stands out because, in contrast to her normally subtle allusions, she stages a debate about Austen's literary merits that makes explicit the positions underpinning her article. Rachel's dislike of Austen – 'so like a tight plait'– combines with Richard Dalloway's patriarchal approval to map out the restrictiveness of her reputation: 'She is incomparably the greatest female writer we possess [ . . . ] for this reason: she does not attempt to write like a man' (*VO* 67, 70). Reducing Austen to her symbolic power as ideal woman writer and author of (overly) neat courtship plots, this approval rings doubly hollow given the soporific effect of her fiction on Richard Dalloway: although Clarissa begins to read *Persuasion* to Richard and gifts it to a reluctant Rachel, none of the characters finishes the novel, leaving its continued relevance questionable. '[D]etermined that Sir Walter [Elliott] should take her husband's mind off the guns of Britain, and divert him in an exquisite, quaint, sprightly, and slightly ridiculous world' (*VO* 71), Clarissa appreciates *Persuasion* at least partly because it guarantees an opportunity to pursue her own interests while her husband is asleep: as Simpson notes, '[w]hile ostensibly Clarissa is in many ways the epitome of the ideal wife, she also carves out space for her own independence and freedom and Austen facilitates this duality'.³⁷ Describing *Persuasion* as 'a little less threadbare than the others', she too assumes the sceptical position that links Austen's last and least traditional courtship novel with the plot of *The Voyage Out*. Tracing a series of homoerotic and sexually ambiguous encounters between Rachel and her aunt, Clarissa Dalloway and several spinsters, Kathryn Simpson posits that

> If *Persuasion* begins to challenge established structures of authority – of class, gender, and generation – through the process of testing the 'tight plait' of the courtship plot, *The Voyage Out* unravels these more fully as it opens up a far more complex set of questions about male and female relationships, about gendered roles and identities and about what it is possible to think, feel and say about women's desires.³⁸

Jane de Gay similarly argues that although Woolf uses Austenian irony and satire to insert veiled social criticisms into her novel, she only partially adapts her neat courtship narratives. Rachel's death prevents a traditional marriage ending for her narrative, but also 'affirms what Austen hints at: that marital happiness is easier to assert in a conclusion than to demonstrate in a developed narrative'.³⁹

Yet if this encounter seems to lament Austen's exemplary femininity, Woolf offers a more positive assessment of it in 'A Scribbling Dame' (*TLS*, 1916), a review of *The Life and Romances of Mrs Eliza Haywood* by George Frisbie Whicher, PhD. Invoking 'dusty books from desolate museums', Woolf takes a rather scathing approach to a study of 'this faded and antique specimen of the domestic house fly with all her seventy volumes orderly arrayed around her': 'She is dead, she is old, she wrote books, and nobody has yet written a book about her' (*E* 2.23). Woolf's engagement with the actress, writer, and editor Eliza Haywood, 'who played a key role in the novel's evolution and defined central issues in the portrayal of eighteenth-century female subjectivity', follows a familiar pattern:⁴⁰ although she laments the scarcity of known facts about Haywood's life and condemns Pope's 'disgusting stanzas in *The Dunciad*', she also dismisses the 'mass of unreadable journalism which by its form and by the inferiority of the writer's talents throws no light upon her age or upon herself' (*E* 2.23) and is oblivious to the fact 'that Eliza Haywood – a pioneering woman journalist, the editor of *The Female Spectator* and *The Parrot* – warrants recognition'.⁴¹ Both the quality and quantity of Haywood's fiction thus prompt Woolf's firm resistance to Haywood's reinscription into a female literary canon via Austen:

> In what sense Mr Whicher can claim that Mrs Haywood 'prepared the way for [ . . . ] quiet Jane Austen' it is difficult to see, save that one lady was

undeniably born some eighty years in advance of the other. For it would be hard to imagine a less professional woman of letters than the lady who wrote on little slips of paper, hid them when anyone was near, and kept her novels shut up in a desk, and refused to write a romance about the august House of Coburg at the suggestion of Prince Leopold's librarian – behaviour that must have made Mrs Haywood lift her hands in amazement in the grave. (E 2.24–5)

Whicher's identification of Haywood as an important precursor to the modern novel is not as outrageous as Woolf would have it: Paula Backscheider notes Haywood's importance as

> an important experimental novelist who often broke new ground and set trends. As Christopher Flint remarked, 'Haywood, more than any other eighteenth-century writer . . . bridges the fictional narratives of Behn or Defoe and the works of Burney and Austen' (*Family Fictions*, 219).[42]

Notably, Woolf's argument is biographical, not generic. Haywood's prolific professionalism is indeed a far cry from the refined and reclusively feminine mode of writing she ascribes to Austen. Far from presenting a disadvantage, Austen's exemplary femininity here serves to absolve her from Haywood's suspected mercenary vulgarity: as in the various family biographies, Austen's superior artistic motives are guaranteed by her delicacy in concealing her work, evidence of feminine modesty and lack of ambition. Relegating Haywood's part in literary history to 'that of swelling the chorus of sound', Woolf asserts that an Austen of Haywood's period would 'have written not novels but a few exquisite letters', thus prioritising private amateur productions over prolific popularity. It is this dismissive attitude towards the majority of women who supported themselves by writing that causes some of Woolf's encounters with neglected women writers such as Haywood to be less than productive (unlike her imaginative restorations of forgotten predecessors), leading her to wilfully assign them to further oblivion, as Chapter 5 will show in more detail.

Although Woolf effortlessly wields Austen's exemplary reputation to exclude Haywood from female literary traditions, she continues to be ambivalent about her value as a model for the future. Two years later, in 'Mr Howells on Form' (*TLS*, 1918), a review of a reprint of Leonard Merrick's novel *The Actor-Manager. With an Introduction by W. D. Howells* (1898/1918), or rather of Howell's introduction to it, Woolf contrasts Austen's formalism with the aimlessness of current fiction:

> We cannot recognize among ourselves a conception of the art of fiction such as Jane Austen seems to have held so surely and unquestioningly [ . . . ]

It is not that life is more complex and difficult now than at any other period, but that for each generation that point of interest shifts, the old form puts the emphasis on the wrong places, and in searching out the severed and submerged parts of what to us constitutes form we seem to be throwing fragments together at random and disdaining the very thing that we are trying our best to win from chaos. (*E* 2.325–6)

Todd notes that '[o]n her own, Jane Austen most commonly signifies perfection – a hard, forbidding quality', and Woolf conflates literature and biography to create this perception: the formal perfection of Austen's published novels fuses with the myth that '[e]very thing came finished from her pen; for on all subjects she had ideas as clear as her expressions were well chosen'.[43] This certainty further separates Austen from being acknowledged as a model for Woolf's own writing, even though with *Night and Day* (1919) Woolf returns to Austen's speciality, the courtship plot.

*Night and Day*'s engagement with Austen is complex but undeniable: its 'skilful Austen-ticity' lies in its 'apparent preoccupation with tea-table drama and drawing-room minutiae' that covers more subversive impulses.[44] Jane de Gay traces numerous, often parodic, Austenian echoes in *Night and Day*'s courtship plots, suggesting that it can be read as 'a cross-cast version of *Mansfield Park*' with Ralph Denham taking on the role of economically insecure outsider (consequently, Katharine loses status but gains independence through marriage, subverting Austen's pattern), and Mary Datchet deliberately absenting herself from the courtship narrative in the manner of Anne Elliot and Fanny Price.[45] Yet while modern critics see both *Night and Day* and its engagement with Austenian intertexts as inherently subversive, contemporary reviewers saw it as a shorthand for the novel's pre-war setting and formal conservatism: 'Miss Austen up to date'. In a review for the *Athenaeum*, Katherine Mansfield classified *Night and Day* as 'a novel in the tradition of the English novel [ . . . ] it makes us feel old and chill: we had never thought to look at upon its like again'.[46] In the privacy of her diary, Woolf vents her frustration at this comparison:

> K.M. wrote a review which irritated me – I thought I saw spite in it. A decorous elderly dullard she describes me, Jane Austen up to date. Leonard supposes that she let her wish for my failure have its way with her pen. He could see her looking about for a loophole of escape. 'I'm not going to call this a success – or if I must, I'll call it the wrong kind of success.' (*D* 1.314)

Woolf's reaction to Mansfield's review demonstrates how easily Austen's reputation is weaponised: the epitome of the charming female novelist, she represents 'the wrong kind of success' for any ambitious modern writer. However, Woolf's irritated reaction to Mansfield's comparison has frequently overshadowed the actual content of the review, which goes into more detail on the similarities between the two writers. Mansfield praises *Night and Day*'s 'quiet perfection' (surely a backhanded compliment familiar to Woolf) and emphasises the formal and thematic safety of Woolf's novel, 'unaware of what has been happening':

> As in the case of Miss Austen's novels we fall under a little spell; it is as though, realizing our safety, we surrender ourselves to the author, confident that whatever she has shown us, and however strange it may appear, we shall not be frightened or shocked.[47]

Like E. M. Forster and other contemporary critics, who found *Night and Day*'s characters insufficiently compelling (*D* 1.310), Mansfield singles out character as one of the weaker areas of the novel – again in comparison to Austen:

> What is it that carries us away? With Miss Austen, it is first her feeling for life, and then her feeling for writing; but with Mrs. Woolf these feelings are continually giving way the one to the other, so that the urgency of either is impaired.

Like Woolf's 'Jane Austen' review, Mansfield identifies a 'feeling for life' as central and shared interests in their fiction; however, *Night and Day* falls short of Austen's example when it comes to the vividness of characterisation. Woolf's irritation is therefore likely not only at being pigeonholed as a successor to Austen's feminine respectability, but also an inferior one at that: at the end of the year, pitting two differently negative reviews of *Night and Day* against each other, she opted for H. W. Massingham's 'annoyed and abusive' (*L* 2.399) attack on her: 'I'd rather write in my own way of "four passionate snails" than be, as K.M. maintains, Jane Austen over again' (*WD* 22).

One last example of Woolf's inability to envision a more progressive or relevant Jane Austen is her review of Mary Augusta Austen-Leigh's *Personal Aspects of Jane Austen* (1920), in 'Jane Austen and the Geese' (*TLS*, 1920). Mary Augusta, the daughter of James Edward Austen-Leigh (author of the 1870 *Memoir*), offers the first female perspective on a great-aunt she never knew. Unfortunately, her rambling biography, dedicated to 'all true lovers of Jane Austen' and intended to silence all critics forever, follows the family tradition in trying to cement her position as a paragon of virtue, domesticity and morality.[48] Woolf's review is scathing and dismissive of M. A. Austen-Leigh's concerns about critical misconceptions of Austen's works and persona: 'Never have we had before us such certain proof of the incorrigible stupidity of reviewers. [ . . . ] Ever since Jane Austen became famous they have been hissing inanity in chorus' (*E* 3.268). Noting her position as one of the most tightly controlled and exemplary figures of literary biography, Woolf asserts that

> Of all writers Jane Austen is the one, so we should have thought, who has had the least cause to complain of her critics. Her chief admirers have always been those who write novels themselves, and from the time of Sir Walter Scott to the time of George Moore she has been praised with unusual discrimination. (*E* 3.268)

In asserting her position as literary favourite, Woolf prioritises the early Victorian Jane Austen over her later popular iterations, and slyly implies the impartiality of her own previous criticism. Interestingly, Woolf's overall acceptance of the family version of Austen means that she accepts Mary Augusta Austen-Leigh's assertions concerning Jane's domestic happiness unquestioningly, but is highly resistant to her attempts to situate her more firmly with the political life of her times. The biography is innovative in emphasising the wider Austen family's connections to India and Warren Hastings via Jane's aunt Philadelphia Austen, the French Revolution (the husband of Philadelphia's daughter Eliza was a French aristocrat, guillotined in 1794), as well as Jane's strong interest in the Navy, which employed two of her brothers, thus introducing a key argument of modern feminist interpretations of Austen's life, which frequently assert that she 'was deeply involved in, and cognisant of, the major ideological debates of her time'.[49] However, Woolf strongly resists this more worldly writer and ridicules Austen-Leigh's widening of Austen's English horizon:

> It is, therefore, undeniable that Jane Austen might have 'indulged in romantic flights of fancy with India and France for a background', but it is equally undeniable that Jane Austen never did. Yet it is difficult to deny that had she been not only Jane Austen but Lord Byron and Captain Marryat into the bargain her works might have possessed merits which, as it is, we cannot truthfully say that we find in them. (*E* 3.269)

Woolf's eagerness to dismiss this construction of Austen rather than explore its potential sees her misquoting Austen-Leigh's hackneyed argument that patriotism, not a lack of awareness of contemporary politics, influenced Austen in setting her novels in the English countryside and suggests the strong hold of Leslie Stephen's apolitical writer on her imagination.

As before, Woolf is most interested in Austen's development as a writer, and settles on the inclusion of the marginal notes that teenaged Jane Austen left in Goldsmith's *History of England* as the biography's only redeeming feature. Although they are 'slight and childish' (*E* 3.269) and say nothing of substance – other than Jane Austen was a reader with a keen sense of humour even at a young age – Woolf utilises these notes to silence both Austen's critics and those who want to reinvent her:

> Only to hear Jane Austen say nothing when the critics have been debating whether she was a lady, whether she told the truth, whether she could read, and whether she had personal experience of hunting a fox is positively upsetting. We remember that Jane Austen wrote novels. It might be worth while for her critics to read them. (*E* 3.270)

This forceful dismissal of biographical speculation makes a memorable last line, even if it could not be further from her own subsequent proceeding: as the rest of this chapter demonstrates, public access to Austen's private and juvenile writings causes her Victorian image to crumble and leads Woolf to re-evaluate even the supposedly static perfection of her novels.

### Jane Austen Practising – Modernism?

*Love and Freindship and Other Early Works*, the first collection of Austen juvenilia, was published in 1922, making it the first substantial addition to Austen's oeuvre since the publication of *Persuasion* roughly 100 years earlier. 'Jane Austen Practising' (*New Statesman*, 1922*)* is thus the first of Woolf's reviews that actually deals with Austen's fiction first and foremost. Yet image and work are so tightly connected that Woolf begins with a tour de force of the biographical myths that have padded and softened Austen into a reassuring maiden aunt:

> All over England for the past ten or twenty years the reputation of Jane Austen has been accumulating on top of us like these same quilts and blankets. The voices of the elderly and distinguished, of the clergy and the squirearchy, have droned in unison praising and petting, capping quotations, telling little anecdotes, raking up little facts. She is the most perfect artist in English literature. And one of her cousins had his head cut off in the French Revolution. [ . . . ] So they pile up the quilts and counterpanes until the comfort becomes oppressive. (*E* 3.331–2)

The fusion of author and work continues throughout the rest of the review: drawing on the contents of Austen's notebook of juvenilia, *Volume the Second*, Woolf instead sketches a portrait of an irreverent and satirical teenager who mocks the literary and social conventions of the day. She indulges in the sense of having unmediated textual access to a more authentic, less heavily edited Jane from 'long before she was the great Jane Austen of mythology' and emphasises the freshness of the manuscripts collected in the volume: 'Nobody (for we may leave Mr Chesterton [the editor] to the end) has been here before us and so we may really read Jane Austen by ourselves for the first time' (*E* 3.332). Woolf's sense of intimacy and delight at the apparent discovery of a private manuscript is the result of strategic editorial decisions: Sutherland observes that none of the 'print editors of the early manuscript notebooks attempt to regulate them for publication to such a degree as to suggest that their proper textual state is print'.[50] Instead, the edition painstakingly replicated the hand-painted watercolour illustrations as well as Austen's mock-solemn dedications, which imperfectly (and thus even more successfully) imitate the appearance of eighteenth-century novels. The choice to preserve Austen's eccentric spelling in the titular short story 'Love and Freindship' heightens the sense of secrecy and transgression: unlike the formal perfection of the novels, this manuscript reveals that in private, even Jane Austen made spelling mistakes.

The juvenilia offers Woolf all the ammunition needed to topple the respectable Aunt Jane of the Victorian tradition. Her impeccable morals and utmost respectability are revealed as little more than myths: Austen's sketches, novelistic fragments and stories burst with illegitimate children, seductions, adultery, and openly selfish, manipulatively fainting heroines and satirise morality and decorum, suffering femininity, and the literature of the period. Most importantly, they allow Woolf to rewrite the narrative of Austen's childhood. No longer set in a sheltered Victorian parsonage and brought up with great care, Austen becomes an eighteenth-century writer again:

> [t]he eighteenth century still persisted. The little Austens had the freedom of the house as no other children would have it for a century at least. Money and marriage would no doubt be jokes in the nursery as they were, much more coarsely, on the stage. And clever children, beginning to laugh at their elders, would in the year 1790 pick up the latest new novel and make fun of its heroine. (*E* 3.332)

No longer a sheltered maiden aunt, Woolf's Austen now shares fully in the adult life of the period; and her raunchy sketches meet with an enthusiastic family audience. Woolf also uses the juvenilia to revisit the myths surrounding the act of writing itself: 'The authoress of these lines had, if not a whole sitting room to herself, some private corner of the common parlour where she was allowed to write without interruption' (*E* 3.333). This encouraging and supportive environment of course differs fundamentally from the discreet and unobtrusive writing idealised by later biographers: although the adult writer may have hidden the minute pages of her novels at the creak of a door, the teenager compiled her manuscripts in volumes and dedicated them to family and friends, writing without censorship or shame.

Woolf's review also offers a literary assessment of Austen's juvenilia. The essay title emphasises its imperfect state, and Todd reads the review as an attempt to gain the upper hand in a critical struggle with her predecessor. However, this neglects the complexity of Austen's well-established perfection on a critical and biographical level: Woolf grapples with this last remaining myth throughout the review, and questions her own impulse to assert the juvenilia's significance because of it. As before, Woolf's review thrives on imagining the writing process behind the finished work. She imagines Austen writing for herself, to fulfil a deep-seated need for creative self-expression: 'She is writing for everybody, for nobody, for our age, for her own; in short, is writing' (E 3.332). Woolf takes the exuberance of 'Love and Freindship' – '[s]pirited, easy, fun, verging with freedom upon sheer nonsense' – as evidence for an effortless composition process involving no struggle and little reflection: 'taking up her pen again she wrote, it is clear, as fast as she could write, and faster than she could spell', 'in the enviable position of having one page to fill and a bubbling fancy capable of filling half a dozen' (E 3.333). Todd reads this passage as further evidence of Woolf's arrogance, 'render[ing] Jane Austen a precocious child and her critic a kindly aunt reporting on her progress'.[51] Yet contrasted with the tight formal control of the mature novels and the negative implications of female 'perfection' as used by Mansfield and Woolf, this spontaneity and lack of attention to detail appear more as a humanising of Austen than a denigration; particularly as Woolf goes on to argue that Austen's fundamental development as a satirist between juvenilia and novels was insignificant. Focusing largely on the more measured social satire of a 'Collection of Letters', Woolf finds evidence of Austen's idiosyncratic impersonality:

> Girls of seventeen [ . . . ] have no fixed point from which they see that there is something eternally laughable in human nature. [ . . . ] But Jane Austen knew it. [ . . . ] Whatever she writes is finished and turned and set in its relation to the universe like a work of art. (E 3.333–4)

Asserting that Austen instinctively knew her proper sphere as a writer – courtship, marriage and society – and readily accepted her limitations in eschewing experiments with other forms, Woolf returns to a self-fulfilling prophecy of perfection that declares the 'Collection of Letters' representative of three volumes of surviving fair copies (themselves likely to have undergone a selection process of some sort). Picturing an infant Austen entering a contract with a fairy godmother – 'She had agreed that if she might rule over that territory she would covet no other' (*E* 3.334) – the review thus promotes a narrative of perfection not unlike that promoted in the family biographies. Woolf acknowledges 'the influence of the quilts and counterpanes' on her judgement:

> But just as we determine to shake ourselves free – and, after all, she was a limited, tart, rather conventional woman for all her genius – we hear a snatch of music. [ . . . ] we are content to listen all day long to Jane Austen practising. (*E* 3.334)

Although Woolf tries to safeguard herself against overpraising the juvenilia, her brief outline suggests a limitation in the opposite direction, as her belief in Austen's status as an entirely apolitical writer remains unchallenged. Austen's mockery of the sentimental heroines of romances and their excessive artificial sensibility reveals a writer who even at a young age was highly critical of unrealistic representations of women, and her novels abound with subtle attacks on patriarchal society: *Pride and Prejudice* satirises contemporary conduct books, *Northanger Abbey* provides a chilling portrait of General Tilney's domestic tyranny and defends novels despite their association with female reading, and *Persuasion* criticises the inherent male bias in literary representations of women.[52] As readers, Douglas Murray suggests, 'we realize how [Austen's] fiction systematically dramatizes the dangers – both physical and psychological – of growing up female in a patriarchal society'.[53] Given this range of potential areas for identification, Woolf's lack of response is puzzling. Jean Long suggests that 'Austen's subtle jabs so resembled Woolf's own that she was oblivious to them'.[54] However, Margaret Kirkham points to the role of biography in obscuring Austen's feminism: 'the received "life" of Jane Austen, together with general ignorance about the development of feminist ideas from the beginning of the eighteenth century, has obscured her importance as a feminist moralist of the age of Enlightenment'.[55] Woolf's patriarchal blind spot for Austen's more radical dimension therefore remains intact: as in 'Jane Austen and the Geese', she strongly rejected attempts to turn Austen into a more political writer.

This reluctance stands out all the more against Woolf's increasing interest in claiming Austen as an important 'lost' Modernist predecessor. 'Jane Austen at Sixty', written in December 1923 as a review of R. W. Chapman's *The Works of Jane Austen* (5 vols, Oxford University Press) for the *Nation & Athenaeum*, represents a turning point in Woolf's engagement with Austen. Woolf substitutes speculative biography and the unwritten proto-Modernist novels of Austen's future for a review of the works at hand, and so casts their author as 'a nineteenth-century caterpillar about to emerge as a modernist butterfly'.[56] In spite of its transformative status, 'Jane Austen at Sixty' is rarely considered as an essay in its own right: even the *Essays of Virginia Woolf* present it as a footnote to the *Common Reader* essay 'Jane Austen', into which Woolf later incorporated it. However, 'Jane Austen at Sixty' deserves to be considered as an independent piece of criticism: while gender and Austen's reputation for feminine perfection had been important factors in Woolf's previous reviews, this is the first of her essays that explicitly addresses their impact on her popularity. Paying the customarily conflicted tribute to Austen's talent – 'of all great writers she is the most difficult to catch in the act of greatness' – Woolf examines the patriarchal and paternalistic dynamics of her well-guarded reputation:

> It would be interesting, indeed, to inquire how much of her present celebrity Jane Austen owes to masculine sensibility; to the fact that her dress was becoming, her eyes bright, and her age the antithesis in all matters of female charm to our own. (*E* 4.155n)

Recalling the enduring image of the serenely smiling young woman of Austen-Leigh's memoir, Woolf suggestively links Austen with a nostalgic retreat to an idealised past of pleasing and presumably anti-feminist women. This chivalric impulse extends even to the editor of these 'splendid', 'authoritative' and 'exquisitely illustrated' volumes (*E* 4.155n), Chapman himself. Kathryn Sutherland argues that '[i]n some senses, Chapman's Austen is chiefly a vehicle for annotation': paradoxically, his patronising editorial approach imitated the process of emending classical texts to "improve" the grammar and style of Austen's novels to the high levels expected from her.[57] Woolf's distrust of the scholarly apparatus and what Sutherland terms the volumes' 'faux-Regency presentation – old-fashioned binding with marbled paper sides, type-facsimile first-edition title-pages' suggest that these too are just another attempt to create a particularly quaint and old-fashioned Austen at the expense of her works.[58]

By dedicating an entire review to the novels which Austen could have written had she not died at forty-two, Woolf sidesteps the question of editorial legacies and substitutes an entirely new and authentic – because fictional – writer. As in 'Jane Austen Practising', Woolf moves beyond asserting Austen's perfection and explores her potential for development:

> Enough attention perhaps has never yet been paid to the novels that Jane Austen did not write. Owing to that peculiar finish and perfection of her art,

we tend to forget that she died at forty-two, at the height of her powers, still subject to all those changes which often make the final period of a writer's career the most interesting of them all. (*E* 4.155n)

This sudden interest in Austen's future is no coincidence: she wrote 'Jane Austen at Sixty' when she herself was forty-one, only a year younger than Austen at the time of her death. While Austen at that age could point to her 'six neat volumes', Woolf was only just establishing a reputation as a Modernist writer, and her diaries show that she saw herself as a writer just discovering how to write: on finishing *Jacob's Room* in July 1922, she wrote that '[t]here's no doubt in my mind that I have found out how to begin (at 40) to say something in my own voice; & that interests me so that I can go ahead without praise' (*D* 2.186). In 'Jane Austen at Sixty', *Persuasion* takes on a prophetic role for Austen's future development, as for Woolf *Jacob's Room* did: 'Jacob was a necessary step, for me, in working free' (*D* 2.208). That Austen was on Woolf's mind during this time is evident from her first sketches for the *Common Reader*: even half a year before the publication of 'Jane Austen at Sixty', she was the first author in a list of potential chapter headings, suggesting Woolf's strong interest in revisiting her.

Austen thus becomes 'a character in whom [Woolf] inscribes some of her own aesthetic and psychological assumptions', as Judith Lee has noted.[59] No longer a woman content within a limited sphere, Woolf's diagnosis of discontent is the last step in a revision of the Victorian Jane Austen into a role model for Woolf herself. Her analysis of *Persuasion* discovers an Austen who is, much like herself, actively experimenting with new ways of fictional representation: its 'peculiar beauty and [ . . . ] peculiar dullness' now lead the critic to argue that 'while we feel that Jane Austen has done this before, and done it better, we also feel that she is trying to do something which she has never yet attempted' (*E* 4.153). Woolf's reading of *Persuasion* combines literary criticism with biographical and psychological conjecture to argue for the novel's deeper emotionality:

> Her attitude to life itself is altered. She is seeing it, for the greater part of the book, through the eyes of a woman who, unhappy herself, has a special sympathy for the happiness and unhappiness of others [ . . . ] There is an expressed emotion in the scene at the concert and in the famous talk about women's constancy which proves not merely the biographical fact that Jane Austen had loved, but the aesthetic fact that she was no longer afraid to say so. Experience, when it was of a serious kind, had to sink very deep, and to be thoroughly disinfected by the passage of time, before she allowed herself to deal with it in fiction. (*E* 4.154)

Woolf's analysis strikes a careful balance between asserting the biographical basis of *Persuasion*'s emotional landscape and maintaining Austen's impersonality as a writer. While Austen's documented flirtation with Tom Lefroy or the mysterious seaside admirer recorded by Cassandra Austen offer a basis for speculation,[60] Woolf focuses on Austen's process of fictionalising life and presumed emotions into art, again aligning her with her own interests in the period. *Persuasion* thus emerges as an intertext for *Mrs Dalloway*, subtly following the character from *The Voyage Out*. Austen's 'strikingly innovative depiction of consciousness in *Persuasion*' appears particularly influential: as a 'simultaneous comprehension of and response to a single moment alive with multiple forces: social interaction, physical location, cultural implications and a flux of bodily and emotional sensations', it suggests an important influence on Woolf's 'tunnelling' structure which merges past and present, interior and exterior world.[61] Although Woolf's criticism here and elsewhere 'largely ignores Austen's story matter', as Morris observes,[62] both novels also explore the consequences of disappointed lovers reuniting, and Mrs Dalloway's party offers an interesting parallel to *Persuasion*'s emotionally charged meeting at a public concert: yet where Austen ultimately reunites her lovers, Woolf allows Peter Walsh a moment's ecstasy but leaves the Dalloways' marriage intact. In Woolf's reading, both texts also share the experience of transforming personal emotions into an impersonal and fictional truth. On writing Septimus's narrative in June 1923, Woolf had questioned

> Am I writing The Hours from deep emotion? Of course the mad part tries me so much, makes my mind squint so badly that I can hardly face spending the next weeks at it. [ . . . ] Have I the power of conveying the true reality? Or do I write essays about myself? (*D* 2.248)

Retrospectively, Austen thus becomes a model of another such transformation of personal experience into impersonal fiction, as in another example of a self-fulfilling prophecy, Woolf projects Anne Elliot's experience onto her author.

Woolf aligns Austen's imagined future with her own life, envisioning that '[s]he would have stayed in London, dined out, lunched out, met famous people, made new friends, read, travelled, and carried back to the quiet country cottage a hoard of observations to feast upon at leisure' (*E* 4.154). Moving between a stimulating life in the capital and a rural retreat, this Austen does not resemble any figure from the various biographies, not least because her income from her novels would have been unlikely to offer complete financial independence with frequent travel. At the core of Woolf's vision of Austen's future is the fiction she would have written: even with more experience of life and her sense of security shaken, Woolf argues that Austen would have continued to explore life akin to her own 'ordinary mind on an ordinary day' (*E* 4.160). Stylistically, likewise, Woolf's predicted developments align Austen with herself: a turn from dialogue and towards interiority would have made her a predecessor to Henry James and psychological realism. Woolf suggests that

> She would have devised a method, clear and composed as ever, but deeper and more suggestive, for conveying not only what people say, but what they leave unsaid; not only what they are, but what life is. She would have stood farther away from her characters, and seen them more as a group, less as individuals. Her satire, while it played less incessantly, would have been more stringent and severe. (*E* 4.155)

In noting the gradual shift of Austen's novels from dialogue to the representation of interior thought, Woolf's speculation is based on perceptive literary criticism: Sutherland similarly notes that '[t]he hybrid idiom of free indirect discourse, [Austen's] particular contribution to the development of the English novel, allowed her to write at the same time from within and from without a character'.[63] Ultimately, however, the future of Austen's writing also expresses Woolf's own interest in conveying the unsaid and 'what life is', 'the central things' (*D* 2.249). 'Jane Austen at Sixty' therefore rewrites the usual pattern of literary tradition: instead of adapting Austen's writing into a more modern form, Woolf remakes Austen into a lost proto-Modernist predecessor. Although the essay ends with an admission of futility – 'Vain are these speculations' (*E* 4.155) – Woolf's acknowledgement of Austen as an important predecessor paves the way for her exalted position in the community of women writers established in *A Room of One's Own*.

### 'What genius, what integrity': Jane Austen and the Woman's Sentence

After the publication of Austen's juvenilia and the revisions of 'Jane Austen at Sixty', Woolf's Austen remains relatively stable. Instead, as a textual collage composed of extracts of the previous essays, the *Common Reader* 'Jane Austen' seeks to reconcile the various personas proposed during the previous decade:

> Charming but perpendicular, loved at home but feared by strangers, biting of tongue but tender of heart – these contrasts are by no means incompatible,

and when we turn to the novels we shall find ourselves stumbling there too over the same complexities in the writer. (*E* 4.146)

Like Austen's oeuvre, which has expanded from 'six neat volumes' to include juvenilia, novel fragments and unwritten novels, her persona has grown beyond the Victorian epitome of feminine perfection introduced in Woolf's first essay to become more complex and multi-dimensional.

The essay completes this informal survey of Austen's writing by investigating her creative method through the novel fragments *Sanditon* and *The Watsons*. With no surviving manuscripts for the published novels and very little information from eyewitnesses, Austen's composition process remains mysterious, yet access to an unrevised novel in an early draft stage finally lets Woolf imagine her at work: '[t]he second-rate works of a great writer are worth reading because they offer the best criticism of his masterpiece. Here her difficulties are more apparent, and the method she took to overcome them less artfully concealed' (*E* 4.149). Woolf's change of pronouns once again reminds the reader of Austen's anomalous canonical status. The fragments reveal deletions and paragraph substitutions and dispel all lingering myths by showing that not '[e]very thing came finished from her pen'. Most of all, they reveal the extensive revision that must have gone into the published novels:

> To begin with, the stiffness and bareness of the first chapters prove that she was one of those writers who lay their facts out rather badly in the first version and then go back and back and back and cover them with flesh and atmosphere. (*E* 4.149)

Fully breaking with the Victorian tradition of a ladylike writer who intuitively and effortlessly created works of perfection, Woolf professionalises Austen's writing by turning it into a serious endeavour requiring hard work and failure. As novelists, they now see eye to eye: again, Woolf uses her newly gained insight to strengthen the similarities between Austen and herself. The novel fragments, 'outwardly trivial' and flawed, link Austen's 'pages of preliminary drudgery' (*E* 4.149) with Woolf's own 'devil of a struggle' (*D* 2.249) in writing *Mrs Dalloway*. Again, Woolf retrospectively aligns Austen's method in fiction with her own:

> Jane Austen is thus a mistress of much deeper emotion than appears upon the surface. She stimulates us to supply what is not there. What she offers is, apparently, a trifle, yet is composed of something that expands in the reader's mind and endows with the most enduring form of life scenes which are outwardly trivial. (*E* 4.149)

It is no coincidence that Wolfgang Iser chose this quotation to illustrate the process at the core of reader response theory:[64] Woolf's analysis of Austen shows how her restraint in writing invites readers to engage with the text and supply its deeper meaning. Austen's ability to evoke strong emotional responses by means of ordinary life provides an example for Woolf's quest for 'deep emotion' (D 2.248) in *Mrs Dalloway*. While Woolf's ultimate solution, to 'dig out beautiful caves behind my characters; I think that gives exactly what I want; humanity, humour, depth' (D 2.263), differs from the form of Austen's novels, it achieves a similar purpose in supplying ordinary life with deep imaginative meaning. This discussion of Austen's failures and methods demonstrates how radically Woolf had revised her image since the 1913 essay; however, vestiges of Victorian legacies become apparent whenever Woolf attempts to characterise the woman, not the writer. In addition to her previously discussed resistance to a politically invested Austen, her brief character sketch assumes a moralistic tone not too far from that of the family biographies and Leslie Stephen's *Dictionary of National Biography* entry: 'the wit of Jane Austen has for partner the perfection of her taste', and '[i]t is against the disc of an unerring heart, an unfailing good taste, an almost stern morality, that she shows up those deviations from kindness, truth, and sincerity which are amongst the most delightful things in the English language' (E 4.152). Linking this moral dimension to 'the depth, the beauty, the complexity of her scenes', Woolf thus retains the fundamental fusion of personal virtue and literary value that is characteristic of the Victorian Austen.

While the *Common Reader* consolidates Woolf's Austen by reconciling her complexities, *A Room of One's Own* universalises her position as proto-Modernist predecessor to foremother of women's writing. Woolf has come full circle, beginning and ending with an exemplary woman writer, but Austen has been transformed from a representative of a limiting Victorian ideal of femininity into the originator of the woman's sentence. However, this heavily symbolical Austen also loses the more distinctive personality she had acquired from 'Jane Austen Practising' onwards: as idealised representative of all women, Woolf streamlines her image to facilitate her integration into a community of women writers.

The history of women's writing in chapter 4 of *A Room of One's Own* revolves around the Victorian household and three of Woolf's four great novelists are Victorians, yet Austen undoubtedly belongs to a culture and generation that predates the Brontës and George Eliot. Woolf subtly covers Austen's previously asserted origins in the eighteenth century and aligns her with a later, firmly Victorian period. In an otherwise baffling change from the manuscript version's 'tomb of Aphra Behn' (W&F 100), she suggests that 'Jane Austen should have laid a wreath upon the grave of Fanny Burney' (*AROO* 60), acknowledging Burney's influence on Austen, but obscuring both the inconvenient fact that Burney survived Austen by twenty-three years as well as Austen's multiple literary tributes to her.[65] Likewise, although Woolf's close reading of the juvenilia had uncovered the freedom and supportiveness of Austen's eighteenth-century childhood home, in *A Room of One's Own*, Woolf returns to Austen-Leigh's famous anecdote of Austen's secretive composition habits to illustrate middle-class women's lack of privacy:

> [M]ost of the work must have been done in the general sitting-room, subject to all kinds of interruptions. She was careful that her occupation should not be suspected by servants or visitors or any persons beyond her own family party. (*AROO* 60–1)

Austen therefore once again becomes both the representative and the ideal of the Victorian woman writer: deprived of space and limited to an education in 'people's feelings' and 'personal relations' (*AROO* 61), she is nevertheless perfectly adapted to her situation and transcends these obstacles in her writing. Again, she has to undergo some editing to achieve this serenity. Isaac Gewirtz draws attention to one particularly significant deletion on the proofs of *A Room of One's Own*:

> 'If a woman wrote, she would have to write in the common sitting-room. And **though it must always be difficult to write in the common sitting-room with people going in and out,** still it would be easier to write prose and fiction there than to write poetry or a play. Less concentration is required. **One would not lose one's temper so violently if interrupted.** Jane Austen wrote like that to the end of her days' (Proof, 100–101). Woolf cannot know that Austen would have lost her temper violently had she written poetry instead of fiction. Note that Woolf says 'so violently,' implying that Austen must have lost her temper at least a little when she was writing her novels.[66]

Woolf's assumption of anger seems insignificant compared to the more extensive speculation of 'Jane Austen at Sixty', but again highlights the subtle manipulation required to uphold Austen's idealised status. With Charlotte Brontë disqualified by just this kind of unbecoming anger and George Eliot and Emily Brontë by their choice of uncongenial medium, Austen emerges as the only successful novelist of the four and the ideal of the woman writer:

> I could not find any signs that her circumstances had harmed her work in the slightest. That, perhaps, was the chief miracle about it. Here was a woman about the year 1800 writing without hate, without bitterness, without fear, without protest, without preaching. (*AROO* 61)

Both impersonal and distinctly female, Austen's impersonality, alternately cursed and praised by Woolf, returns as a marker of excellence. In 'Jane Austen Practising', Woolf had applauded Austen for transforming personal snubs into universal satire, but now expands this to patriarchal society as a whole. Jean Long notes that 'it is odd that not a word of Austen's prose is quoted by Woolf to illustrate its perceived faultlessness' yet this comes as no surprise given her previous approach.[67] Here as elsewhere, Austen's prose loses out against biographical speculations about its composition process. However, this need not be an automatic devaluation of Austen's novels: the afterlife of the 'awkward break' of Charlotte Brontë's writing shows that that approach is not without its own dangers. By focusing on an intangible quality that exists independent of subject matters, Woolf sidesteps the well-established discussion of Austen's limited sphere – the 'little bit (two inches wide) of ivory' – and places her with Shakespeare in the first ranks of English literature.

In her abstract impersonality and idealisation, Woolf's Jane Austen bears an uncanny resemblance to her relative of the family biographies: there too, 'it was in the nature of Jane Austen not to want what she had not. Her gift and her circumstances matched completely' (*AROO* 62). Again, Woolf's edits are revealing: the proofs' 'Jane Austen *was so perfectly adapted that she never wanted* what she had not' alerts us that this was a process (conscious or not) instead of the perfect organic match the final version suggests.[68] At the core of Woolf's argument is therefore a return to patriarchal uses of Austen: not only does Woolf approve of Austen's ideological conformity, she also uses her to censure a more rebellious writer like Charlotte Brontë whose nature is less fortunately matched with her age. This paradox, and the question of Austen's conscious adaptation to external expectations haunts Woolf's argument and resurfaces throughout the passage:

> What genius, what integrity it must have required in the face of all that criticism, in the midst of that purely patriarchal society, to hold fast to the thing as they saw it without shrinking. Only Jane Austen did it and Emily Brontë. [ . . . ] They wrote as women write, not as men write. (*AROO* 68)

Although Woolf refrains from the more explicit Modernist re-alignment of her previous articles, Austen's absolute imperviousness to misogynist criticism here functions as a stand-in for Woolf's own. She recalls the pervasive sexism facing any woman writer, 'that persistent voice, now grumbling, now patronising, [ . . . ]; admonishing them [ . . . ] to keep within certain limits which the gentleman in question thinks suitable – " . . . female novelists should only aspire to excellence by courageously acknowledging the limitations of their sex"' (*AROO* 68). Revealing that this, 'rather to your surprise', is a contemporary review, the full quotation, taken from Desmond MacCarthy's journal *Life and Letters*, explicitly aligns Woolf and Austen in their acceptance of feminine 'limitations':

> If, like the reporter, you believe that female novelists should only aspire to excellence by courageously acknowledging the limitations of their sex (Jane Austen *and, in our own time, Mrs Virginia Woolf*, have demonstrated how gracefully this gesture can be accomplished). (*AROO* 68n; see also 111 n13, my emphasis)

Again, Woolf's edits reveal that integrity in the face of misogyny is a conscious and complicated process of adaptation: she only removed the explicit reference to her own fiction at the proof stage.[69]

MacCarthy thus joins the many critics who extol Austen's virtuous acceptance of her limitations, but this backhanded compliment also recalls Katherine Mansfield's review of *Night and Day*, 'Miss Austen up to date'.[70] However, Woolf now responds with the knowledge of her powers as a writer, rejecting MacCarthy's sexism but embracing the comparison with Austen: 'I was amused to find that when Rebecca West says "men are snobs" she gets an instant rise out of Desmond; so I retorted on him with the condescending phrase used about women novelists "limitations" in Life & Letters' (*D* 3.195). The reappearance of MacCarthy's review in *A Room of One's Own* as well as Woolf's repeated ironical references to Rebecca West's 'arrant feminism' (*AROO* 32, 53) condemn his misogyny as part of a fundamentally patriarchal literary establishment; and Woolf's celebration of Austen's imperviousness to such attacks also asserts her own sense of resistance. By making Austen the originator of the woman's sentence, Woolf not only embraces her own literary heritage, she also presents a history of women's writing that culminates in her own work. Woolf traces Austen's literary innovation, the 'perfectly natural, shapely sentence proper for her own use' to a more generalised future of female writing:

> The novel alone was young enough to be soft in her hands – another reason, perhaps, why she wrote novels. Yet who shall say that even now 'the novel' (I give it inverted commas to mark my sense of the word's inadequacy), who shall say that even this most pliable of all forms is rightly shaped for her use? No doubt we shall find her knocking that into shape for herself when she has the free use of her limbs; and, providing some new vehicle, not necessarily in verse, for the poetry in her. (*AROO* 70)

The ambiguity of Woolf's pronouns allows a seamless transition from Austen to the women writers of the future, achieving a sense of community across literary periods and genres. Yet her musings on the future of women's poetry also point towards *The Waves*, already gestating as *The Moths*: Woolf's 'abstract mystical eyeless book: a playpoem' (*D* 3.303) suggests that at the centre of women's writing is Woolf herself, taking on Austen's legacy and carrying it into the future.

## 'The Coarseness of Jane Austen': The Sexual Life of Women

Although she is not 'one of the obscure women of the past, of whom I wish I knew more' (*AROO* 97), Woolf's engagement with Austen nevertheless thrives on the discovery of private manuscripts, literary fragments and letters which had been suppressed by her family to preserve the image of a domestic saint. Woolf's slow recovery of a multi-dimensional Austen is therefore exactly the rewriting of history which she encouraged her female audience in *A Room of One's Own* to perform. Yet having transformed an oppressive Victorian legacy into a mystical feminist foremother, Woolf's interest in Austen quickly waned: *A Room of One's Own* is her last substantial piece of writing on Austen, and subsequent comments suggest that Woolf struggled to find much use for a figure who, in spite of all revisions, signalled a ladylike decorum and lack of political engagement.

In the spirit of 'Jane Austen at Sixty', Woolf's letters provide an insight into what her own unwritten essays on Austen might have looked like. Her epistolary discussions of Austen continue to free her from Victorian legacies by re-examining her gentility and character, which had previously resisted attacks. In a 1936 note to Austen's editor R. W. Chapman, Woolf writes that 'I have often thought of writing an article on the coarseness of J.A. The people who talk of her as if she were a niminy piminy spinster always annoy me. But I suppose I should annoy them' (*L* 6.87). Given the context, it is plausible that Woolf's article would have drawn on Austen's letters as evidence for her claims, particularly as one such review had already been attributed to her. The front-page review of the two volumes of letters, written by E. M. Forster, was published in the *Times Literary Supplement* in 1932, and laments Austen's lost gentility and criticises the 'catalogues of trivialities' assembled in the two volumes:

> In the letters, how Miss Austen's occasional comments on expectant motherhood do jar! She faces the facts, but they are not her facts, and her lapses of taste over carnality can be deplorable, no doubt because they arise from lack of feeling. She can write, for instance, and write it as a jolly joke, that

'Mrs. Hall of Sherborne was brought to bed yesterday of a dead child, some weeks before she expected, owing to a fright. I suppose she happened unawares to look at her husband.' Did Cassandra laugh? Probably, but all that we catch at this distance is the whinnying of harpies.[71]

Forster's horror and disappointment are palpable: the letters destroy all illusions of Austen's gentility and virtue, they revel in local gossip and daily life instead of offering serious discussion of literature, and record the troubles and tribulations of women's lives in the early nineteenth century with cynicism and no illusions. As Forster's review was misattributed to Woolf by several acquaintances, she defends the letters all the more forcefully for the insights into Austen's character they offer. Thus, she writes to Ethel Smyth that

> I bought Jane Austen, and find as I suspected that the man or woman is entirely flatly and absolutely wrong, and that the Austen letters are so important and interesting that I fear I shall have to write about them one of these days myself [ . . . ] What I shall proceed to find out, from her letters, when I've time, is why she failed to be much better than she was. Something to do with sex, I expect; the letters are full of hints already that she suppressed half of her in her novels – Now why? (L 5.127)

Woolf's question finds an obvious answer in Forster's misogynist attack on the 'whinnying of harpies': her exploration of Austen and sex would likely have come to the conclusion that Austen employed self-censorship because, like the narrator of 'Professions for Women', she knew 'what men will say of a woman who speaks the truth about her passions' (E 6.482).

Ultimately, Woolf's exploration of Austen's half-suppressed coarseness was never written. Coming shortly after the 'pivotal' early months of 1931 identified by Alice Wood and the conception of 'an entire new book [ . . . ] about the sex life of women: to be called Professions for Women perhaps' (D 4.6), it matches the focus of her early planning stages.[72] However, Woolf's increasing interest in the interconnections between patriarchy and fascism, feminism and pacifism, clearly found little to relate to in a writer she continued to view as entirely apolitical. Jean Long notes that Austen's 'anger and her means of inoffensively leaching it out through irony, were of diminishing use to Woolf since they only mirrored her own, and confined her inside the decorously limited world in which she had grown up'.[73] Woolf's increasing politicisation, and Austen's lack of purchase in her last decade as a writer are borne out in one of the few remaining allusions to her:

> If Jane Austen had lain as a child on the landing to prevent her father from thrashing her mother, her soul might have burnt with such a passion

against tyranny that all her novels might have been consumed in one cry for justice

she speculated in the second *Common Reader* essay on 'Mary Wollstonecraft' (*E* 5.472). Woolf's anecdote is apocryphal, but shows that Austen has no place in *Three Guineas*, or its increasingly polarised world. Austen remained a model of successful adaptation to patriarchal society, and, from Woolf's vantage point, more antiquated than ever before.

## Notes

1. Maitland, p. 475.
2. Unlike most of the other critics cited in this chapter, who focus on Woolf and Austen's engagement with the courtship novel, Morris convincingly argues that both writers are linked by their scepticism towards idealism, and promote a more egalitarian view of the relationship between people, things and the physical and social world, thereby expanding our understanding of what is representable in fiction. Pam Morris, *Jane Austen, Virginia Woolf and Worldly Realism* (Edinburgh: Edinburgh University Press, 2017), p. 55.
3. Jane de Gay, *Virginia Woolf's Novels and the Literary Past* (Edinburgh: Edinburgh University Press, 2006), p. 25; Kathryn Simpson, 'Persuading Rachel: Woolf and Austen's "Little Voyage of Discovery"', in *Virginia Woolf and Heritage*, ed. by Jane de Gay, Tom Breckin and Anne Reus (Clemson, SC: Clemson University Press/Liverpool University Press, 2017), pp. 141–7 (p. 142); Nick Smart similarly argues for Woolf's continued engagement with Austen in *The Voyage Out* in '"Never see Rachel again": Virginia Woolf and the End of Domestic Fiction', in *Voyages Out, Voyages Home: Selected Papers from the Eleventh Annual Conference on Virginia Woolf*, ed. by Jane de Gay and Marion Dell (Clemson, SC: Clemson University Digital Press, 2010), pp. 62–69.
4. Jean Long, 'The Awkward Break: Woolf's Reading of Brontë and Austen in A Room of One's Own', *Woolf Studies Annual*, 3 (1997), 76–94.
5. Todd, p. 113.
6. Cheryl A. Wilson, *Jane Austen and the Victorian Heroine* (Basingstoke: Palgrave Macmillan, 2017), pp. 9; 127–9, quotation on p. 127.
7. Simpson, p. 142.
8. Wilson, p. 24.
9. Hermione Lee, *Virginia Woolf's Nose: Essays on Biography* (Princeton, NJ: Princeton University Press, 2005), p. 65.
10. Jane Austen and Edward Hugessen Knatchbull-Hugessen Brabourne, *Letters of Jane Austen. Edited, with an Introduction and Critical Remarks* (London: R. Bentley, 1884), p. xii <http://archive.org/details/lettersofjaneaus01austuoft> (accessed 27 September 2021).

11. Juliette Wells notes that this attribution, though established, is entirely speculative and disregards the possibility of Cassandra Austen's involvement in the commemoration of her sister. 'A Note on Henry Austen's Authorship of the "Biographical Notice"', *Persuasions: Journal of the Jane Austen Society of North America*, 38.1 (2017), <http://jasna.org/publications-2/persuasions-online/vol38no1/wells/> (accessed 3 July 2020).
12. Henry Austen, 'Biographical Notice of the Author', in *A Memoir of Jane Austen and Other Family Recollections*, ed. by Kathryn Sutherland (Oxford: Oxford University Press, 2008), pp. 135–41 (pp. 137 and 141).
13. Austen, p. 141.
14. Austen, p. 140.
15. Kathryn Sutherland, 'Introduction', in *A Memoir of Jane Austen and Other Family Recollections* (Oxford: Oxford University Press, 2008), pp. xiii–xlviii (p. xxv).
16. Sutherland quoted by Wilson, p. 21.
17. Larger omissions from this narrative are Austen's mentally disabled brother George, her brother Henry's bankruptcy as well as two brief romantic attachments which did not conclude in marriage. See Joanne Shattock, 'Jane Austen and George Eliot: Afterlives and Letters', *George Eliot Review: Journal of the George Eliot Fellowship*, 34 (2003), 7–20 (p. 13); Kathryn Sutherland, 'Introduction', p. xv.
18. James Edward Austen-Leigh, *A Memoir of Jane Austen and Other Family Recollections*, ed. by Kathryn Sutherland (Oxford: Oxford University Press, 2008), pp. 70–71, quotations on pp. 70 and 72.
19. Kathryn Sutherland, *Jane Austen's Textual Lives: From Aeschylus to Bollywood* (Oxford: Oxford University Press, 2005), p. 86.
20. Emily Auerbach, 'Searching for Jane Austen: Restoring the "Fleas" and "Bad Breath"', *Persuasions: The Jane Austen Journal*, 27 (2005), 31–8 (pp. 34–6, quotation on p. 33).
21. Bank of England, '£10 Note', 2020 <http://www.bankofengland.co.uk/banknotes/polymer-10-pound-note> (accessed 6 July 2020).
22. Margaret Kirkham, 'The Austen Portraits and the Received Biography', in *Jane Austen: New Perspectives*, Women & Literature series (New York and London: Holmes & Meier, 1983), pp. 29–38 (p. 29).
23. James Edward Austen-Leigh, p. 192.
24. William Austen-Leigh was the son of James Edward Austen-Leigh and therefore Jane Austen's grand-nephew; Richard Arthur was the son of his brother Cholmeley and thus Austen's great-grand-nephew. Neither ever met Jane Austen, as she died several decades before their births.
25. Deirdre Le Faye considers it 'the first proper biography' because it combines all information, anecdotes and letters previously held by the different branches of the Austen family. 'Introduction', in *Selected Letters*, by Jane Austen (Oxford: Oxford University Press, 2004), pp. ix–xxxv (p. xi).
26. See Wilson, pp. 203–5.
27. Elizabeth Gaskell, *The Life of Charlotte Bronte* (Oxford: Oxford University Press, 2009), pp. 273–75.
28. Wilson, p. 4; de Gay, *Virginia Woolf's Novels and the Literary Past*, p. 25.
29. Leslie Stephen, 'Austen, Jane', *Dictionary of National Biography Archive*, 1885 <https://doi.org/10.1093/odnb/9780192683120.013.904>

30. Leslie Stephen, 'Humour.', *The Cornhill Magazine*, 33.195 (1876), 318–26 (p. 324).
31. Stephen, 'Humour.', p. 325.
32. Rose O'Malley, 'Sororal Generations: Fanny Price's Sister Strategy', *Nineteenth Century Gender Studies*, 14.3 (2018) <http://ncgsjournal.com/issue143/omalley.html> (accessed 12 November 2021).
33. Morris, p. 141.
34. Ibid.
35. Stephen, 'Humour.', pp. 324–5.
36. Wilson, p. 21.
37. Simpson, p. 144.
38. Simpson, p. 146.
39. De Gay, *Virginia Woolf's Novels and the Literary Past*, pp. 24–33; quotation on p. 31.
40. Christine Blouch, 'Eliza Haywood and the Romance of Obscurity', *Studies in English Literature, 1500–1900*, 31.3 (1991), 535–52 (p. 536). Blouch also notes that Whicher, although mistaken about Haywood's marriage to a clergyman, remained the main biographical source for Haywood scholars throughout the century (p.536), making his claim to 'a contribution to knowledge worthy of publication' (preliminary pages, quoted in *E* 2.23) more plausible than Woolf gives him credit for.
41. Fernald, p. 95.
42. Paula R. Backscheider, 'Haywood [Née Fowler], Eliza (1693?–1756), Author and Actress', *Oxford Dictionary of National Biography* <https://doi.org/10.1093/ref:odnb/12798> (accessed 13 July 2020).
43. Todd, p. 111; James Edward Austen-Leigh, p. 147.
44. Susan Hudson Fox, 'Woolf's Austen/Boston Tea Party: The Revolt against Literary Empire in Night and Day', in *Virginia Woolf: Emerging Perspectives*, ed. by Mark Hussey, Vara Neverow, and Jane Lilienfeld (New York: Pace University Press, 1994), pp. 259–65 (p. 260).
45. De Gay, *Virginia Woolf's Novels and the Literary Past*, pp. 49–51.
46. Katherine Mansfield, 'A Ship Comes Into The Harbour', *The Athenaeum*, 21 November 1919, p. 1227.
47. Mansfield.
48. Mary Augusta Austen-Leigh, *Personal Aspects of Jane Austen* (London: John Murray, 1920).
49. Hermione Lee, *Virginia Woolf's Nose*, p. 75.
50. Kathryn Sutherland, *Jane Austen's Textual Lives*, p. 211.
51. Todd, p. 115.
52. Emily Auerbach, *Searching for Jane Austen* (Madison: University of Wisconsin Press, 2004), p. 142; Miriam Rheingold Fuller, '"Let me go, Mr. Thorpe; Isabella, do not hold me!": Northanger Abbey and the Domestic Gothic', *Persuasions: The Jane Austen Journal*, 32 (2010), 90–104; Chapter 5 of *Northanger Abbey* consists almost entirely of the narrator's defence of the novel, see also Long, pp. 87–9.
53. Douglas Murray, '"She could not repent her resistance": *Northanger Abbey* and the #MeToo Movement', *Nineteenth Century Gender Studies*, 16.2 (2020), para. 4.
54. Long, p. 88.

55. Kirkham, p. 32.
56. Todd, p. 116.
57. Kathryn Sutherland, *Jane Austen's Textual Lives*, p. 45.
58. Kathryn Sutherland, *Jane Austen's Textual Lives*, p. 36.
59. Judith Lee, '"Without hate, without bitterness, without fear, without protest, without preaching": Virginia Woolf Reads Jane Austen', *Persuasions: Journal of the Jane Austen Society of North America*, 12 (1990), 111–16 (p. 111); Morris makes a similar observation, p. 55.
60. Hermione Lee, 'Jane Austen Faints', in *Virginia Woolf's Nose: Essays on Biography*, pp. 67–9.
61. Morris, pp. 163, 164.
62. Morris, p. 30.
63. Kathryn Sutherland, *Jane Austen's Textual Lives*, p. 174; Austen's use of free indirect discourse remains an important aspect in modern analysis of her work, see, for example, Laura Mooneyham White and Carmen Smith, 'Discerning Voice through *Austen Said*: Free Indirect Discourse, Coding, and Interpretive (Un)Certainty', *Persuasions: The Jane Austen Journal On-Line*, 37.1 (2016) <http://www.jasna.org/publications/persuasions-online/vol37no1/white-smith/> (accessed 8 March 2018); Mary Beth Tegan, 'Training the Picturesque Eye: The Point of Views in Jane Austen's Persuasion', *The Eighteenth Century*, 58.1 (2017), 39–58; Rebecca Richardson, 'Dramatizing Intimacy: Confessions and Free Indirect Discourse in Sense and Sensibility', *ELH*, 81.1 (2014), 225–44.
64. Wolfgang Iser, 'The Reading Process: A Phenomenological Approach', *New Literary History*, 3.2 (1972), 279–99 (p. 280).
65. Woolf neglects the fact that Austen's novels do pay tribute to Frances Burney's early work: *Pride and Prejudice* (1813) in particular borrows its title from a passage in Burney's *Cecilia, or Memoirs of an Heiress* (1782) and shares important thematic concerns such as family pride and undesirable marriages; and in *Northanger Abbey*, Austen's defence of the novel singles out Burney's contributions to the genre. See also Claire Harman, *Fanny Burney: A Biography* (London: Harper Collins Publisher, 2000), pp. 268–9.
66. Bolded as in the original to indicate the deleted sentences. Isaac Gewirtz, '"With anger and emphasis": The Proof Copy of A Room of One's Own', *Woolf Studies Annual*, 17 (2011), 1–76 (p. 16).
67. Long, p. 90.
68. Gewirtz, p. 58.
69. Gewirtz, p. 59.
70. Jane Goldman plausibly argues that Woolf's spat might have been with *Life and Letter*'s regular reviewer, Peter Quennell, whose (signed) review of *A Room of One's Own* concedes that 'the reviewer was horrified to see quoted there, amid acid commentary, a sentence, part of an anonymous criticism, which he remembers having contributed last year to the columns of *Life and Letters*. [ . . . ] And yet, curiously enough, my unhappy sentence was inspired by a wholehearted admiration of Mrs Woolf!' However, Quennell and MacCarthy's belief in the intellectual limitations of women is representative of the generally misogynist slant of the magazine. 'Desmond MacCarthy, Life and Letters (1928–35), and Bloomsbury

Modernism', in *The Oxford Critical and Cultural History of Modernist Magazines, Volume I: Britain and Ireland 1880–1955*, ed. by Peter Brooker and Andrew Thacker (Oxford: Oxford University Press, 2009), pp. 428–52 (pp. 442–451 (quotation on pp. 446–7)); Mansfield.
71. E. M. Forster, 'Miss Austen and Jane Austen', *The Times Literary Supplement* (London, 10 November 1932), No. 1606 edition, p. 821; 'E. M. Forster on the Letters of Jane Austen - Then and Now, 1932', <https://www.the-tls.co.uk/articles/public/e-m-forster-jane-austen/> (accessed 8 March 2018).
72. Alice Wood, p. 32.
73. Long, p. 92.

Chapter 3

# 'Even a lady sometimes raises her voice': Mary Russell Mitford and Elizabeth Barrett Browning

In 1920, Virginia Woolf archly summarises the life of nineteenth-century woman of letters Mary Russell Mitford (1787–1855): 'Her loves were vegetable, and her lanes were shady' (*E* 3.211). Twenty-five years earlier, the *Dictionary of National Biography* had credited Mitford with laying 'the foundation of a branch of literature hitherto untried' with *Our Village*, a collection of sketches of rural life, yet now, the wish of the narrator of *A Room of One's Own* has come true: 'the homes and haunts of Mary Russell Mitford [have been] closed to the public for a century at least' (*AROO* 42).[1] Yet Woolf's review, ominously entitled 'An Imperfect Lady', challenged Mitford's rural idyll by centring on the figure of her emotional and financially abusive father, an experience she shared with her friend (and erstwhile protégée) Elizabeth Barrett Browning (1806–61), convicted 'of some complicity in the development of modern poetry' by Woolf (*F* 109 n2). Although both women were bestselling canonical writers in their lifetimes, their literary fortunes were waning when Woolf was most drawn to their lives. Woolf's critical attention at once presents a canonical intervention – she advocates for Barrett Browning but condemns Mitford to obscurity – but also sidesteps discussions of their literary merit. Most famously, Woolf is drawn to the life of the spaniel Flush, Mitford's gift to Barrett Browning; yet her earlier reviews of both women's lives and work centre on their shared position as victims of a patriarchal society, 'triply imprisoned by sex, health, and her father' (*E* 5.262), and constitute some of her most sustained journalistic engagement with aspects of the central arguments of *A Room of One's Own* and *Three Guineas*.

Neither woman has been studied extensively in relation to Woolf. Mary Russell Mitford is most commonly acknowledged as the first owner of Flush, while to date, Anna Snaith is the only critic to acknowledge Barrett Browning's fundamental importance to Woolf's thinking in the 1930s.[2] This chapter builds on Snaith's article to argue that both writers played a fundamental role in the development of Woolf's feminism in the 1920s and 1930s. If Woolf's engagement with Austen highlights that biography fundamentally shaped her reception of individual writers, her writing on Mitford and Barrett Browning makes legible the extent to which her fiction and journalism are mutually constitutive projects. An unwelcome series of reviews of Constance Hill's *Mary Russell Mitford and Her Surroundings* (1920) prompts Woolf into articulating the foundations of her New Biography in an intertextual spoof of Mitford's life, while maintaining a critical stance on professional authorship in a patriarchal society that will evolve into *Three Guineas*' interrogation of women writers' involuntary collusion with it. Over the next decade, Mitford's role is taken over by Barrett Browning's more sensational suffering. Woolf builds on the popular stage play *The Barretts of Wimpole Street* (1930) to reintroduce *Aurora Leigh* (1856) and its eloquent discussion of women's place in Victorian society to a wider reading public, but also capitalises on its success with *Flush* (1933). *Flush* is the culmination of Woolf's fictionalising of the blank spaces in Mitford's life, and playfully continues her analysis of patriarchy's desire to dominate women, dogs and servants from Flush's perspective, yet as a text that foregrounds a non-verbal animal's perspective over that of two celebrated writers, it also epitomises how Woolf's interest in her predecessors frequently works to their detriment.

## 'A good daughter': Mary Russell Mitford

Mary Russell Mitford's early career was almost contemporaneous with that of Jane Austen, yet unlike her, she lived and worked well into the Victorian period: both her cultural impact and her literary networks span at least the first half of the nineteenth century. Mitford began to publish poetry in the Regency era, wrote several successful historical tragedies in the 1820s and 1830s, and later worked as an editor. She also cultivated an active network of literary correspondents and frequently mentored younger (male and female) writers.[3] Most importantly, however, she gained international fame as the author of a series of sketches of rural English village life, *Our Village*. Originally written for *Lady's Magazine* in 1822, with 'sales of the magazine increasing dramatically' due to its popularity, five volumes of *Our Village: Sketches of Rural Character and Scenery* were published in 1824, 1826, 1828, 1830 and 1832, and reissued throughout the century.[4]

As with Austen, these volumes gained an independent Victorian afterlife. Mitford's cottage in the village of Three Mile Cross quickly became a popular destination for literary tourists: '[d]istinguished visitors crowded to her cottage. Passing coachmen and post-boys pointed out to travellers the localities in the village described in the book, and children were named after Miss Mitford's village urchins and pet greyhounds'.[5] Cheryl Wilson notes that *Our Village* is situated in a transitional temporal space: it 'both reaches forward to an increasingly industrial Victorian society and back to the Austen novels by which she was inspired' to offer an illusion of a simpler, more stable past.[6] Yet Barbara Onslow defends Mitford from 'a rather unfair reputation for romanticization', arguing that this nationalistically tinged nostalgia for '*Our Village* as rural idyll is as much a construct of later Victorian readings and volume illustrations as it is hers'.[7] Kevin Morrison similarly asserts that the earliest sketches in their original magazine context were 'ambivalently torn between idyll and real world and conflicted about how best to respond to the social turmoil afflicting the English countryside in the 1820s'. Only the later additional volumes of books, reissued with lavish illustrations for a growing middle-class market, 'become invitations to nostalgia' that help shape 'a national consciousness through shared images of rural England'.[8] This phenomenon further intensified towards the end of the century: Mitford's sketches' 'afterlives as a publishing phenomenon' included 'amply illustrated, newly kitschified editions' that became 'props for rituals of homesickness, vehicles securing the continuity of everyday Englishness across cultural divides' for readers throughout the British Empire.

Much like Austen, Woolf's Mitford was therefore a Victorian product – and part of her ancestral literary networks. Anny Thackeray Ritchie edited and introduced a lavishly illustrated edition of *Our Village* in 1893 that, Onslow suggests, 'fixed readers' idea of *Our Village* for generations to come'.[9] In common with other Victorian editions, Ritchie's introduction to the volume locates Mitford firmly in the literary circles of a romanticised past, but her brief sketch of Mitford's life gains poignancy by acknowledging the frequent anxiety and suffering which Dr Mitford caused his daughter.[10] Yet Mitford's Victorian reach is evident in her mentorship of *Cornhill* contributor and subsequent editor James Payn, a college friend and colleague of Leslie Stephen.[11] Payn's memoir *Some Literary Recollections* (1884) offers a drastically different take on Mitford: in spite of poverty and illness, she is a quaint but powerful mentor who 'had considerable influence in the world of letters, which was always at the service of her friends'.[12] Alison Booth notes the detrimental effects of genre and gender on Mitford's afterlife:

> biographical portraiture almost invariably pictured her at home, though the interior of that very small house hardly invited many to linger. Homes and

haunts writing both made Mitford and did her in; [ . . . ] her works and persona were interpreted through the spirit of a genre that matches the locale.[13]

Consequently, contemporary criticism often struggles to locate Mitford near (if not within) the literary canon. Booth argues for Mitford's relevance to modern critics 'as part of the current recovery of successful women writers between Austen and the Brontës'.[14] Mitford was a writer in a transitional period, as Linda Peterson argues: for the first time in literary history, the financial success of the magazine market made professional authorship, male as well as female, possible and profitable.[15] 'But for her father, she would have been rich': Dr Mitford squandered his wife's fortune of £28,000 as well as his daughter's £20,000 winnings in the Irish lottery on 'gambling, speculation, greyhounds, entertaining, and whig [sic] electioneering'.[16] Mitford's professional success was therefore considerably double-edged:

> [s]he told Elizabeth Barrett Browning she was never without 'pecuniary care' pressing on her thoughts last thing at night; waking every morning 'with a dreary sense of pain and pressure'. [ . . . ] Only her parents' needs 'reconcile me to the perpetual labour, the feverish anxieties and the miserable notoriety of such a career'.[17]

Woolf's quip about Mitford's vegetable loves therefore contains a grain of truth: as a self-sacrificing 'Good Daughter' (as another of her reviews was titled), Mitford's life was shaped by her parents' needs. She never married and her father's substantial debts survived him, requiring a subscription organised by friends to be paid off in full.[18]

In Constance Hill's *Mary Russell Mitford and Her Surroundings* (1920), these elements of Mitford's life fade into the background. Hill encourages literary tourism and a nostalgic immersion in the past by glossing over the unpleasant aspects of Mitford's life – her father, poverty and incessant work – and eschews psychological depth: her Mitford resembles the narrator of *Our Village*, always cheerful and radiating 'peace and good-will upon all who surround her'.[19] With chapters organised around various sites of interest, and lengthy extracts from Mitford's sketches and letters merging with Hill's own descriptions, the text encourages readerly immersion: as Wilson notes of the companion volume on Austen, 'to be in "[Mitford]-Land" is to travel, both geographically across England and historically across time'.[20] Highly uncharacteristically, Woolf – in the midst of writing *Jacob's Room* – reviewed this travel-book-cum-biography not just once, but three times in total: first in the *Times Literary Supplement* ('An Imperfect Lady', 6 May), then in the *Daily Herald* ('A Good Daughter', 26 May), and finally in the *Athenaeum* ('The Wrong Way of Reading', 28 May).[21] What is more, all three reviews take distinctly different approaches to *Mary Russell Mitford and Her Surroundings* and therefore offer a sense of a dynamic development in Woolf's engagement with Mitford: although they are all dismissive of the biography (it is as such that Woolf reviews it), they introduce themes ranging from biographical representation and the female canon, money and domestic tyranny, to fiction and veracity in biographical writing. Mitford thus comes to function much like Anny Thackeray Ritchie, Woolf's 'transparent medium' for the nineteenth century, a process which, as Marion Dell notes, ultimately renders the medium invisible: Woolf 'reveals her appreciation by using them, albeit without acknowledgement'.[22]

Woolf's subtle project of effacement begins in the *TLS* review 'An Imperfect Lady' with a sustained attack, which pits her own status as modern novelist and reviewer against Hill's oeuvre of nostalgic female biography:

> [w]e are trying to find out what considerations had weight with Miss Hill when she decided to write *Mary Russell Mitford and her Surroundings*. [ . . . ] In the first place, Miss Mitford was a lady; in the second, she was born in the year 1787. (*E* 3.210)

Given Mitford's current obscurity. Woolf's surprise appears halfway authentic to a modern reader, yet Alison Booth notes that Mitford remained popular well into the 1930s: she therefore presented a sensible choice for the genteel biographer.[23] Woolf's pointed dismissal of Constance Hill's previous works – *Jane Austen: Her Homes and Her Friends* (1902), *Maria Edgeworth and Her Circle in the Days of Buonaparte and Bourbon* (1910), and *Fanny Burney at the Court of Queen Charlotte* (1912), all with (no doubt picturesque) illustrations by Ellen Hill – distances herself from any suspicion of female solidarity with such mass-market productions: in spite of the feminist slant of Woolf's analysis, she does not participate in Hill's nostalgia. This includes a deliberate shift of perspective from the surroundings of Mitford's cottage in Three Mile Cross to the household dynamics inside it, suggesting that in spite of Woolf's well-established interest in literary tourism, gender, not genre, proves the determining factor in her reading of Mitford's life. Indeed, Woolf begins by uncovering Hill's nostalgia as part of a deeply patriarchal project:

> It is undoubtedly because of their reticence that Miss Hill is on the side of the ladies. They sigh things off and they smile things off, but they never seize the silver table by the legs or dash the teacups on the floor. It is in many ways

a great convenience to have a subject who can be trusted to live a long life without once raising her voice. (*E* 3.211)

Class, as Peterson notes, is another determining factor for Mitford's persona and consequently, the success of *Our Village* and Hill's nostalgic project:[24] Mitford may have lived in close proximity to agricultural labourers and indeed in a workman's cottage, but she is the daughter of a gentleman; thus positioned, she can safely interpret the rural population and their customs to her middle-class readers. Like the saintly Jane Austen of the previous chapter, Hill's Mitford never fell in love and lived a quiet country life, an illusion which Woolf is impatient to destroy to recover a more complex biographical subject.

Woolf's review challenges Hill's reading of Mitford's cottage home as merely a picturesque house. Hill describes (via quotations from Mitford) a domestic idyll; a delightful flower-bedecked

> cottage – no – a miniature house, with many additions, little odds and ends of places, pantries, and what not; all angles and of a charming in-and-outness ; [ . . . ] the closets . . . full of contrivances and corner cupboards; [ . . . ] That house was built on purpose to show in what an exceedingly small compass comfort may be packed.[25]

The review takes up this imagery, but offers a tongue-in-cheek reinterpretation of the Homes and Haunts genre:

> Can one be sure that anything not wholly made of mahogany will to the very end stand empty in the sun? Even cupboards have their secret springs, and when, inadvertently we are sure Miss Hill touches this one, out, terrible to relate, topples a stout old gentleman. (*E* 3.211)

Using gothic tropes to introduce the spectre of Dr Mitford, Woolf offers a suggestive and broadly period-appropriate reinterpretation of the Mitford family dynamics. Paralleling Catherine Morland's anticlimactic discovery of an old laundry bill in an imposing Gothic wardrobe, Woolf's imagery borrows from Austen's *Northanger Abbey*, itself derived from Ann Radcliffe's female gothic and its narratives of female imprisonment and persecution. Austen's General Tilney may not have murdered his wife, but he is controlling, irascible and isolates his daughter from female companions; and Woolf similarly established Dr Mitford as a domestic tyrant. Like his gothic counterparts, he 'has gambled and speculated [ . . . ] in old age he has lain upon a sofa and insisted that fresh air is bad for daughters; [ . . . ] dying at lengths, he has left debts that can only be paid by selling everything you have (*E* 3.212). In Woolf's feminist reinterpretation, this history of exploitation and abuse has been absorbed into the domestic spaces Mitford inhabited and bursts forth at the slightest provocation to transform the snug cottage into a gothic prison, and a material witness to the past. Much as, two years later, she would recollect 22 Hyde Park Gate 'tangled and matted with emotion', the Mitfords 'had permeated the whole vast fabric [ . . . ] with [their] family history' (*MoB* 45).

Faced with a biographical subject who refuses to complain about her situation, as well as a biographer who will happily collude with this aim, Woolf subtly incorporates her critique into a superficially comical review. Hill, intent on emotional harmony, suggests that 'Miss Mitford's biographers have justly censured her father's evil courses, some considering him as altogether worthless; but surely there must have been many redeeming qualities in one who called forth such love from such a daughter?'[26] Woolf instead includes Mitford's poignant lament at leaving her cottage, 'It was grief to go; there I had toiled and striven and tasted as deeply of bitter anxiety, of fear, and of hope as often falls to the lot of woman' (*E* 3.212), thus allowing her profound unhappiness to break through the review's comic mode. Yet reminding her readers that '[m]any women have had fathers' (*E* 3.212), Woolf also hints at the wider repercussions of Mitford's suffering. In the *TLS* review, this remains a brief gesture at Mitford's case as symptomatic of nineteenth-century patriarchal society: Woolf joins Mitford and Hill in their lady-like reticence by sighing things off and smiling things off and burying her criticisms in comical brief asides and literary allusions. Using the 'surface manner' of her own Victorian tea-table training, which allowed her 'to slip in things that would be inaudible if one marched straight up and spoke out loud' (*MoB* 152), Woolf smuggles a brief feminist critique past her editor, but ends the review by repeating her attack on Hill's failures as a biographer rather than Dr Mitford's as a father:

> That is the worst of writing about ladies; they have fathers as well as teapots. On the other hand, some pieces of Dr Mitford's Wedgwood dinner service are still in existence [ . . . ] If there is nothing improper in the suggestion, might not the next book be devoted entirely to them? (*E* 3.212).[27]

Woolf's interest in recovering Mitford as a more eloquent biographical subject dominates her next review, more provocatively entitled 'A Good Daughter', in the socialist and reform-oriented *Daily Herald*. Focusing on the interrelation of Mitford's private and public personas, Woolf's review offers a supplement to Hill's

> portrait of an amiable and distinguished lady, who [ . . . ] had presumably an infinity of feelings which are now only to be guessed at. We can scarcely go

wrong if we suppose them to refer in about equal proportions to her father and to her money. (*E* 3.213)

While 'the florid gentleman' (*E* 3.214) remains an easy target for Woolf's detached amusement, her reading of Mitford remains speculative: as the biography is composed 'chiefly by means of quotation' (*E* 3.213), its supreme reticence originates with Mitford. In an echo of her early Austen criticism, Woolf's most detailed discussion of Mitford's work focuses on her perfect presentation in print:

> To be a popular writer in the year 1850 it was very necessary to write well. [ . . . ] Presumably the ordeal of appearing in print was then so severe that no lady went through it without taking pains with her deportment. Jane Austen, moreover, had set the fashion. [ . . . ] The result is that Miss Mitford is still readable – well preserved, as we say of some trim, hale, old spinster who has never been ravaged by passion or lost her figure in bearing children. (*E* 3.214)

Woolf locates Mitford in a vaguely defined past. Both a disciple of Austen and at the peak of her popularity in the 1850s, this shifting temporality transforms her into a ghost of past femininity and reduces her professional achievements to a flawless deportment on paper. Linking Mitford to Austen situates her geographically, socially and canonically: Woolf's 'trim, hale, old spinster' recalls Mitford's own anecdote (via an acquaintance on visiting terms) of Austen as 'the most perpendicular, precise, taciturn piece of "single blessedness" that ever existed' (*E* 2.10). However, Mitford determined to 'copy as closely as I can Nature and Miss Austen, keeping, like her, to genteel country life'.[28] Austen offered a successful model of English pastoral writing, as Wilson notes, and *Our Village* makes this explicit in its first instalment: 'nothing is so delightful as to sit down in a country village in one of Miss Austen's delicious novels, quite sure before we leave to become intimate with every spot and every person it contains'.[29]

Woolf's reflections on early nineteenth-century female authorship echo Anny Thackeray Ritchie's 1893 introduction to *Our Village*. Ritchie's summary of Mitford's life indulges in nostalgia for the loss of ease and certainty that accompany female emancipation:

> The literary ladies of the early part of the century in some ways had a very good time of it. A copy of verses, a small volume of travels, a few tea-parties, a harp in one corner of the room, and a hat and feathers worn to one side, seemed to be all that was wanted to establish a claim to fashion and inspiration. [ . . . ] *They* were dolls perhaps, and lived in dolls' houses; we are ghosts without houses at all; [ . . . ]

> Miss Mitford, notwithstanding all her troubles (she had been known to say she had rather be a washerwoman than a literary lady), had opportunities such as few women can now obtain.[30]

Ritchie's New Woman-influenced sense of disorientation ('We do not belong to the old world any more! The new world is not yet ready for us'[31]) draws attention to the increasing professionalisation of the world of literature over the course of the century and recasts Mitford as an accidental amateur writer, yet like Woolf (and Hill), she is reluctant to acknowledge the full extent of Mitford's literary activities: in a fusion of Ibsen and genre writing, Mitford remains a doll in a doll's house. Mitford not only belonged to the first generation of professional writers, male or female, whose income was solely derived from the literary marketplace, she made a fortune from writing *Our Village* (and lost it to her father). Peterson argues that '[f]or women in the 1830s, as for men, the key aspects of professional authorship were respectable social status, genius or genial wit, and silence about earnings': Mitford therefore functioned as a model woman writer since she 'trumpets neither her earnings nor her father's faults – and hence earns *Fraser's* [*Magazine's*] praise' in a discussion of literary luminaries.[32]

Mitford's skilful adherence to this code of conduct almost certainly influences later representations of her career, such as Hill's biography, Ritchie's retrospective and even Woolf's brief summary: it allows her genteel authorship to be accepted as a matter of course. Where female literary biographies like Gaskell's *Life of Charlotte Brontë* (1857) and Austen-Leigh's *A Memoir of Jane Austen* (1870) focus on the conflicting demands on a woman writer's attention, Mitford's writerly activity can be read as an extension of her daughterly position: because she does not seek independence and her income is never truly hers, it does not challenge patriarchal hierarchies in the way Ritchie implies that later women's writing does. The same logic runs through Hill's representation of Mitford's writing. Only briefly acknowledging that Mitford was the family's main earner, Hill limits her critical evaluation to admiring clichés – 'Miss Mitford's capacity of throwing herself heart and soul into the widely varying subjects upon which she was engaged was truly remarkable'[33] – and instead emphasises the social aspect of Mitford's activities by situating her in the centre of an epistolary network of famous mid-century writers. Additionally, Mitford's writing itself assumes an indeterminate status between public and private: written in a tone which assumes familiarity between reader and narrator, her sketches often revolve around mundane domestic matters like a comically unsuccessful shopping trip to Reading, country rambles with her dogs, or quaint encounters with neighbours, and make a firm distinction between private life and public appearance impossible. Hill adds to this by indiscriminately quoting from Mitford's private correspondence and her various publications, further adding to this apparently complete cohesion between public and private persona. Ultimately, Mitford's literary work therefore appears like a private and personal activity: the actual acts of composition, revision and publication are effaced by the content of her pieces, all differences between personal experience and final publication submerged and Mitford's narration taken at face value.

Woolf's review participates in this making domestic of Mitford's professional activities. This tendency is particularly striking given the general focus on female authorship in a patriarchal society in Woolf's 1920s writing: outside of the flippant reference to the 'ordeal of appearing in print', Mitford's professional self-sufficiency goes largely unremarked in what approaches a retrospective imposition of an amateur status on Mitford. However, as in the previous review, this reorientation towards the private sphere allows Woolf to examine the impact of Dr Mitford's exploitation of his daughter: the well-preserved spinster appearing in print leads inwards to Mitford's drawing room self, a 'sentimental, conservative, impulsive English lady with a deep respect for conventions, property, the classics and the church', before Woolf locates a private Miss Mitford in 'a little room to herself up in the roof'. There, 'she did her accounts, waited for the door to slam, wrote about her greyhounds, and sighed pretty frequently' (*E* 3.214). Countering Mitford's natural outdoors setting, Woolf prioritises the room of one's own as the setting for both self-reflection and literary activity: it allows Mitford to distance herself from the constant demands on her attention by family and literary tourists alike. Yet Woolf also already undermines this logic of retreat by emphasising the impossibility of escaping from external constraints. Anna Snaith argues that

> [c]ontrary to Elaine Showalter's formulation, a room of one's own does not mean withdrawal or exile. It is a liberating private space, an active choice, and, importantly, it is from the room that the woman will gain access to the public sphere through writing.[34]

Mitford's room emphasises the necessity of this element of active choice: neither room, profession, nor income can liberate Mitford from the demands of her father. The review therefore gestures forwards to the more pessimistic analysis of *Three Guineas* in emphasising the impossibility of challenging this system from within. *Our Village* merely helps Mitford 'follow and repeat and score deeper the old worn ruts in which society, like a gramophone whose needle has stuck, is grinding out'

(3G 231): the complete self-sacrifice of the 'Good Daughter' relies on a sense of complete entitlement on the part of Dr Mitford which differs from Woolf's 'infantile fixation' only in its manifestation (3G 258).

'A Good Daughter' only hints at the analysis that *Three Guineas* states outright and explores in greater detail, and ultimately blames Mitford for her lack of rebellion: 'But what is the use of scolding her now? It was none of his fault, she said; had all the gold of Peru been poured into her lap she would not have exchanged him for another' (*E* 3.214). Notably, this is a rephrasing of Mitford's original: 'I would not exchange my father, even though we toiled together for our daily bread, for any man on earth, though he could pour the gold of Peru in my lap' (*E* 3.223 n13), which in its more explicit rejection of a husband offers even more grounds for a Freudian reading, but also – with the Mitfords' loss of home and fortune still two years away – envisions herself toiling alongside her father, not by herself for him. Like 'An Imperfect Lady', 'A Good Daughter' therefore ends in complicity: with the focus squarely on Mitford's willingness to sacrifice herself, Woolf's review complicates the cheerful pastoral of *Mary Russell Mitford and Her Surroundings*, but does not disrupt it.

This only happens in the final review of the three, 'The Wrong Way of Reading', in the *Athenaeum*: more experimental than the preceding two, it breaks almost entirely with the pretence of assessing the merits of *Mary Russell Mitford and Her Surroundings*. Written concurrently with *Jacob's Room*, Woolf's interest in juxtaposing different perspectives on Mitford resembles her approach to characterisation in her novel. On 8 May, she had complained about the onslaught of Mitford reviews: 'Partly [owing] to the horror of writing 1,2,3,4, reviews on end, 3 concerning Mitford too, I've been groaning & grumbling, & seeing myself caged, & all my desired ends – Jacob's Room that is – vanishing down avenues' (*D* 2.35). While each previous review had added at least one carefully extrapolated new perspective on Mitford, 'The Wrong Way of Reading' combines profound meditation on the shortcomings of biography with a fantastical rewriting of Mitford's life. The resulting review reads like a missing link between the exuberant parody of 'Friendship's Gallery' and the more measured approach of *Orlando*. Both nonsensical and a serious commentary that anticipates 'The New Biography', the review demonstrates how productive Woolf's journalistic engagement with bad writing could be: 'the great merit of these scrapbooks, for they can scarcely be called biographies, is that they licence mendacity' (*E* 3.218).

Woolf's parody of Hill begins at the beginning, with the moment of Mitford's birth. Hill had briefly informed her reader that '[h]ere [in

Alresford] it was that [ . . . ] on the 16th December, 1787, Mary, also an only child, was born', but quickly moved from such intimate details to the interior design of the house in which she spent the 'happy happy days' of childhood: 'The breakfast-room . . . was a lofty and spacious apartment literally lined with books, which, with its Turkey carpet, its glowing fire, its sofas and its easy-chairs, seemed, what it indeed was, a very English nest of comfort'.[35] Retaining the subversive use of domestic spaces from her previous reviews, Woolf's retelling parodies the concept of this 'English nest of comfort':

> So Miss Mitford was born in the breakfast room about eight-thirty in a snowy morning between the Doctor's second and third cup of tea. 'Pardon me,' said Mrs Mitford, turning a little pale, but not omitting to add the right quantity of cream to her husband's tea, 'I feel . . . ' [ . . . ] 'Observe,' says Mendacity, 'with what an air the Doctor drinks his tea, and how she, poor lady, contrives to curtsey as she leaves the room.' Tea? I inquire, for the Doctor, though a fine figure of a man, is already purple and profuse, and foams like a crimson cock over the frill of his fine lace shirt. 'Since the ladies have left the room,' Mendacity begins, and goes on to make up a pack of lies with the sole object of proving that Dr Mitford kept a mistress in the purlieus of Reading. (*E* 3.218)

In modelling her brief history of Mitford's birth after Sterne's scandalously explicit *Tristram Shandy*, Woolf provides another rebuttal to Hill's genteel reticence. The grotesque scenario of Mrs Mitford's unflagging attention to her husband – even while giving birth – broadcasts the skewed hierarchies and priorities of a family that sacrificed the health and comfort of its female members to keep the Doctor entertained and in money.

Woolf humorously justifies her invention's factual basis, noting that 'The touch about the cream, for instance, might be called historical, for it is well known that when Mary won £20,000 in the Lottery, the Doctor spent it all upon Wedgwood china' (*E* 3.218). This is another parodic revision of *Mary Russell Mitford and Her Surroundings* that inserts domestic horror into Hill's superficial commentary. The Mitfords' Wedgwood china was commissioned to celebrate Mary winning the Irish lottery on her tenth birthday (Woolf's chronology is therefore strictly not historical). The prize money enabled the family to move from 'dingy' London lodgings to a country house in Reading, yet, as Mitford herself reflected, the china outlasted the fortune considerably:

> In less than twenty years what was left of the produce of the ticket [no. 2224] so strangely chosen? What? except a Wedgwood dinner-service that my father had had made to commemorate the event, with the Irish harp within the

border on one side and his family crest on the other! That fragile and perishable ware outlasted the more perishable money.³⁶

Although Hill acknowledged the emotional significance of the dinner service by including this account in her biography, she is more interested in the tangible link to the past it offers:

> The writer of a graceful article entitled, "In Miss Mitford's Country" which appeared in a magazine several years ago, saw at a friend's house in Reading some odd pieces of this very dinner-service. [ . . . ]
> She supposed [2224] to be the Wedgwoods' private number, and it was not until she came upon the passage just quoted in Miss Mitford's *Recollections of a Literary Life* that the mystery was solved.³⁷

Hill's self-important account renders the service devoid of the subtle irony which Mitford ascribed to it: the mystery of the number 2224 resolved by the assiduous biographer, it fades into insignificance. Woolf, on the other hand, is highly attuned to its emotional significance. In reverting to the Wedgwood china as a witness to the household's skewed dynamics, she draws on a long tradition of Victorian object biographies in reminding her readers that objects 'are nearly always in the process of escaping from consumer cycles of exchange, affixing themselves instead to the identities, memories, affections, and aspirations of the characters they possess'.³⁸ Elaine Freedgood argues that 'from the margins of culture', the Victorian object narrative 'can try on ideas in public that would be scandalous in other generic locations'. Objects

> see and hear that to which traditional human (or humanoid) narrators may not be privy. In these tales, the commodity exerts a certain ownership in that it 'holds' the stories of so many of its owners in reserve; it is a universal heirloom, a keepsake that keeps its owners rather than being kept by them.³⁹

Although Woolf's jug of cream is not an object narrator in a conventional sense, it functions in a similar way: the Wedgwood china regains its original significance as unlikely sole survivor of a profoundly unjust situation, and a witness that continues to speak out over time, imbued with its owners' emotions and memories. Woolf's historical touch therefore reveals the potential inherent in writing the lives 'some pieces of Dr Mitford's Wedgwood dinner service' (*E* 3.212).

The rest of the review follows a similar pattern: Woolf turns Hill's disregard for time, structure and major life events into playful protests against the strict form of traditional biography and parodies Hill's ineptitude in a display of her own skill as a writer and critic. She mimics Hill's haphazard style, and her tendency to introduce largely irrelevant information on the history of buildings, localities or ancient families; while Mendacity's failure to keep an eye on its chronology – 'Poor Mrs Mitford! Twenty-one years ago she left the breakfast-room and no news has yet been received of her child' (*E* 3.219) – is a pointed reference to Hill's failure to do the same for much of her biography, which drifts aimlessly between the 1820s and 1840s. Although these scenes are even funnier where they are matched to elements of Hill's rambling biography, they do not rely on this recognition on the reader's part: by weaving her fictions around the facts of Mitford's life, or at the very least, the facts that Hill assembles in her biography, Woolf is already practising humorously the form she would suggest in earnest in 'The New Biography', an 'amalgamation of rainbow and granite', of fact and fiction.

This parody stretches to include Mitford's sketches as well. Prompted by one of Hill's more tangential digressions, the account of a severe snowstorm that Mitford did not experience, Woolf observes that

> [t]here is something very charming in an ancient snowstorm. The weather has varied almost as much in the course of generations as mankind. The snow of those days was more formally shaped and a good deal softer than the snow of ours, just as an eighteenth-century cow was no more like our cows than she was like the florid and fiery cows of Elizabethan pasture. (*E* 3.219)

The formal snowstorms of Hill's biography are of a piece with Mitford's own well-controlled and regulated landscape, which obligingly supplies her with monthly topics for her sketches and consequently an income, but in 'The Wrong Way of Reading' they function as a further illustration of Hill's shortcomings. Although her biography abounds with natural scenes, she never utilises them beyond the stereotypical evocation of a nostalgic rural past. Paula Maggio notes of the *Common Reader* version of Woolf's essay that it is only one of a series of contributions to a theory on weather articulated in Woolf's non-fiction:

> She maintains that weather and literature are linked in a manner that parallels the symbiotic connection between the human world and the natural world, a view that allows her to disavow the commonly held belief that the two operated within an independent duality.[40]

This playful engagement with *Mary Russell Mitford and Her Surroundings* eventually prompts a serious enquiry into the problems of biography, and particularly the problem of knowing people, which is of central importance to *Jacob's Room*. Woolf relates a condensed version of Hill's 'Chapter V. Lyme Regis', which focuses largely on the King of Saxony's visit to Lyme Regis, where he gathered fossils with Mary Anning and 'an old woman seated herself in the King's coach – was she Mary Mitford?' (*E* 3.220). Since she was not, Woolf concludes that

> [i]n the year 1844 Mary Russell Mitford was fifty-seven years of age, and so far what we know of her is curiously negative; she had not known Mary Anning, she had not found an ichthyosaurus; she had not been out in the snowstorm, and she had not seen the King of France (*E* 3.220).

Blurring the boundaries between philosophical enquiry and bad writing, Woolf uses Hill's ineptitude as a biographer to argue for the fundamental difficulties of a truthful representation of character and mind:

> when we come to say what anyone is like we often find ourselves in Miss Hill's predicament without her excuse and merely reply that an anonymous old woman once sat in the King of Saxony's coach. If this is so with the living, what can we know about the dead? (*E* 3.220)

Woolf's ultimate conclusion is therefore slightly more sympathetic towards Hill's struggles: while the key facts of Mitford's life are known, the fundamental incomprehensibility and inaccessibility of her true character condemn any biographical endeavour to failure. With this conclusion, the review also echoes themes at the heart of *Jacob's Room*. Woolf implicitly demonstrates that 'what [people] are depends on what we are' by presenting multiple points of view on Jacob which nevertheless preserve the central mystery of his being. Linda Martin notes that 'Woolf employs an experimental, externalized mode of narration that cultivates in readers the odd sensation that Jacob is already absent or out of reach, even though he is alive and before our eyes until the very last pages'.[41] Like the anonymous old woman in a coach, the novel's omnibus passengers remain fundamentally unreadable to each other: 'Each had his past shut in him like the leaves of a book known to him by heart; and his friends could only read the title, [ . . . ] and the passengers going the opposite way could read nothing at all' (*JR* 85). Consequently, Woolf cannot bridge the gap between the desire to capture Mitford and the knowledge that it is impossible: 'Poor Miss Mitford – but how "poor Miss Mitford" if we know nothing about her?' (*E* 3.220–1).

Instead, the review ends with a thorough rejection of Mitford as a symbol of English national identity. Shifting the terms of engagement from the nostalgic pastoral of countryside rambles to the stasis of a bestselling literary formula, Woolf offers a brief moment of rebellion on behalf of her subject:

> if we consider what it must be like to sit at the same window, year in, year out, hoping that a dog may trip up an old woman, or that the cobbler's little

girl may break the jug in which she is carrying him his beer in order that the Americans may rejoice in the simplicity of rural England, one feels that to smash the window, strangle the doctor, and hamstring all the ponies in Berkshire would, as they say in novels, be the work of a moment. (*E* 3.221)

Woolf's pointed juxtaposition of the literary realism of *Our Village* and the actual reality of life in Three Mile Cross provides an eloquent commentary on the practice of naïve readers like Constance Hill, who take Mitford's words and images at face value. However, her assumption of Mitford's point of view also suggests the extent to which biography relies on the invention of an interior life which, however plausible, cannot always be verified – given that Mitford's only known revolt lies in the quiet sadness of her letters. The violent disruption of this nostalgic rural idyll through Woolf's imaginary revolt continues her feminist critique of Mitford's life: as Bonnie Kime Scott notes, '[a]s she became increasingly aware of feminist and pacifist standpoints, Woolf grew skeptical of "Englishness" – national identification with a place often used to promote patriarchal and national projects, including war'.[42]

'The Wrong Way of Reading' ends with an image of Mitford in old age, finally living on her own in a book-stuffed apartment borrowed from Payn's *Literary Recollections*: 'though she was undoubtedly dressed, no one could tell what she was dressed in; or know from looking at her as she lay on two chairs which was tiny Miss Mitford and which was rug, quilt, skirt, or dressing-gown' (*E* 3.222).[43] Mitford's ghostly disappearance into her own soft furnishings acts as an apt metaphor for Woolf's tendency to make her a background character in her own life. In a short review of a new edition of *The Letters of Mary Russell Mitford* (1925), Woolf complains that 'one would like occasionally to feel that Miss Mitford was in a hurry, or in a temper, or had something very urgent to say' (*E* 4.15): the letters conceal Mitford's true self as efficiently as Hill's ineptitude as a writer had done. Woolf's disappointment with Mitford also finds its expression in her revised *Common Reader* essay of the same year. One of a series of 'Outlines', the essay combines the first part of 'The Wrong Way of Reading' with most of 'An Imperfect Lady' with very minor modifications. Notably, it therefore excludes the explicitly feminist analysis of 'A Good Daughter', even though the *Common Reader* was entirely under Woolf's editorial control, giving her the freedom to raise her voice on behalf of Mitford. *A Room of One's Own* goes even further, beginning with Woolf's dismissal of conventional histories of women's writing, including 'some witticisms if possible about Miss Mitford' (*AROO* 3). Yet by publicly excising Mitford from her own literary history twice, Woolf acknowledges her lingering influence: as I will argue at the end of this chapter, Mitford's reappearance in *Flush* is evidence of her continued importance in shaping Woolf's thinking on women and patriarchy as well as a catalyst for experimental biography.

## 'A bad poet': Elizabeth Barrett Browning

The catalogue of unsuitable women writers in 'An Imperfect Lady' had also featured Elizabeth Barrett Browning: 'Mrs Browning was a married woman' (*E* 3.210) and therefore disqualified from treatment by a lady biographer like Hill. While Hill might have had reservations about prying into the private life of a married woman, the general public did not. By the 1930s, Barrett Browning, once a 'behind-the-scenes contender for the prize position of England's Poet Laureate in 1850', whose portrayal of female authorship in *Aurora Leigh* had inspired generations of Victorian women writers, had been transformed into a damsel in distress.[44] Her imprisonment by a tyrannical father and subsequent elopement with fellow poet Robert Browning by far overshadowed any lingering remembrance of her reputation as a poet. Marjorie Stone suggests that unease with women's literary achievements was a major factor in this loss of popularity:

> While many late Victorian critics continued to approach EBB as one of the century's major poets, those hostile to the implications of her achievement increasingly carried the day [ . . . ] By the early twentieth century, hostility to the author of *Aurora Leigh* had subsided, but at the cost of reducing EBB to an appendage of her husband.[45]

Barrett Browning thus presented to Woolf a case study of women's lives in patriarchal society in several respects: through her own experiences, through her politically engaged poetry, and in her afterlife and loss of literary prestige. As Snaith notes, Woolf was highly attuned to her importance: 'Woolf's interest in Barrett Browning was all to do with context [ . . . ] Woolf understood that the fascination with Barrett Browning's life had prevented readers from fully appreciating the politics of her writing'.[46]

This understanding of the fascination of Barrett Browning's life is all the deeper because Woolf frequently falls prey to it herself: from the refutation of Leslie Stephen's views on privacy in 'Poets' Letters' (1906) to her renewed attention in the wake of the sensational play *The Barretts of Wimpole Street* (1930), her interest in Barrett Browning's personal life dominates her articles. Her review of Percy Lubbock's *Elizabeth Barrett Browning in Her Letters* (1906) coincides with the lowest point of

Barrett Browning's popularity; it therefore, not unreasonably, questions her relevance to a modern readership. While Woolf celebrates the volume for interpreting Barrett Browning for a new century, she is ambivalent about the literary merit of her poetry. Making her an example of the worst excesses of the nineteenth century, Woolf appropriates Barrett Browning to continue the revision of her late-Victorian legacies that also shapes her short fiction of the same period: 'our fathers were strangely mistaken when they exalted her to the place which she holds, in theory at least, at the present day. [ . . . ] Mrs Browning, as a poet, has ceased to play much part in our lives' (*E* 1.101). The review engages in an intertextual debate with Leslie Stephen's 'The Browning Letters' (*National Review* in 1899, expanded for *Studies of a Biographer*, vol. III (1902)), which revolves around 'the claim of men of genius to posthumous privacy'.[47] Woolf begins with humorous praise for Lubbock's double service to readers in tactfully selecting extracts from Barrett Browning's letters, and trimming their excessive language and sentiment to meet a modern audience's taste:

> It was dreadful, the sensitive said, to overhear; but if one did sin, the more callous suggested, it was as well to be guilty of a pleasant crime. And the eavesdropper became so weary of those emphatic voices, protesting and asseverating, uttering commonplaces with dreadful distortion of the lips and drowning even the simple emotions in a twisted torrent of language, that he might surely consider that his fault was expiated as soon as committed. (*E* 1.101–2)

Here, she directly responds to Leslie Stephen's ethical unease in reading a married couple's private correspondence:

> The sense of impropriety which besets one every now and then in reading – that uncomfortable suspicion that one is, after all, an eavesdropper – is purely due to the following all the little ins and outs through so long a correspondence, and the feeling that one is looking over the shoulders of the writers at a moment when they would have shown the door to an intruder.[48]

Although Stephen admits that Barrett Browning herself believed letters to be the 'most vital part of biography' without which the 'dead would be deader', ultimately, his own concerns about the demoralising effect of publicity prevail.[49] Woolf's mockery of this 'sensitivity' and her comical conflation of Stephen's ethical concerns with the (Barrett) Brownings' excessively verbose sentimentality at once publicly establish her as a critic of such outdated concerns, but also obscure the fact that privately, her own treatment of her parents' correspondence would have appeased the most conservative of critics.

As in her contemporaneous short stories, Woolf introduces an explicitly gendered element into this generational revision. Barrett Browning's letters offer an insight into the excesses of patriarchal society; as in her later reading of Mitford, a reckoning with fathers' influences on their daughters therefore shapes Woolf's review. Stephen had suggested that writers' letters were of value to the literary critic because 'A man's infirmities are, after all, part of him; [ . . . ] and very often they suggest the only excuse for his shortcomings'.[50] Woolf expands this line of argument from the personal to the political in an exploration of Barrett Browning's existence as 'a life-long prisoner in a London house, guarded by a mad gaoler in the person of her father, and nourished almost solely upon books and writing' (*E* 1.102). The letters therefore serve as documentary evidence of the tyranny of the private household:

> In hands less just and discriminating the story becomes so monstrous that its real effect upon Mrs Browning is obscured. But as it is told here, with the perpetual illustration of the letters, it becomes clearly a thing that did really happen. (*E* 1.102)

She would return to Mr Barrett's tyranny as a case study in *Three Guineas*, but in 1906, this documentary use of Barrett Browning's life prevents any serious consideration of her writing. Although 'the only life that was free to her' (*E* 1.103) gains value as an act of self-assertion and defiance, poetry (like the dog Flush) is a coping mechanism and merely a substitute for suppressed emotions and lack of social interactions. The review thus serves as an elegy for Barrett Browning's lost potential: with 'sane poetry' made impossible by her circumstances, she becomes collateral damage in Woolf's attempt to distance herself from her father's biographical ethics.

If Woolf's lack of interest in Barrett Browning's works needed further proof, it lies in the two-and-a-half decades of silence that follow this review. However, when Barrett Browning returns, she does so with full force, and as Snaith remarks, her 'writing, her life, her reputation, and of course her dog, Flush, are behind much of Woolf's thinking throughout the 1930s'.[51] Although Woolf claimed that she had read *Aurora Leigh* 'by chance with great interest' in 1931, it is more likely that *The Barretts of Wimpole Street: A Comedy in Five Acts* (1930) caused the sudden return of her interest (*L* 4.301). Julia Novak notes that the play depicts 'Barrett Browning as an entirely relational creature, defined through and dependent on, first, her possessive father and, later, increasingly, her "life-giving" bridegroom'.[52] Woolf confessed to being 'rather disappointed, though amused by the astonishing story – which is not an exaggeration' and thought the play 'rather feeble': 'they might have made it hit harder I thought. However the Barretts themselves are furious, threatening libel actions as it is' (*L* 4.351, 349). Yet its popular success clearly inspired Woolf to return to the author she had so willingly dismissed in 1906 to offer a competing and corrective life narrative, which highlights *Aurora Leigh*'s relevance as a genre-defying experimental poem and an important social commentary on women's position in Victorian society. While Woolf had previously tacitly condoned Barrett Browning's fall from grace at the end of the nineteenth century, 'Aurora Leigh' (published June 1931 in the *Yale Review* (signed), July 1931 in the *TLS* and with minor changes in the *Common Reader II* (1932)) more explicitly challenges the misogyny that drives it. Asserting – with full awareness of her own gentility – that 'the only place in the mansion of literature that is assigned [Barrett Browning] is downstairs in the servants' quarters, where [ . . . ] she bangs the crockery about and eats vast handfuls of peas on the point of her knife' (*E* 5.258), Woolf's vivid imagery comically exaggerates the condescension of the anonymous male critic she quotes: 'Her importance, they say, "has now become merely historical. Neither education nor association with her husband ever succeeded in teaching her the value of words and a sense of form"' (*E* 5.258). Woolf thus perfectly sets the scenes for a discussion of Aurora Leigh's struggles as a female writer, yet continues to undercut the book's contemporary relevance by 'mus[ing] with kindly condescension over this token of bygone fashion': 'it is not a book but a dusty mantle with fringes and furbelows that our grandmothers actually wore; a cluster of wax fruit that they stood in a glass case' (*E* 5.258, 259). *Aurora Leigh* thus joins the Mitfords' Wedgwood china and the 'conglomeration [ . . . ] of the most heterogeneous and ill-assorted objects, piled higgledy-piggledy in a vast mound' (*O* 160) in *Orlando* as eloquent witnesses of the past. However, Woolf's assortment of Victorian objects also invokes the heterogeneity of *Aurora Leigh*, one of its most striking features. Thus, Kerry McSweeney notes that Barrett Browning

> unscrupulously mixes genres (novel, autobiography, social satire, tract for the times, treatise on poetics, theodicy), subjects (geographically ranging from the slums of London to the New Jerusalem), and themes (sexual, vocational, aesthetic, social, religious), and holds them all suspended in a cornucopian fluency of discourse.[53]

What Woolf encounters in *Aurora Leigh* – Victorian experiences of womanhood, educational disparity and the struggle for creative expression in a suitable genre – therefore reveals as much about her own preoccupations in the early 1930s as it does about Barrett Browning's in the 1850s.

Woolf's strong and immediate response to *Aurora Leigh* as a personal, almost autobiographical, narrative aligns her with Victorian women's responses to the text: Stone notes that 'EBB had a particularly powerful effect on women writers and reformers' in the nineteenth century.[54] Woolf's review includes a detailed summary of Book 1, but none of the others, suggesting that Aurora's Victorian childhood and education resonated most strongly with her own interests: after losing her parents, Woolf summarises, Aurora returns from Italy to England and 'suffered the education that was thought proper for women', memorising assorted facts and doing needlework in preparation for marriage (E 5.260). Woolf treats Aurora's passionate exclamation against this feminine education with slight amusement, yet Aurora's survival strategies clearly resonate with Woolf's own use of private spaces in *A Room of One's Own*. Woolf's review notes the private retreat offered by Aurora's green bedroom and the freedom provided by 'books, books, books!' (E 5.260/ *Aurora Leigh* 1.833): as Anne Wallace argues, 'the green fabrics of Aurora's domestic space [ . . . ] become continuous with the green plants of the outdoor world, the province of the male pedestrian poet' and thereby enable Aurora's poetic development through a symbolical escape from the rules of her aunt's household.[55]

By her own admission, Woolf read *Aurora Leigh* for the first time in 1931, three years after the publication of *A Room of One's Own*, therefore ruling out any direct influence (although she could have read Laura Stephen's 1873 edition, with a dedication from Robert Browning, much earlier). Yet these and other similarities suggest that despite being born at opposite ends of the century, Woolf was finding Aurora's experience directly relevant to her own thinking. As Christine Chaney notes,

> [w]hat is distinctive and important about the discourses that Barrett Browning 'joins' in *Aurora Leigh* is the way they present the unique life story of a single woman in such a way as to compellingly witness and argue for what society should allow for *all* women – a place for both work and love, marriage and equality.[56]

Barrett Browning's stance on education and literature likewise shows strong similarities to many of Woolf's conclusions in *Three Guineas*, yet Woolf does not name her as an influence: Julia Briggs therefore generously suggests that those 'parallels now seem obvious, but were perhaps so much at the forefront of her mind as to have been almost invisible to her'.[57] In spite of their gender-based exclusion from formal education, Aurora, Woolf and Barrett Browning are united by a distrust of universities and instead advocate for the value of alternative forms of instruction, like their own unrestricted access to their fathers' libraries.[58] Woolf quotes Aurora's description of her unstructured literary education, which rejects a conscious searching for virtue and utilitarian approaches to reading:

> It is rather when
> We gloriously forget ourselves and plunge
> Soul-forward, headlong, into a book's profound,
> Impassioned for its beauty and salt of truth –
> 'Tis then we get the right good from a book. (*E* 5.260/*Aurora Leigh* l.705–9)

Sheila Cordner notes Barrett Browning's rejection of university education in a letter to Mitford – 'a worn-out plaything in the hands of one sex already, & need not be *transferred* in order to be proved ridiculous' – and argues that the failure of Romney's schemes for social reform lie in his inability to understand human nature, an art not taught at university.[59] Woolf cultivated a similar lifelong scepticism towards university education, and in *Three Guineas* accuses universities of contributing to social division and oppression: 'Do [facts] not prove that education, the finest education in the world, does not teach people to hate force, but to use it?' (*3G* 150–1). Woolf's critique ends with the proposal of a different set of values for education: envisioning a new college which teaches the 'art of understanding other people's lives and minds', she returns to the literary education and intuitive reading which her own schooling had focused on and *Aurora Leigh* also advocates for (*3G* 155).

Although *Aurora Leigh* extensively examines widespread obstacles to female authorship in the nineteenth century, and in spite of its many resonances with her own thinking in *Three Guineas*, Woolf treats the book predominantly as a personal, quasi-autobiographical narrative: 'Aurora the fictitious seems to be throwing light upon Elizabeth the actual' (*E* 5.261). Barrett Browning's domestic life doesn't require the subtle teasing of Mitford's to reveal itself, and therefore, her poetry cannot be judged without taking into account her virtual imprisonment by her father: 'Mrs Browning could no more conceal herself than she could control herself, a sign no doubt of imperfection in an artist, but a sign also that life has impinged upon art more than life should' (*E* 5.261). The review therefore offers a pessimistic commentary on Aurora's escape through her green bedroom's literary sanctuary: neither literature nor Italian exile offers a complete escape from paternal oppression. Barrett Browning's sick-room also recalls the similarly divided nature of Mitford's little attic bedroom and her literary career, equally successful and oppressive: in both cases, fathers' control over their daughters extends far beyond the household into every aspect of their public and private lives and leaves its traces in their works. Woolf answers Barrett Browning's rhetorical question, 'And do you also know what a disadvantage this ignorance [of real life] has been to my art?' emphatically: 'it is not surprising that even in the depths of her sick-room her mind turned to modern life as a subject for poetry. [ . . . ] She had lived shut off, guessing at what was outside, and inevitably magnifying what was within' (*E* 5.261–2, 262–3).

However, Barrett Browning's turn to modern life is her poem's biggest strength, and offers another reason for Woolf's suddenly re-awakened interest: although it is only 'a masterpiece in embryo; a work whose genius floats diffused and fluctuating in some pre-natal stage waiting the final stroke of creative power to bring it into being' (*E* 5.263), and lacks the subtlety of novelistic character development, its vividness and heightened intensity also convince her that 'the street, the drawing-room, are promising subjects; modern life is worthy of the muse' (*E* 5.267). Woolf's praise for Barrett Browning's innovation in writing a book-length, genre-defying poem coincides with the completion of the first draft of *The Waves*, her own masterpiece and 'the greatest opportunity I have yet been able to give myself' (*D* 3.312). Unlike most of the articles discussed here, 'Aurora Leigh' was not commissioned: Woolf offered her 'study of *Aurora Leigh*' (*L* 4.301) to the *Yale Review* and it was reprinted in the *TLS* before being included in the *Second Common Reader*. It therefore functions as a rare spontaneous tribute to a female predecessor: unlike Barrett Browning, who had complained that 'I look everywhere for grandmothers and see none',[60] Woolf could clearly identify with this ambition to transcend generic boundaries and create a new kind of poetry for her generation. Although she approached the challenge of the generically hybrid novel poem from a radically different angle, *The Waves* presents a Modernist view on her age and *The Pargiters* struggles with finding a form that could combine political essay and fiction. Woolf's self-assessment that 'Yet I respect myself for writing this book. Yes – even though it exhibits my congenital faults' (*D* 3.312) sounds very similar to her final verdict on *Aurora Leigh* as the form most suited to Barrett Browning's own peculiar flaws and gifts as a writer.

## 'A joke': Flush

If *The Waves* prompted Woolf's sudden desire to write about *Aurora Leigh*, it also inspired her to turn to the spaniel Flush, Mary Russell

Mitford's gift to Elizabeth Barrett Browning. Writing to Ottoline Morrell in 1933, Woolf explained that

> I was so tired after the Waves, that I lay in the garden and read the Browning love letters, and the figure of their dog made me laugh so I couldn't resist making him a Life. I wanted to play a joke on Lytton – it was to parody him. (*L* 5.161–2)

However, two years earlier, she had already confessed to Vita Sackville-West that *Flush* was 'a little escapade by means of wh. I hope to stem the ruin we shall suffer from the failure of The Waves. This is the worst publishing season on record. No bookseller dares buy' (*L* 4.380). Like the Mitford reviews and 'Aurora Leigh', *Flush* therefore continues Woolf's engagement with a middlebrow readership. As Book Society and Book-of-the-Month Club selection, *Flush* became a bestseller as intended; yet it also continues Woolf's analysis of Victorian structures of oppression and, as Snaith has persuasively shown, alerted contemporary readers to the dangers of fascism in Italy and the UK.[61] Jane Goldman summarises that its 'very transgression and destabilisation of the categories of "high" and "low" art make it a satirical allegory of canon formation. [ . . . ] [*Flush*] was considered a fall from high-brow grace by some contemporary reviewers and most subsequent Woolf critics'.[62] But although animal and biographical studies have done much to recover *Flush* (and Flush) as an 'attempt to exercise modernist literary techniques in the mapping of a canine subjectivity', his owners have increasingly faded from view.[63] Yet *Flush* also continues Woolf's playful exploration of the gaps in Mitford's recorded life, moving from her dinner service to her dog, and contextualises the Browning romance within a wider political narrative that emphasises the systemic nature of Mr Barrett's domestic tyranny. *Flush* therefore unites the previous strands of analysis but again showcases how Woolf prioritises experimentation and popularity over an extensive engagement with both women's work.

*Flush* works against the relational view of Barrett Browning by restoring Mitford as an important figure in Barrett Browning's life, thus countering the excessive focus on her love life, which Woolf had lamented in 'Aurora Leigh'. After Mary Russell Mitford and Elizabeth Barrett Browning were introduced to each other in 1836, Mitford quickly 'came to act as a literary mother to EBB': she encouraged her poetic talent and '[t]heir letters teem with discussions of English, American, and European authors, particularly women writers such as Mary Wollstonecraft and Jane Austen, and writers of the day such as Tennyson and George Sand'.[64] Mitford witnessed Barrett Browning's second prolonged illness as well as the loss of her favourite brother and tried to 'revive EBB's interest in life after Bro's death [ . . . ] with the gift of the spaniel Flush in January 1841'.[65] Although Mitford's publication of the intimate details of this death in her *Recollections of a Literary Life* (1851) created a rift between them, there is little doubt that Mitford (and Flush) were among Barrett Browning's most important relationships during her imprisonment in London and offer a challenge to heteronormative approaches to her life. Thus, Morrison observes that Barrett Browning's biographers generally struggle to adequately define their relationship with its 'intense emotional intimacy' centred on a shared interest in Flush:

> These seemingly trivial discussions do not fit with the current understanding of Barrett Browning as a serious poet and thinker who tackled complex philosophical and social issues. [ . . . ] Additionally, the shared pet was often central to female marriages and romantic friendships. [ . . . ] As such, any consideration of the triangulated relationship of Barrett, Mitford, and Flush would detract from the spectacular love story of Elizabeth and Robert with which so much criticism is invested.[66]

Although *Flush* balances this interest in queer, non-heteronormative relationships with the love story at the centre of the plot, Woolf preserves this triangulated relationship by prioritising Flush's perspective as the bond between both women. Although 'very little is known about him, and I have had to invent a great deal' (*L* 5.167), Flush is one of the better recorded dogs in history. Drawing on the (Barrett) Brownings' correspondence and Mitford's letters for details of Flush's life, Woolf preserves the animalistic focus of both (she had already drawn attention to the prominent role of household pets in 'The Letters of Mary Russell Mitford' (1925)). Woolf herself possessed a highly developed animal fantasy life in her own relationships: Scott summarises that '[a]nimal identities, reaching well into Woolf's maturity, might comment lightly on regrettable behavior, or work into fantasies that facilitated disclosures about the body and sexual desire – otherwise subjects of reticence and coding for Woolf'.[67] Small changes, such as Mitford's personal delivery of Flush on a lead (*F* 13–19), rather than his actual journey via train and coach in a hamper, serve to cement this relationship and emphasise Flush's symbolical and emotional value at the nexus of the relationship between Barrett Browning and Mitford.[68] However, Woolf removes any obviously queer aspects from their relationship by making Barrett Browning 'more like a daughter than a friend' (*F* 13) to Mitford. Mitford and her friendship with Barrett Browning frame the series of threatening male figures which otherwise dominate Flush's life. Dr Mitford, Mr Barrett and the dog snatcher aim to control and dominate dogs and women, and from Flush's jealous point of view, even Robert Browning is characterised largely by his ability to take Barrett Browning away from him. *Flush* therefore sets a nourishing and supportive female relationship against male tyranny, rewriting both Mitford's and Barrett Browning's biographies.

Woolf's expansion of the limits of biographical representation with *Flush* have been discussed extensively. *Flush* transcends barriers between species: thus, Thomas Lewis notes that 'through the dog's sensations and most especially through his olfactory nerve Woolf was able to go beyond the limitations of biography', while David Herman argues that *Flush*, by using 'modes of consciousness presentation conventionally associated with fictional narratives', destabilises conventional boundaries between human and non-human minds.[69] Flush also disrupts assumptions about who makes a worthy biographical subject: Scott notes that '*Flush* sustains Woolf's interests in biography and lives of the obscure. Flush and Miss Barrett's loyal maid, Wilson, pose comparable challenges of depicting marginality to the biographer'.[70] What is more, Christine Reynier proposes that Flush's aristocratic descent exposes not just Victorian biography's preference for noble subjects to ridicule: Woolf's satire 'may well extend to Lytton Strachey's own biographies which, for all their irony and iconoclasm, still focus on Queen Victoria, Cardinal Manning and other well-known figures'.[71] It is, however, worthwhile to consider how this approach intersects with the lives of Flush's human characters. Moving from object biography to animal biography, *Flush* continues Woolf's experimentation with different but equally occluding perspectives on Mitford's life. Craig Smith reminds us that although *Flush* is most commonly read allegorically, it is without a doubt also a story about a dog: as such, it belongs to a genre of animal narratives that originates with Anna Sewell's *Black Beauty: His Grooms and Companions, the Autobiography of a Horse* (1877). Although I disagree with his reading of *Flush* as a story that lacks a moral or political agenda, his larger point, that *Flush* is fundamentally about the life of Flush the dog, highlights that Mitford and Barrett Browning are a necessary casualty in any non-anthropocentric reading of *Flush*.[72]

Choosing the perspective of a dog, Woolf conveniently and humorously resolves Leslie Stephen's biographical dilemma of being present 'at a moment when [the Brownings] would have shown the door to an intruder'.[73] Consequently, Flush's lifespan and physical location dictate much of the narrative focus: Mitford is a marginal figure, present in Flush's early youth and deathbed memories, and by necessity, the narrative overlaps with the famous story of Barrett Browning's courtship, elopement and marriage. Given that Woolf envisioned *Flush* as a popular bestseller, this was clearly a calculated risk; however, it also means that both women's professional activities go largely unnoticed as Flush neither understands poetry nor is particularly interested in literature. Their literary careers become implicit background activities left for the knowing reader to substitute. Woolf draws strongly on Barrett Browning's 'To Flush, My Dog' and 'Flush or Faunus' as well as Mitford's *Our Village* to fill in the blanks of Flush's existence, but moves all direct references to Barrett Browning's poetry to her endnotes. A similar loss of detail is evident in her depiction of Barrett Browning's mind: the reader is denied access to her thoughts due to the limits of Flush's understanding and much of the brilliance and intelligence which Woolf had observed in 'Aurora Leigh' is therefore lost. Novak likewise notes how Woolf's narrative skews away from Barrett Browning's success as a poet to 'the private woman, with all her personal tragedies and joys': 'While Barrett Browning is never shown working on her poetry, she is, in fact, repeatedly depicted as an avid letter-writer, and *Flush* contains several such quotations from the letters'.[74]

Woolf similarly domesticates Mitford. Although the account of Flush's rambles through the fields strongly resembles Mitford's walks with Mayflower and succeeding generations of dogs in *Our Village* in tone and content (F 10–11), she effectively contrasts Flush's delight in his freedom with Mitford's imprisonment by her father. As in her earlier reviews, Woolf couches her criticisms of Dr Mitford with humour; however, she also uses Flush's lack of socialisation to dispel any romanticised notions about the genteel poverty of life in a rural cottage, vividly contrasting it with the material wealth of Wimpole Street:

> Until this moment he had set foot into no house but the working man's cottage at Three Mile Cross. The boards were bare, the mats were frayed; the chairs were cheap. Here there was nothing bare, nothing frayed, nothing cheap [ . . . ] Up the funnel of the staircase came warm whiffs of joints roasting, of fowls basting, of soups simmering – ravishing almost as food itself to nostrils used to the meagre savour of Kerenhappock's penurious fries and hashes. (F 14–15)

Mitford herself provides a pessimistic coda to *Flush*'s narrative of liberation: in contrast to Flush's escape to material prosperity and ultimately freedom in Italy, she remains 'still sitting in her greenhouse at Three Mile Cross' (F 88), denied a similar happy ending by her enduring devotion to an undeserving father.

Woolf uses *Flush* to unequivocally condemn the domestic tyranny of Dr Mitford and Mr Barrett, but also offers a last rebuttal to Leslie Stephen's advocacy for discretion on domestic matters. Mitford's obvious tragedy is complemented by the more subtle one of Nero, the

Carlyles' dog: '[i]t was common knowledge that Mrs Carlyle's dog Nero had leapt from a top storey window with the intention of committing suicide. He had found the strain of life in Cheyne Row intolerable, it was said' (F 92). In 'The Browning Letters', Stephen draws extensively on Froude's publication of Carlyle's *Reminiscences of Jane Welsh Carlyle* (1881) and his *Life of Carlyle* (1882–84), both revealing Carlyle's inconsideration and irritability in his relationship with his wife, to ponder whether there exists a moral obligation to reveal biographical truth.[75] Woolf's footnote answers by innocently wondering whether Nero was 'driven to desperate melancholy by associating with Mr Carlyle' (F 114 n8): only by exposing the domestic tyranny suffered by Elizabeth Barrett Browning, Mary Russell Mitford and Jane Carlyle can the full damage of patriarchal society be exposed and women's points of view be made accessible.[76]

This revelatory impulse also drives Woolf's representation of Victorian slums. Thus, Reynier sees *Flush* as a direct response to Barrett Browning's call for political poetry by women in 'A Curse for a Nation' (1860) and argues that *Aurora Leigh* and *Casa Guidi Windows* are 'woven into Woolf's text' through her depictions of women's domestic imprisonment and Italy's classless society.[77] However, *Aurora Leigh* and *Flush* also share an interest in the ills of Victorian society, revealing both women's social awareness, but also their own limitations as middle-class women. Where Barrett Browning argues for a more compassionate approach to poverty by charting the failure of Romney's schemes to reform and unite two apparently separate classes through marriage, Woolf goes a step further by exposing the links between the surface respectability of Wimpole Street and its slums. The dog snatchers represent the complex systems of economy and power that joins the two: 'The terms upon which Wimpole Street lived cheek by jowl with St Giles's were well known. St Giles's stole what St Giles's could; Wimpole Street paid what Wimpole Street must' (F 53–4). Woolf's footnote to the passage singles out Barrett Browning's complicity in this system:

> Readers of *Aurora Leigh* – but since such persons are non-existent it must be explained that Mrs Browning wrote a poem of this name, one of the most vivid passages in which (though it suffers from distortion natural to an artist who sees the object once only from a four-wheeler, with Wilson tugging at her skirts) is the description of a London slum. (F 109 n5)

Yet Woolf here appears to be projecting some of her own discomfort on Barrett Browning: Snaith notes that Woolf too 'had trouble with the Whitechapel chapter, rewriting it three times in January 1933. She was confronting her own privilege and her own experience of otherness'.[78]

In recognising the absence of simple solutions to complex societal problems, Woolf's political analysis in *Flush* points forwards to *Three Guineas*. Scott notes that 'Flush has impressed numerous critics as a study of women's conditioning under patriarchy', but not all of these interpretations account for the complexity of Woolf's political position.[79] Thus, Susan Squier provides a straightforward reading of *Flush* as 'a physical and psychological journey from imprisonment in London to freedom in the foreign cities of Pisa and Florence: archetype for the woman writer's development' and points out the parallels between Flush's imprisonment and that of Barrett Browning, yet this reading fails to account for victims of patriarchal oppression like Mitford and Jane Carlyle, who never escape from their domestic tyrants.[80] Additionally, Woolf depicts a more complex interrelationship between tyranny and love than this reading suggests. Flush conquers his hatred of Robert Browning out of love for Elizabeth Barrett Browning, a parallel to Mitford's and Barrett Browning's disturbing decision to accept their fathers' abuse as an expression of love. Woolf therefore strongly hints at Barrett Browning's own capacity for tyranny by forcing Flush to submit to her will. *Flush*, like *Three Guineas*, therefore cannot establish simple dichotomies and demonstrates that there are few uncompromised positions in society. Pamela Caughie similarly argues that 'Flush resembles less the woman writer than the writer's servant Wilson': both lack any meaningful agency and are completely dependent on Barrett Browning.[81] Yet as a male dog, Flush also gains social and sexual freedoms that none of the women around him could ever possess.

Woolf's increasing awareness of the interconnections of tyranny and fascism, and the lack of real alternatives therefore provides a strong link between *Flush* and the pessimism of *Three Guineas*. Mitford and Barrett Browning's lives demonstrate that even with a room of their own and financial independence, they could at most exchange the men who controlled their lives, not exist entirely independently, yet Woolf also uses Barrett Browning to show middle-class women's complicity in this system, as oppressors of the poor, dogs and servants. Woolf had described *Aurora Leigh* as presenting 'people who are unmistakably Victorian, wrestling with the problems of their own time' (*E* 5.526), but the political scope of *Flush* shows that these problems transcend the Victorian period. *Flush* therefore anticipates *Three Guineas* in its reading of contemporary political developments through the lens of nineteenth-century politics. Woolf's playful mockery of Flush's pride in his racial purity and superior breeding parodies the increasing nationalist and anti-Semitic political discourses of the 1930s, and her use of Barrett Browning to highlight the pervasiveness of domestic and social oppression translates easily to a larger-scale analysis of contemporary society.[82]

In *Three Guineas*, Woolf uses Barrett Browning, not Mitford, to delineate the 'infantile fixation' that leads Victorian fathers to desire absolute control over their daughters' lives. *The Barretts of Wimpole Street* had already introduced Mr Barrett as a popular figure associated with paternal abuses of power, and his literal imprisonment of his daughter offers a more clear-cut example of tyranny than Dr Mitford's financial control – not least because Mitford's successful career would undermine Woolf's argument about women's lack of professional options. While Woolf therefore returns to a more simplistic view of Barrett Browning as solely a victim of society, her previous analysis of Mitford's and Barrett Browning's lives informs the contours of her argument. As in *Flush* and 'A Good Daughter', Woolf cannot envision a way of reforming society from within: the idealistic, but entirely imaginary Outsiders' Society is a manifestation of this problem rather than a solution. Julia Briggs observes that

> [a] sense of frustration and helplessness, a recognition that some problems might have no solutions, is never far beneath the surface of *Three Guineas*, contributing to the complex twists and turns of the arguments, the occasional moments of defeat, the reluctance to give the guineas, and the non-involvement of the members of the Outsiders' Society – their roles as observers rather than agents.[83]

While Woolf never managed to resolve this dilemma, it helps to demonstrate the immense value of non-canonical or underappreciated women writers to her work: from her earliest reviews to *Flush*, Woolf uses neglected women writers' lives to explore the interconnections of patriarchy, tyranny and society, presenting a trajectory which culminates in the arguments of *Three Guineas*. However, Mitford's gradual disappearance from her own life, and the unacknowledged similarities between Barrett Browning's thinking and Woolf's own also highlight that this reappraisal is driven by Woolf's artistic needs: any benefit for the writers at its centre is merely coincidental.

## Notes

1. Elizabeth Lee, 'Mitford, Mary Russell', *Dictionary of National Biography Archive*, 1894 <https://doi.org/10.1093/odnb/9780192683120.013.18859>.
2. Anna Snaith, 'Of Fanciers, Footnotes, and Fascism: Virginia Woolf's Flush', *MFS Modern Fiction Studies*, 48.3 (2002), 614–36 <https://doi.org/10.1353/mfs.2002.0070>.

3. See Katie Halsey, ''Tell me of some booklings: Mary Russell Mitford's Female Literary Networks', *Women's Writing*, 18.1 (2011), 121–36.
4. Martin Garrett, 'Mitford, Mary Russell', *Oxford Dictionary of National Biography* <http://www.oxforddnb.com/view/article/18859> (accessed 1 February 2017).
5. Elizabeth Lee.
6. Wilson, p. 182.
7. Barbara Onslow, *Women of the Press in Nineteenth-Century Britain* (Basingstoke: Palgrave Macmillan, 2000), p. 91.
8. Kevin A. Morrison, 'Foregrounding Nationalism: Mary Russell Mitford's *Our Village* and the Effects of Publication Context', *European Romantic Review*, 19.3 (2008), 275–87 (pp. 277, 283).
9. Deidre Lynch, 'Homes and Haunts: Austen's and Mitford's English Idylls', *PMLA*, 115.5 (2000), 1103–8 (p. 1106); Barbara Onslow, quoted in Morrison, 'Foregrounding Nationalism', p. 283.
10. Anny Thackeray Ritchie, 'Introduction', in *Our Village; By Miss Mitford; With an Introduction by Anne Thackeray Ritchie; and One Hundred Illustrations by Hugh Thomson*, by Mary Russell Mitford (London: Macmillan and Co., 1893), pp. vii–liiii.
11. Leslie Stephen, *Sir Leslie Stephen's Mausoleum Book*, ed. by Alan Bell (Oxford: Clarendon Press, 1977), p. 85.
12. James Payn, *Some Literary Recollections* (London: Smith Elder & Co., 1884), p. 93.
13. Alison Booth, *Homes and Haunts: Touring Writers' Shrines and Countries* (Oxford: Oxford University Press, 2016), p. 104.
14. Alison Booth, 'Revisiting the Homes and Haunts of Mary Russell Mitford', *Nineteenth-Century Contexts*, 30.1 (2008), 39–65 (p. 40).
15. Linda H. Peterson, *Becoming a Woman of Letters: Myths of Authorship and Facts of the Victorian Market* (Princeton, NJ: Princeton University Press, 2009), pp. 1–4.
16. Garrett.
17. Onslow, p. 91.
18. Booth, *Homes and Haunts: Touring Writers' Shrines and Countries*, p. 113.
19. Constance Hill, *Mary Russell Mitford and Her Surroundings* (London: John Lane, The Bodley Head, 1920), p. v.
20. Wilson, p. 186.
21. I have not managed to find another instance of this in Woolf's journalism; and Woolf's diary offers no clue as to why she would agree to review a work she clearly found frustrating multiple times.
22. Dell, pp. 4, 9.
23. Booth, *Homes and Haunts: Touring Writers' Shrines and Countries*, pp. 105–6.
24. Peterson, p. 33.
25. Constance Hill, p. 171.
26. Constance Hill, p. 140.
27. Hill's second to last chapter, 'Farewell to Three Mile Cross', ends with an illustration of a teapot that has no obvious connection to any of the previous pages. Constance Hill, p. 359.

28. Constance Hill, p. 207.
29. Wilson, pp. 180–5; Mary Russell Mitford, *Our Village; By Miss Mitford; With an Introduction by Anne Thackeray Ritchie; and One Hundred Illustrations by Hugh Thomson*, ed. by Anny Thackeray Ritchie (London: Macmillan and Co., 1893), p. 4, Archive.org.
30. Ritchie, 'Introduction', pp. xxi–xxii.
31. Ritchie, Introduction, p. xxii.
32. Peterson, p. 33.
33. Constance Hill, p. 230.
34. Snaith, *Virginia Woolf*, p. 2.
35. Constance Hill, pp. 5, 4, 5.
36. Constance Hill, p. 55.
37. Constance Hill, p. 54.
38. Jennifer Sattaur, 'Thinking Objectively: An Overview of "Thing Theory" in Victorian Studies', *Victorian Literature and Culture*, 40.1 (2012), 347–57 (p. 348).
39. Elaine Freedgood, 'What Objects Know: Circulation, Omniscience and the Comedy of Dispossession in Victorian It-Narratives', *Journal of Victorian Culture*, 15.1 (2010), 83–100 (p. 84).
40. Paula Maggio, 'Digging for Buried Treasure: Theories about Weather and Fiction in Virginia Woolf's Essays', *Virginia Woolf Miscellany*, 78 (2010), 23–6 (p. 24).
41. Linda Martin, 'Elegy and the Unknowable Mind in Jacob's Room', *Studies in the Novel*, 47.2 (2015), 176–92 (p. 176).
42. Bonnie Kime Scott, *In the Hollow of the Wave: Virginia Woolf and Modernist Uses of Nature* (Charlottesville: University of Virginia Press, 2012), p. 114.
43. See Payn, p. 77.
44. Carol Hanbery MacKay, 'Emerging Selves: The Autobiographical Impulse in Elizabeth Barrett Browning, Anne Thackeray Ritchie, and Annie Wood Besant', in *A History of English Autobiography*, ed. by Adam Smyth (Cambridge: Cambridge University Press, 2016), pp. 207–20 (p. 209).
45. Marjorie Stone, 'Browning [Née Moulton Barrett], Elizabeth Barrett (1806–1861)', *Oxford Dictionary of National Biography* (Oxford: Oxford University Press) <http://www.oxforddnb.com/view/article/3711?docPos=1> (accessed 2 March 2017).
46. Snaith, 'Of Fanciers, Footnotes, and Fascism', p. 615.
47. Leslie Stephen, 'The Browning Letters', in *Studies of a Biographer, Volume III* (London: Duckworth & Co., 1902), pp. 1–35 (pp. 1, 12).
48. Stephen, 'The Browning Letters', p. 32.
49. Stephen, 'The Browning Letters', pp. 14, 26.
50. Stephen, 'The Browning Letters', p. 7.
51. Snaith, 'Of Fanciers, Footnotes, and Fascism', p. 614.
52. Julia Novak, 'The Notable Woman in Fiction: The Afterlives of Elizabeth Barrett Browning', *A/b: Auto/Biography Studies*, 1, 2016, 83–107 (p. 88).
53. Kelly McSweeney, 'Introduction', in *Aurora Leigh*, by Elizabeth Barrett Browning (Oxford: Oxford University Press, 1993), pp. ix–xxxv (p. xx).
54. Stone.

55. Anne D. Wallace, '"Nor in Fading silks compose": Sewing, Walking, and Poetic Labor in Aurora Leigh', *ELH*, 64.1 (1997), 223–56 (p. 244) <https://doi.org/10.1353/elh.1997.0010>.
56. Christine Chaney, 'The "Prophet-Poet's Book"', *Studies in English Literature, 1500–1900*, 48.4 (2008), 791–9 (p. 794).
57. Julia Briggs, *Virginia Woolf: An Inner Life* (London: Penguin Books, 2006), p. 272.
58. Woolf's retrospective may have exaggerated how unguided her reading really was, as Corbett suggests: more plausibly, Leslie Stephen supervised her choices during her teenage years. *Behind the Times: Virginia Woolf in Late-Victorian Contexts*, pp. 77–8.
59. Sheila Cordner, 'Radical Education in Aurora Leigh', *Victorian Review*, 40.1 (2015), 233–49 (p. 234) <https://doi.org/10.1353/vcr.2014.0005>.
60. Quoted in McSweeney, p. xvii.
61. Snaith, 'Of Fanciers, Footnotes, and Fascism', pp. 625–26; Pamela L. Caughie, 'Flush and the Literary Canon: Oh Where Oh Where Has That Little Dog Gone?', *Tulsa Studies in Women's Literature*, 10.1 (1991), 47–66 (pp. 56–57).
62. Jane Goldman, *The Cambridge Introduction to Virginia Woolf* (Cambridge: Cambridge University Press, 2006), p. 75.
63. See, for example, Craig Smith, 'Across the Widest Gulf: Nonhuman Subjectivity in Virginia Woolf's "Flush"', *Twentieth Century Literature*, 48.3 (2002), 348–61; Jane Goldman, '"Ce Chien est à moi": Virginia Woolf and the Signifying Dog', *Woolf Studies Annual*, 13 (2007), 49–86; David Herman, 'Modernist Life Writing and Nonhuman Lives: Ecologies of Experience in Virginia Woolf's Flush', *MFS Modern Fiction Studies*, 59.3 (2013), 547–68.
64. Stone.
65. Stone. Snaith sets the date slightly earlier and quotes EBB thanking Mitford for Flush in a letter from December 1840 (*F* 9n), however, EBB had not yet received Flush when she wrote this letter: 'there is nothing to be done but to be ready to receive him at the earliest moment, & to love him at all moments, for your sake [ . . . ] will you write to mention the very day he sets out – so that the coachman may be prepared?': Elizabeth Barrett Browning, '779. EBB to Mary Russell Mitford', *The Brownings' Correspondence: An Online Edition* <https://www.browningscorrespondence.com/correspondence/884/?rsId=204445&returnPage=1> (accessed 10 September 2020).
66. Kevin A. Morrison, 'Elizabeth Barrett Browning's Dog Days', *Tulsa Studies in Women's Literature*, 30.1 (2012), 93–115 (p. 98).
67. Scott, p. 155.
68. Barrett Browning.
69. Thomas S. W. Lewis, 'Combining "the advantages of fact and fiction": Virginia Woolf's Biographies of Vita Sackville-West, Flush and Roger Fry', in *Virginia Woolf: Centennial Essays* (Troy, NY: The Whitston Publishing Company, 1983), pp. 295–324 (p. 307); Herman, pp. 553–4.
70. Scott, pp. 170–1.
71. Christine Reynier, 'The Impure Art of Biography: Virginia Woolf's Flush', in *Mapping the Self: Space, Identity, Discourse in British Auto/Biography*

(Saint-Etienne: Publications de l'Université de Saint-Etienne, 2003), pp. 187–202 (p. 191).
72. Craig Smith, pp. 348, 350.
73. Stephen, 'The Browning Letters', p. 32.
74. Novak, p. 94.
75. Stephen, 'The Browning Letters', p. 10.
76. Woolf follows a similar train of thought in 'The London Scene: Great Men's Houses': 'One hour spent in 5 Cheyne Row will tell us more about them and their lives than we can learn from all the biographies': namely, the Carlyles had no running water or gas and only one maid. 'Thus number 5 Cheyne Row is not so much a dwellingplace as a battlefield – the scene of labour, effort and perpetual struggle' (*LS* 31, 34).
77. Reynier, pp. 192–3, 197.
78. Snaith, 'Of Fanciers, Footnotes, and Fascism', pp. 623–4.
79. Scott, p. 172.
80. Susan M. Squier, *Virginia Woolf and London: The Sexual Politics Of the City* (Chapel Hill and London: University of North Carolina Press, 1985), p. 122.
81. Caughie, pp. 60–1.
82. Snaith, 'Of Fanciers, Footnotes, and Fascism', pp. 629–30.
83. Julia Briggs, *Reading Virginia Woolf* (Edinburgh: Edinburgh University Press, 2006), p. 328.

# Chapter 4

# 'That indefinable something': Charlotte Brontë and Protest

Virginia Woolf's engagement with Charlotte Brontë (1816–55) often revolves around distance. In a 1916 *TLS* leader on the centenary of her birth, she emphasises above all Brontë's remoteness – geographical, social and temporal – from modern metropolitan society:

> When we think of her we have to imagine someone who had no lot in our modern world; we have to cast our minds back to the fifties of the last century, to a remote parsonage upon the wild Yorkshire moors. Very few now are those who saw her and spoke to her; and her posthumous reputation has not been prolonged by any circle of friends. (*E* 2.26)

However, she admits, this distance is mediated by a flourishing afterlife which brings before the modern reader 'a picture of Charlotte Brontë, which is as definite as that of a living person, and one may venture to say that to place her name at the head of a page will cause a more genuine interest than almost any other inscription' (*E* 2.26–7). Virginia Woolf was well qualified to judge Brontë's interest to a modern readership: her discussions of Charlotte Brontë span her career, and range from her first published article, 'Haworth, November 1904', two centenary reviews (1916 and 1917), and a *Common Reader* essay to prominent discussion in *A Room of One's Own* and *Three Guineas*. These texts demonstrate the continued relevance of Brontë's life and work to her audience as well as her own reading and writing, and grapple with female authorship, Victorian womanhood and biographical legacies.

It is no coincidence that Woolf prioritises Charlotte over her sisters. The only one of the Brontës to cultivate strong friendships outside of her family, and subject of a biography by fellow novelist Elizabeth Gaskell, Charlotte's more extensively documented life offers itself as a case study for a number of issues, while Emily's incontestable genius becomes a trope of its own and Anne remains largely ignored. Cora Kaplan notes of more recent feminist debates about women's subjectivity and experience that '*Jane Eyre*, its heroine and its author (the distinctions between book character and writer are frequently blurred) have acted as a kind of cultural magnet [ . . . ], drawing widely dispersed issues into the novel's field of meaning'.[1] Woolf's essays fall into a similar pattern: prone to conflating Charlotte Brontë and her heroines, they mix literary criticism and biographical speculation to systematically analyse women's position in Victorian society, as well as to criticise Brontë's individual response to her marginalised position. Over the course of her writing life, Woolf's engagement with Charlotte Brontë shifts from exploration of an individual life towards a larger study of the patterns dominating women's lives: from the detailed examination of Haworth and the personal relics, and a character study of the writer, she moves to a dissection of Brontë as a provincial woman writer, and finally just a nineteenth-century woman.

Woolf's writing on Charlotte Brontë is divisive: virtually all critics focus on her condemnation of Brontë's anger in *A Room of One's Own*, but interpretations range from Andrea Zemguly's liberating manifestation of a Modernist aesthetic of impersonality to Kaplan's class-based attack on a literary outsider. Jane Marcus on the other hand sees Woolf's disavowal of Brontë as a part of the text's fundamentally feminist rhetoric, while Jean Long takes a middle road, reading Woolf's juxtaposition of Austen and Brontë as symbolical of the unresolved binary of anger and irony in her feminism.[2] Fewer critics consider how far Woolf might have identified with a writer she attacked so vigorously: Jane Lilienfeld's queer reading constitutes the only larger-scale investigation of Woolf's Brontë beyond *A Room of One's Own*.[3] Yet many of Woolf's essays are deeply personal: at stake are not only Brontë's femininity and right to protest, but also her own. Particularly in the early articles, Brontë emerges as a model for strength in the face of adversity, as well as outspoken, if unfeminine, protest; linking this phase of Woolf's writing closely with the negotiation of tone in *A Room of One's Own*, as well as the uncompromised criticism of *Three Guineas*. This fascination with Charlotte Brontë is complicated by Woolf's negotiation of her Victorian afterlife: although new biographies were being published by Brontë enthusiasts and fellow writers alike,[4] Woolf's essays instead explore the lasting legacies of Elizabeth Gaskell's *The Life of Charlotte Brontë* (1857) and Leslie Stephen's criticism, rendering her liable to discuss Brontë within the same parameters as these texts and resort to the same tropes and stereotypes.

## Parallel Currents? 'Haworth, November 1904'

Virginia Woolf's career as a professional writer begins with a pilgrimage to the Brontë parsonage: 'Haworth, November 1904' is the first essay she ever wrote for publication.[5] Written during her stay with Madge Vaughan in Giggleswick after Leslie Stephen's death, Woolf accompanies her fairly conventional description of a trip to Haworth with a reflection on the purpose and value of literary tourism. The essay pits her own experience of 'Brontë country' against Gaskell's iconic descriptions of Yorkshire in the *Life of Charlotte Brontë*, yet also shows the lasting impact of her narrative and its division of Brontë's domestic and literary life into parallel currents.

Woolf's uneasy dialogue is with the Victorian period as much as with Gaskell's biography: literary tourism and an increased interest in heritage sites were relatively recent phenomena. As Nicola Watson shows, 'readers were seized en masse by a newly powerful desire to visit the graves, the birthplaces, and the carefully preserved homes of dead poets and men and women of letters' throughout the nineteenth century.[6] Gaskell's *Life of Charlotte Brontë* contributed to this development by positing a close connection between the sisters' unconventional writing and their residence in Yorkshire. After lingering on the slow approach to Haworth parsonage in the first chapter, the second chapter presents a brief and selective history of Yorkshire, arguing that

> [f]or a right understanding of the life of my dear friend, Charlotte Brontë, it appears to me more necessary in her case than in most others, that the reader should be made acquainted with the peculiar forms of population and society amidst which her earliest years were passed.[7]

Haworth's isolation and the wild hostility of Yorkshire and its natives are therefore recurring themes in Gaskell's biography, and eventually become part of a larger myth of 'Brontë country', 'an amalgam of biographical and ambiguously real and fictive locations', at the centre of which was Haworth Parsonage, 'a narrative space which compacts together inextricably the Gothic of the sisters' lives and of their novels'.[8]

By 1904, it was impossible to approach Haworth without expectations shaped by a half-century of Brontë mythology, but Woolf deliberately breaks with some of the most common tropes of the genre. 'Haworth, November 1904' begins with a slightly awkward condemnation of such 'pilgrimages to the shrines of famous men' as 'sentimental journeys'. Woolf's interest in understanding the Brontës as writers leads to her refusal to perform the customary reactions to Brontë country as part of a wider interrogation of the value of literary tourism (*E* 1.5). Although she draws on Gaskell to assert that 'Haworth expresses the Brontës; the Brontës express Haworth; they fit like a snail to its shell' (*E* 1.5), Woolf undercuts the trope of a sublimely Gothic Yorkshire. Instead of Gaskell's 'wild, bleak moors – grand from the ideas of solitude and loneliness which they suggest, or oppressive from the feeling which they give of being pent-up by some monotonous and illimitable barrier',[9] crucial to maintaining the biography's 'myth of martyred feminine creativity',[10] Woolf encounters 'a very cheerful land, which might be likened to a vast wedding cake, of which the icing was slightly undulating; the earth was bridal in its virgin snow' (*E* 1.6). Andrea Zemgulys similarly notes that Woolf is 'pointedly unsentimental in her stance':[11] ironically distancing herself from Gaskell's dramatic hyperbole ('fifty years ago there were few fine days at Haworth' (*E* 1.6)), she finds Haworth itself 'dingy and commonplace' (*E* 1.6) and the recently opened Brontë museum a sad 'mausoleum' with a 'pallid and inanimate collection of objects' (*E* 1.7).[12]

However, Woolf's sceptical stance breaks down when confronted with Charlotte Brontë's dress:[13]

> The most touching case – so touching that one hardly feels reverent in one's gaze – is that which contains the little personal relics, the dresses and shoes of the dead woman. The natural fate of such things is to die before the body that wore them, and because these, trifling and transient though they are, have survived, Charlotte Brontë the woman comes to life, and one forgets the chiefly memorable fact that she was a great writer. (*E* 1.7)

The intimate nature of the dress, and Woolf's intensely emotional reaction to it, suggest that there is some truth to her ironic identification of Haworth as 'the shrine at which we were to do homage' (*E* 1.6). This moment of personal connection and the dress's ability to recall the physical presence of its wearer suggest that it acts as a secular relic, similar to the way Deborah Lutz has described the function of Victorian hair jewellery: '[t]o pore over the relic is to fall into the reverie of memory, to call to mind the absent being. The object disappears and becomes pure symbol, pointing only outside of itself'.[14]

Zemgulys argues that this moment offers a lesson on the dangers of literary tourism: 'the literary museum teaches Woolf how easily it is to *misread* a heritage site by letting the person eclipse the author.[15] However, Woolf's reaction also reveals the long reach of Gaskell's biography: her ready distinction between the woman and the writer imitates the dominant narrative strategy of *The Life of Charlotte Brontë*. Trying to reconcile Brontë's public and domestic identities, Gaskell devised a model of 'parallel currents' that divided her life after the publication of *Jane Eyre*: 'her life as Currer Bell, the author; her life as Charlotte Brontë, the woman. There were separate duties belonging to each character – not opposing each other; not impossible, but difficult to be reconciled'.[16] Gaskell thus retains Brontë's short lived pseudonym to uphold the division between the scandalous author of *Jane Eyre* and the dutiful daughter and wife, disrupting what Linda Peterson terms the 'oppositional mode of the early nineteenth century'. Moving beyond the singular focus on exemplary domesticity dominant in earlier biographies of women writers, the parallel currents allowed Brontë's artistic genius to coexist with her domestic life.[17] Although the biography above all offers an insight into Brontë's private life at home, Gaskell also allowed readers to witness Currer Bell's performance of 'literary genius in a masculine guise', as D'Albertis calls it, by quoting extensively from 'his' literary correspondence with publisher George Smith, editor W. S. Williams and literary figures like G. H. Lewes, alongside Brontë's more intimate correspondence with Ellen Nussey and other female friends.[18] Amber Pouliot traces how Gaskell's parallel currents impacted subsequent literary tourism:

> pilgrims who desired contact with the writer, Currer Bell, sought the wild landscapes associated with her novels and poetry, while those who wished to mourn the death and commemorate the suffering of the woman, Charlotte Brontë, sought the parsonage, the Brontë Museum, and the Church of St Michael and All Angels – the very spaces Woolf tours in her assumed role as the 'sentimental traveller'.[19]

Woolf's glib dismissal of Brontë country thus further privileges the private woman, and undermines her ability to focus on the genius of the writer.

The continued adherence to Gaskell's parallel currents demonstrates that any form of unmediated access to the Brontë sisters remains impossible. Although her frequent references to Gaskell's authority confirm the relevance of each stop on this literary pilgrimage, Woolf's imitation of Gaskell's narrative structure – a slow approach from Keighley, focusing on the scenery, and an uphill journey to the parsonage that ends at the family's memorial tablets – underscores the futility of her own journey. Where *The Life of Charlotte Brontë* moves from wild and windy moors to an intimate encounter with its protagonist, albeit via anecdotes and letters, Woolf encounters an empty house: 'there is nothing remarkable in a mid-Victorian parsonage, though tenanted by genius' (*E* 1.8). Watson emphasises the importance of the parsonage in Gaskell's narrative as an 'essential mechanism in compacting Charlotte Brontë, clergyman's daughter, eldest sister and lady, confined within a household routine detailed at every juncture, with Currer Bell, celebrated author of "wild", "romantic" and "shocking" tales'.[20] Again, Woolf's essay performs a similar motion: collapsing the division between Charlotte Brontë and Currer Bell, she recalls that in the kitchen, 'the girls tramped as they conceived their work' (*E* 1.8).[21] As before, Gaskell's narrative provides the material for this imaginary encounter, but Woolf's slip of memory, which places the sisters in the kitchen instead of the sitting room, emphasises domestic obstacles to their literary endeavours, foregrounding suffering women over literary genius.

Although Woolf's pilgrimage fails to give new insights into the Brontës' works, it enacts an important *topos* of Victorian female literary biography: the visit to the successful woman writer's home. Linda Peterson notes that 'in the *Life* it specifically functions to reinforce the exemplary domesticity of all three women [Elizabeth Gaskell, Charlotte Brontë and Harriet Martineau] and the high literary goals that they share'.[22] Like Brontë's visits to Martineau, which helped establish her place in the literary world, Woolf's journey to Haworth therefore acquires a double meaning. While the essay largely frames it as an act of ultimately futile literary tourism, Woolf symbolically repeats this ritual of initiation into a female tradition of writing, complete with a lingering legacy of Victorian authorship at odds with domesticity.[23] Of course, Brontë's actual use as a role model for Woolf's early career is limited. Woolf's portrayal of her own emerging professional identity is based on a radically modern and commercial approach to literature. Declaring herself 'a lady in search of a job' and wanting 'to work like a steam engine' (*L* 1.167, 172), her determination to turn to journalism 'did much to confirm her status as an "insider" in the literary world at large', Brosnan argues.[24] From this vantage point, the Brontës' laborious entry into the literary marketplace seems quaint and antiquated, and Woolf's essay ends by emphasising this sense of distance. Concluding that '[t]he circumference of her life was very narrow' (*E* 1.8), Woolf neglects the fact that Charlotte as well as her sisters had travelled beyond Haworth, and even England (unlike Woolf herself), and firmly locates her in a remote Victorian past.

Woolf's next turn to Brontëana proves above all her astuteness in choosing journalism as her future career: having moved on from the clerical journal *Guardian*, where she had published 'Haworth, November 1904', she was now writing a centenary celebration of Charlotte Brontë's 100th birthday for the front page of the *Times Literary Supplement*. 'Charlotte Brontë' (*TLS*, 13 April 1916) leaves behind the material memorabilia that had distracted Woolf from the famous author and turns to her novels instead. Musing on the opportunities lost through Brontë's early death – 'a figure familiarly met with in London and elsewhere, the subject of anecdotes and pictures innumerable', Woolf mobilises the 'remote parsonage upon the wild Yorkshire moors' and the sisters' social isolation to declare that Charlotte had 'no lot in our modern world' (*E* 2.26). Only Gaskell's biography and Haworth remain to recall 'that short and circumscribed life' (*E* 2.27) – and of course her novels.

Although Woolf signals a turn to the author, not the woman, her approach remains intensely personal and makes Brontë a friend and companion: the essay offers a character study alongside literary criticism and collapses the boundaries between the woman and the writer that the previous essay had so insistently asserted under Gaskell's influence. However, Woolf's reading of Brontë's life and novels blurs the boundaries between fact and fiction and suggests that Brontë and her heroines are virtually identical: as before, biography interferes with a purely literary appreciation of Brontë's works. This positions 'Charlotte Brontë' in a transitional phase of Woolf's journalism. Like the 1913 'Jane Austen' article, it is still in close dialogue with Victorian criticism; but also initiates an investigation of the representation of character in fiction, which signals a development of Woolf's Modernist aesthetic and distinctive style as a novelist. This ambivalent positioning aligns it with the contemporaneous 'Hours in a Library', which combines a celebration of canonical classics (implicitly located in Leslie Stephen's library) with a call to go 'along unchartered ways in search of new forms for our new sensations' (*E* 2.60).

Transforming her previous symbolical reverence into actual enquiry, Woolf now takes stock of Brontë's literary qualities: 'Charlotte Brontë' is above all interested in what makes her novels so successful. Arguing that works of art are defined by their ability to transcend the periods of their creation, Woolf posits that

> the novels of Charlotte Brontë must be placed within the same class of living and changing creations, which, as far as we can guess, will serve a generation yet unborn with a glass to measure its varying stature. In their turn they will say how she has changed to them, and what she has given them. (*E* 2.27)

Much like her later *Common Reader* essay on Austen's novels, Woolf's approach here anticipates reader response theory in arguing that 'one text is potentially capable of several different realizations, and no reading can ever exhaust the full potential', with different readers filling in 'the unwritten part of the text' with their unique experiences and realities.[25] This 'dialogic principle [ . . . ] leaves room for her own reader's intervention and response' and foregrounds 'a theoretical approach that is speculative and open-ended rather than definitive and conclusive', as Cuddy-Keane argues: this strategy 'encourage[s] readers to shift from conventional realist reading to modernist self-reflexive practices, perhaps even educating readers for their encounters with modernist fictional texts'.[26]

Biographically, the conflation of Brontë's novels with the author herself offers a more multi-faceted and malleable Charlotte Brontë and allows Woolf to transcend the static mid-Victorian image handed down via Gaskell. Woolf supports this reading by offering her essay as only one of many possible interpretations of Brontë. She resists the temptation of 'assigning her to her final position' and declaring her own reading as authoritative and merely offers her readers 'her little hoard of observations' to complement their own (E 2.27): a nod towards the individuality of readers' responses delivered with all the authority of a centenary review in the *Times Literary Supplement*. This approach is even more prominent in a later review of the essay collection *Charlotte Brontë 1816–1916: A Centenary Memorial* ('Charlotte Brontë', published in the *TLS* 13 December 1917). There, Woolf celebrates the collection's widely divergent and even contradictory interpretations of Brontë: 'although we must resign the comfort of depending upon an infallible support, by this means we get a much richer, more various, and finally, we believe, truer estimate than is usual' (E 2.192–3). Brontë's capacity for multiple identities and meanings points forwards to Woolf's own biofictional experimentation, as for example in the fragmented characterisation of *Jacob's Room* or in Orlando's multiple selves.

In spite of the essay's foray into Modernist methods of reading and the representation of character, Woolf's actual criticism of Brontë is decidedly more conventional. Many of her arguments can be traced back to a variety of Victorian sources, most prominently Leslie Stephen's literary criticism and Gaskell's biography. Particularly Woolf's fusion of Jane Eyre and Charlotte Brontë forms part of a well-established critical tradition. Focusing on the novel's immediacy, Woolf argues that *Jane Eyre* allows readers direct access to its author:

> It is not possible, when you are reading Charlotte Brontë, to lift your eyes from the page. She has you by the hand and forces you along her road, seeing the things she sees and as she sees them. She is never absent for a moment, nor does she attempt to conceal herself or to disguise her voice. At the conclusion of *Jane Eyre* we do not feel so much that we have read a book, as that we have parted from a most singular and eloquent woman. (E 2.28)

Reading *Jane Eyre* means reading Charlotte Brontë: asserting that 'she is herself the heroine of her own novels' (E 2.28), Woolf appears to take the subtitle 'An Autobiography' at face value. Early reviewers like

George Henry Lewes had classified *Jane Eyre* as 'an autobiography, – not perhaps, in the naked facts and circumstances but in the actual suffering and experience' in spite of its author's ungendered pseudonym, and the *Revue des Deux Mondes* thought it 'eminently and vigorously personal'.[27] However, most influential on Woolf is Leslie Stephen's article on Brontë in his *Cornhill* series *Hours in a Library*. Stephen not only identifies Brontë's heroines as 'mouthpieces of her peculiar sentiment', but also suggests that the critic can 'infer her personality more or less accurately from the mode in which she contemplates her neighbours, but it is directly manifest in various avatars of her own spirit [ . . . ] when they speak we are really listening to her voice'.[28] Woolf's description of Brontë's intensity of language and vision echoes Stephen's imagery. In Stephen's words, Brontë's stories

> always give us the impression of a fiery soul imprisoned in too narrow and too frail a tenement. The fire is pure and intense. It is kindled in a nature intensely emotional and yet aided by a heroic sense of duty.[29]

Similarly, Woolf judges that 'her production, whatever its faults, always seems to issue from a deep place where the fire is eternal' (E 2.29–30).

Woolf's essay differs from Stephen in the extent to which she reads this passion biographically. Stephen pursues a heavily analytical reading that focuses on 'what, in a scientific sense, would be an inconsistent theory, and, in an aesthetic sense, an inharmonious presentation of life': the unresolved contrast between individual passions and social conventions in Brontë's novels leads him to argue that she lacks a consistent philosophical framework.[30] Woolf, in contrast, reads passion through a heavily gendered lens: criticising Brontë's lack of professional and emotional experience, she quips that 'to be always in love and always a governess is to go through the world with blinkers on one's eyes' (E 2.29), again drawing on Victorian precedents. Gaskell chronicles the end of Brontë's friendship with Martineau over the latter's review of *Villette*, which emphasised that '[t]here are substantial, heartfelt interests for women of all ages, and under ordinary circumstances, quite apart from love'.[31]

In singling out love as the defining element of Brontë's work, Woolf was also reacting to recent biographical discoveries regarding Brontë's tutor in Brussels, Constantine Heger. In 1913, Heger's heirs had donated four passionate letters from Brontë to the British Library, which were subsequently translated and published in *The Times*.[32] This confirmed longstanding rumours about the autobiographical basis of Brontë's works, as for example Leslie Stephen's speculation that *Villette*'s Paul Emanuel was 'hardly explicable, except as a portrait drawn by a skilful hand guided by love, and by love intensified by the consciousness of some impassable barrier'.³³ Although Woolf remains discreetly silent on the facts of Brontë's illicit desire, it informs her depiction of her literary activity: she pictures her writing in compulsive wish-fulfilment as an almost involuntary reaction to 'the burden of sorrow and shame which life had laid on her' (*E* 2.29). This strong focus on the Heger affair distinguishes Woolf's approach from prominent Brontë biographer Clement Shorter, who emphasised the intellectual importance of Heger's tuition for Brontë's literary development even after having to concede the truth of the rumours, but also May Sinclair, who continued to envision Brontë succeeding *in spite* of her Brussels experience: 'in Haworth her genius found itself at home'.³⁴ Woolf shares with this approach only that she too envisions writing as an act of resistance and a way of exerting control over life:

> Every one of her books seems to be a superb gesture of defiance, bidding her torturers depart and leave her queen of a splendid island of imagination. Like some hard-pressed captain, she summoned her powers together and proudly annihilated the enemy. (*E* 2.29)

This focus on the emotional quality of Brontë's writing leaves little room for ambition or even conscious revision or development, but it is an assertion of genius, leaving Brontë triumphant despite her own and her life's limitations.

This reading in itself suggests the fruitfulness of the personal, reader-response-oriented approach that the essay champions. The purpose and value of writing as a means of self-assertion was intensely relevant to Woolf at this period of time: following a breakdown after her marriage, she had only just resumed her activity as a reviewer after a three-year hiatus. In a 1930 letter to Ethel Smyth, Woolf reflected on the extreme significance of writing during this period:

> I was so tremblingly afraid of my own insanity that I wrote *Night and Day* mainly to prove to my own satisfaction that I could keep entirely off that dangerous ground. I wrote it, lying in bed, allowed to write only for one half hour a day. (*L* 4.231)

As a fellow woman writer whose tendency towards morbidity was documented in detail by Gaskell, Charlotte Brontë therefore offered an example of how to use writing for psychological recovery, while a lead article on a canonical woman writer signalled Woolf's return to a professional position of literary authority.

Woolf's ultimate praise of Brontë 'not only as a writer of genius, but as a very noble human being' (*E* 2.31) suggests a personal identification confirmed by the intimate tone and personal focus of the essay. While in

'Haworth, November 1904', the woman had overshadowed the author, here Woolf defends and deliberately constructs a personal encounter as part of the special relationship between readers and writers: 'we are conscious of something that is greater than one gift or another and is perhaps the quality that attaches us to books as people – the quality, that is, of the writer's mind and personality' (*E* 2.31). Although Zemgulys posits a seamless development from 'Haworth, November 1904' to Woolf's criticism in *A Room of One's Own*,[35] Woolf's celebration of a personal connection with Brontë demonstrates that at least in her centenary article, the woman and the author are equally important, and equally fascinating. The value of this personal connection lessens only during the 1920s: Woolf's increasing focus on Brontë in her social context results in a desire to distance herself from her flawed predecessor.

## 'One must be a lady': Woolf's Feminism and Charlotte Brontë

With the 1920s, Woolf's engagement with Charlotte Brontë returns to more familiar territory: many of her reviews from this period, such as, for example, 'Women Novelists' (1918) and 'An Imperfect Lady' (1920), lay the groundwork for *A Room of One's Own* in their close examination of the material and social context of women's writing. As in the feminist revision of Mary Russell Mitford's life, Woolf's interest moves from a personal reading – Brontë's passionate defiance in the face of adversity – to the symbolical significance of her literary life: as a case study for women's writing in the nineteenth century, Brontë becomes a victim of patriarchal society with whom Woolf no longer identifies closely, as the *Common Reader* essay 'Jane Eyre and Wuthering Heights' (1925) and *A Room of One's Own* demonstrate.

Woolf's 1918 review of R. Brimley Johnson's *The Women Novelists* programmatically introduces some of the key questions that would drive her literary criticism for the decade to come:

> What, for example, was the origin of that extraordinary outburst in the eighteenth century of novel writing by women? Why did it begin then, and not in the time of the Elizabethan renaissance? Was the motive which finally determined them to write a desire to correct the current view of their sex expressed in so many volumes and for so many ages by male writers? (*E* 2.314)

Although Woolf is hesitant about the book's premise – 'experience seems to prove that to criticise the work of a sex as a sex is merely to state with almost invariable acrimony prejudices derived from the fact that you are either a man or a woman' (*E* 2.314) – it clearly serves as a springboard for her own analysis. Johnson traces the development of women's writing through the works of Frances Burney, Jane Austen, Charlotte Brontë and George Eliot as well as the 'minor writers' that came between them and offers a comparative literary analysis and a reading of the cultural context that shaped female authorship. As Woolf's initial questions suggest, she is almost exclusively interested in the latter: while she does not yet offer an answer ('money and a room of her own' (*AROO* 3)) to these questions, she is confident that 'the question is not one merely of literature, but to a large extent of social history' (*E* 2.314). 'Women Novelists' therefore prompts Woolf with an opportunity to re-examine Brontë as a woman writer in a patriarchal society.

Anticipating the focus of *A Room of One's Own*, Woolf's exploration of women's social history focuses mainly on the domestic obstacles they encountered:

> [Miss Burney's] manuscripts were burned by her stepmother's orders, and needlework inflicted as a penance, much as, a few years later, Jane Austen would slip her writing beneath a book if anyone came in, and Charlotte Brontë stopped in the middle of her work to pare the potatoes. (*E* 2.315)

Johnson references the burning of Burney's manuscript several times to illustrate how hostile her environment was to female authorship, but Charlotte Brontë's potatoes are Woolf's own addition. Potatoes are one of the items which Pouliot finds imbued with 'allegorical possibilities' in Gaskell's *Life of Charlotte Brontë*: they come to represent the sisters' physical and social near-starvation as well as their creative 'sprouting', but also indicate 'that of the two parallel currents [of Charlotte Brontë's life], the domestic was strongest'.[36] Gaskell's anecdote has Charlotte interrupt the composition of *Jane Eyre* to stealthily re-peel an ageing servant's imperfectly peeled potatoes, thus demonstrating her humility and exemplary domesticity, as well as the sisters' kindness and loyalty to their employees.[37] The anecdote clearly appealed to Victorian audiences: Lucasta Miller traces its proliferation in late-Victorian collections of exemplary women's lives, where Brontë became a model of domesticity to young girls who were almost certainly forbidden from reading her works – as Woolf herself may have been until August 1897.[38] Although Brontë's paid work as teacher and governess would have offered a more forceful example of outside disruptions to her writing, Woolf flags household interruptions as an obstacle overlooked by Johnson to begin her analysis of the stifling effects of Victorian domesticity and re-evaluation of Brontë's sacrifices.

As in 'Haworth, November 1904', Woolf also subtly downplays the Brontës' economic position in 'Women Novelists'. Brontë's deliberate act of kindness becomes a necessity through the omission of the parsonage servants. This may seem like a trivial change, but it sets the tone for much of Woolf's ensuing criticism. As part of her ironic assessment of women writers' suitability for inclusion in Constance Hill's biographies in 'An Imperfect Lady', Woolf suggests that '[t]he Brontës, however highly we rate their genius, lacked that indefinable something which marks the lady' (*E* 3.210). As Chapter 3 showed, Woolf mocks the code of conduct which causes Hill to prefer Mitford's quiet suffering over potentially more outspoken biographical subjects, but ultimately adheres to the same rules in hiding her analysis of Dr Mitford's abusive behaviour behind a humorous tone. Woolf therefore contrasts not only Austen, but also herself, with Charlotte Brontë when she proclaims that

> [o]ne must be a lady. Yet what that means, and whether we like what it means, may be doubtful. If we say that Jane Austen was a lady and that Charlotte Brontë was not one, we do as much as need be done in the way of definition, and commit ourselves to neither side. (*E* 3.211)

Without a closer dissection of the values and assumptions driving this social division, Woolf invokes Brontë's Victorian reputation as a coarse and unfeminine writer. However, her concern with female voicelessness and repressed anger, which permeates the review, also recalls the defiant captain of the centenary review: Brontë can raise her voice, 'seize the silver table by the legs or dash the teacups on the floor', a more direct and effective form of protest from which genteel women like Woolf, Austen and Mitford are debarred.

By 1925, this is a thing of the past: Woolf's *Common Reader* essay 'Jane Eyre and Wuthering Heights' (1925) asserts above all the difference between their social and geographical positions, but also their literary aims: Brontë's intensely personal mode of writing is increasingly at odds with Woolf's more impersonal Modernist fiction. This shift in Woolf's self-positioning is particularly striking because, like many of the *Common Reader* essays, '"Jane Eyre" and "Wuthering Heights"' is based on a revised version of her earlier enthusiastic centenary essay. Its strong sense of personal identification and the speculative, open-ended reading of Brontë's works and personality have become fixed, and Woolf now presents an image of Brontë defined by her social and geographical isolation in Haworth. This interest in the impact of Brontë's social position on her writing is in keeping with Woolf's move towards a feminist re-evaluation of women's writing, but also signals a return to Gaskell, who first posited the strong link between Brontë and Yorkshire. Woolf's image of Charlotte Brontë 'in that parsonage and on those moors, unhappy and lonely, in her poverty and her exaltation' (CR 155) firmly limits Brontë to an existence in Haworth and ignores her life in Brussels. In strong contrast to her on-going re-evaluation of Austen, Woolf therefore appears to have internalised Gaskell's position, signalling an inevitable return to Victorian ways of interpreting Brontë.

This solidification of Brontë's image is accompanied by a more critical analysis of how '[t]hese circumstances [ . . . ] may have left their traces on her work'. While Woolf still praises the immediacy and timelessness of *Jane Eyre*, her analysis focuses more strongly on Brontë's formation as a writer, particularly her lack of education and literary professionalism. Woolf suggests that Brontë's style 'owed nothing to the reading of many books. She never learnt the smoothness of the professional writer [ . . . ] [S]he writes as a lead writer in a provincial journal might have written' (CR 158). Woolf delivers this verdict with all the force of her own metropolitan professionalism: by now an avant-garde novelist and celebrated essayist, she relegates Brontë to the position of a talented but crude predecessor and ignores the atmosphere of feverish literary production and consumption that characterised life in the Brontë parsonage. While Brontë's 'own authentic voice' remains forceful and poetic, Woolf strongly implies that she never acquired the sophistication which distinguishes her writing from that of the amateur:

> we read Charlotte Brontë not for exquisite observations of character – her characters are vigorous and elementary; not for comedy – hers is grim and crude; not for a philosophic view of life – hers is that of a country parson's daughter; but for her poetry. (CR 158)

Again, Woolf echoes Leslie Stephen in expressing this sense of superiority: he similarly suggested that Brontë's 'mind, with its exceptional powers in certain directions, never broke the fetters by which the parson's daughter of the last generation was restricted'.[39] Where Stephen speaks as a university-educated man of letters, Woolf uses her professional status: as Kaplan notes, it is in 'the disdainful voice of a metropolitan intellectual that Woolf carefully crafts the degradation of Brontë's class status and education – one that willingly distorts the breadth of her reading as well as her experience of other places'.[40]

This widening sense of distance also shapes Woolf's discussion of Brontë's now 'overpowering personality'. Although the intensity of *Jane Eyre* remains praiseworthy to Woolf, she is now more critical of the strong autobiographical identification between Brontë and her heroines, further evidence of her limitations as a writer:

> [s]he does not attempt to solve the problems of human life; she is even unaware that such problems exist; all her force, and it is the more tremendous for being constricted, goes into the assertion, 'I love', 'I hate', 'I suffer'. (CR 159)

Noting Brontë's 'desire to create instantly rather than observe patiently' (CR 158), Woolf's criticism echoes George Henry Lewes's debate about literary femininity with Brontë: she refused 'to finish more and be more subdued' and be like 'observant' Jane Austen.[41] Charlotte's flaws emerge even more clearly in contrast to Emily, who transcends both her limiting environment and personal grievances: 'There is no "I" in *Wuthering Heights*. There are no governesses. There are no employers. [ . . . ] She looked out upon a world cleft into gigantic disorder and felt within her the power to unite it in a book' (CR 159). As in her reappraisal of Austen, Woolf now encounters distinctly Modernist elements in Emily's writing: her ability to 'free life from its dependence on facts, with a few touches indicate the spirit of a face so that it needs no body' (CR 161) is closely aligned with Woolf's own goal to convey life, 'this varying, this unknown and uncircumscribed spirit [ . . . ] with as little mixture of the of the alien and external as possible' (CR 150).

It should come as no surprise, then, that *A Room of One's Own* begins with the outright rejection of 'a tribute to the Brontës'. Woolf dismisses both a plausible Victorian canon – 'a few remarks about Fanny Burney; a few more about Jane Austen; a tribute to the Brontës and a sketch of Haworth Parsonage under snow; some witticisms if possible about Miss Mitford; a respectful allusion to George Eliot; a reference to Mrs Gaskell' (*AROO* 3) – as well as her own previous engagement with her literary predecessors. Yet criticism of Charlotte Brontë is central to the argument of *A Room of One's Own*. Tracing the development of women's writing from the excessively hostile ideological climate of the Early Modern period to its emergence as a respectable means of employment at the end of the eighteenth century, Woolf emphasises how sexism and the limitations of a Victorian middle-class lifestyle continued to restrict women's writing. Suggesting that the narrow confines of female life explain the sudden emergence of the novel as women's medium of choice, Woolf argues that

> all the literary training that a woman had in the early nineteenth century was training in the observation of character, in the analysis of emotion.

> Her sensibility had been educated for centuries by the influences of the common sitting-room. (*AROO* 61)

Woolf's literary history elides women's contributions to other genres, particularly non-fiction, as Chapter 5 will explore in greater detail; but she also ignores large numbers of other nineteenth-century novelists by focusing only on Charlotte Brontë's reaction to this limited sphere.

In contrast to Austen's quiet transcendence of society's constraints, Woolf finds in *Jane Eyre* an example of open rebellion against Victorian gender and class politics. Again conflating Brontë and her heroines, Woolf's extensive quotation includes Jane's programmatic speech on women's desire for a wider sphere:

> It is in vain to say that human beings ought to be satisfied with tranquillity [ . . . ] Women are supposed to be very calm generally: but women feel just as men feel; they need exercise for their faculties and a field for their efforts as much as their brothers do; they suffer from too rigid a constraint, too absolute a stagnation, precisely as men would suffer; and it is narrow-minded in their more privileged fellow creatures to say that they ought to confine themselves to making puddings and knitting stockings, to playing on the piano and embroidering bags. (*AROO* 62–3/*Jane Eyre* ch. 12)

Woolf makes Brontë representative of the Victorian woman: in voicing her anger at her exclusion from public and intellectual life, Brontë 'puts her finger exactly not only upon her own defects as a novelist but upon those of her sex at that time' (*AROO* 63). Her central criticism is that Brontë creates an 'awkward break' (*AROO* 63) in the narrative of *Jane Eyre*:

> [I]t is clear that anger was tempering with the integrity of Charlotte Brontë the novelist. She left her story, to which her entire devotion was due, to attend to some personal grievance. She remembered that she had been starved of her proper due of experience – she had been made to stagnate in a parsonage mending stockings when she wanted to wander free over the world. (*AROO* 66)

Woolf's biographical reading of *Jane Eyre* fits into the pattern of her previous engagement with Brontë, again sidelining her stay in Brussels and substituting household annoyances for her work as governess. However, this fixation on one specific passage also leaves her open to criticism: unlike her more generalised praise of Austen, this critical reading of *Jane Eyre* is not necessarily convincing. Even without drawing on Gilbert and Gubar's famous feminist revision of Bertha as Jane's double,[42] Woolf's 'awkward break' is by no means the only way of reading this passage.

Jane's passionate soliloquy ends by condemning the laughter of those who disparage women's ambitions, and is followed by Bertha's actual laughter: this aligns Bertha with Jane's adversaries, and eases the transition from Jane's internal to her external world, as well as invoking Bertha as cautionary figure against such anger and desires.

Politically, as well, Jane's speech resonates within the political context of the 1840s. Voicing the 'personal grievances' of many Victorian middle-class women but also those of working-class men, Brontë skilfully invokes the social unrest of the Hungry Forties as well as Chartism, then at the heights of its power, by reminding the reader that 'Millions are condemned to a stiller doom than mine, and millions are in silent revolt against their lot. Nobody knows how many rebellions ferment in the masses of life which people earth' (*AROO* 63/*Jane Eyre* ch. 12). As Kaplan notes, Woolf's 'critical strategy goes further to devalue that voice, pre-emptively eroding its ability to speak either universally, for "most people" or for women' despite the universal applicability of this bold political statement.[43] Jane Marcus argues that, far from eroding the socialist potential of this speech, *A Room of One's Own* moves it 'from the realm of history to the realm of art in Woolf's socialist argument that "masterpieces are not single and solitary births"'. Yet while Woolf's denigration of Brontë may be an integral part of 'the internal logic of the historical movement of the text' and allow Woolf to establish herself in a feminist tradition, it undoubtedly happens at the expense of Brontë.[44]

Woolf's discussion of Brontë therefore creates its own awkward break in the argument of *A Room of One's Own*, and her exploration of Brontë's life and death goes beyond the requirements of her argument. Now discarding Gaskell's interpretation of Brontë's exemplary domesticity, Woolf focuses instead on her passionate anger and failure to adapt her writing to the requirements of Victorian femininity:

> The woman who wrote these pages had more genius in her than Jane Austen; but if one reads them over and marks that jerk in them, that indignation, one sees that she will never get her genius expressed whole and entire. Her books will be deformed and twisted. She will write in a rage where she should write calmly. *She will write foolishly where she should write wisely. She will write of herself when she should be writing of her characters.* She is at war with her lot. How could she help but die young, cramped and thwarted? (*AROO* 63)

This entire passage changed surprisingly little between manuscript and print copy: in contrast to the surrounding paragraphs, it contains no deletions or emendations; the only substantial changes are the completion of the first sentence and the addition of the two italicised sentences to replace the repetition of 'She will be at war with herself'.⁴⁵ One reason for this may be that Woolf's critique happens through the perpetuation of a critical tradition that chastises Brontë for her imperfect femininity. Thus, Jean Long notes that 'the Victorians were particularly exercised by the combination of anger and femininity in an author. With a different emphasis this is also what informs Woolf's objections to Charlotte Brontë's writing'.⁴⁶

Specifically, Woolf's criticism draws on Leslie Stephen's *Hours in a Library* to resituate his verdicts in a larger feminist argument. Stephen argues that Brontë is fundamentally conflicted because she advocates for individual passions as well as duty as the commanding principles of life:

> The imprisonment is not merely that of a feeble body in uncongenial regions, but that of a narrow circle of thought, and consequently of a mind which has never worked itself clear by reflection, or developed a harmonious or consistent view of life. There is a certain feverish disquiet which is marked by the peculiar mannerism of the style. [ . . . ] At its worst, it is strangely contorted, crowded by rather awkward personifications [ . . . ] We feel an aspiration after more than can be accomplished, an unsatisfied yearning for potent excitement, which is sometimes more fretful than forcible.⁴⁷

Like Woolf in *A Room of One's Own*, Stephen firmly links Brontë's personal shortcomings to her stylistic mannerisms: his 'contorted' style, full of 'feverish disquiet' and 'unsatisfied yearning for potent excitement' are echoed in her image of 'deformed and twisted' books and Brontë's 'cramped and thwarted' life. Clearly, both believe that Brontë is 'at war' – yet Woolf amends the manuscript's 'at war with herself' (*W&F* 105), more closely aligned with Stephen's interpretation, to 'at war with her lot' (*AROO* 63), thus re-contextualising his verdict to argue that Brontë is hampered by a patriarchal society, not her own philosophical shortcomings. In spite of this revision, Woolf's analysis remains deeply personal and targets Brontë's early death as well as her poverty. Thus, she chastises Brontë in a voice that echoes the angry male critic she otherwise dissects throughout the essay:

> One could not but play for a moment with the thought of what might have happened if Charlotte Brontë had possessed say three hundred a year – but the foolish woman sold the copyright of her novels outright for fifteen hundred pounds. (*AROO* 63)

Woolf highlights that Brontë's publisher made a fortune at her expense, yet ignores the fact that she was following standard mid-Victorian practice: as in 'Jane Austen at Sixty', this uncharacteristically profit-oriented approach to literature unrealistically implies that writing fiction would easily have funded a life of travel in metropolitan society. Gualtieri draws attention to the 'vicious circle' in Woolf's argument

> whereby the five hundred pounds a year become both the precondition of a woman's writing (since she 'must have money and a room of her own' (4) in order to write fiction) and its final outcome (as 'money dignifies what is frivolous if unpaid for (84)'.⁴⁸

Condemning Brontë either way (as she failed both to have and earn significant amounts of money), this passage may be an instance of 'Woolf's multilevel discourse [which] allows these different readers to enter her text from different positions', reaching out to those readers who locate Brontë's struggles in life squarely on her own shoulders. Yet '[t]o understand Woolf's rhetoric is therefore not always to see it as successful', Cuddy-Keane concedes.⁴⁹ Here, the reception speaks for itself: as one of the most contested passages of *A Room of One's Own*, the rhetoric of Woolf's criticism of Brontë clearly fails for many of her readers.

Yet Woolf's decision to devote multiple pages of analysis to Brontë's protest against the lot of Victorian women suggests that just like Austen, she is more than just a negative example. Although Woolf aggressively distances herself from Brontë, she also strongly identifies with her anger: as in 'An Imperfect Lady', Brontë suggests the freedom to express her feelings directly and presents Woolf with an opportunity to examine her own anxieties regarding women's voices, anger and femininity. These dominate the narrative structure of *A Room of One's Own*: Woolf's fictional autobiographical narrative balances the insistence of a firsthand account of women's exclusion from institutions of culture and learning with the possibility of distancing herself to maintain a ladylike indifference. Gewirtz notes that *A Room of One's Own*'s 'proof copy is rife with examples of Woolf attempting to erase from the text any evidence of her untransmuted anger, or of what might be called an aggrieved sensibility'.⁵⁰ Long likewise flags that 'Woolf's work was similarly compromised at this stage in her career by her uneasy mediation between [ . . . ] the general dispossession of women and, on the other, her barely-acknowledged tendency to heed [ . . . ] the male reader'.⁵¹ Woolf's reflections on the reception of *A Room of One's Own* show her attempts to mediate these extremes:

> It is a little ominous that Morgan won't review it. It makes me suspect that there is a shrill feminine tone in it which my intimate friends will dislike. I forecast, then, that I shall get no criticism, except of the evasive jocular kind, from Lytton, Roger and Morgan; that the press will be kind and talk of its charm and sprightliness; also I shall be attacked for a feminist and hinted at for a Sapphist; [ . . . ] I shall get a good many letters from young women. I am

afraid it will not be taken seriously. Mrs Woolf is so accomplished a writer that all she says makes easy reading ... this very feminine logic ... a book to be put in the hands of girls. I doubt that I mind very much. (*WD* 148)

Fearing both to alienate male friends with 'a shrill feminine tone' and that her 'charm and sprightliness' would undermine the force of her argument, Woolf charts the impossibility of her situation, but also reveals her hesitancy to fully commit to the feminist position of *A Room of One's Own*. Her objection to its hypothetical classification as 'a book to be put in the hands of girls' anticipates male critics' dismissal of her essay, but also shows how much she still accepted and internalised this implicit devaluation. Yet given its genesis as a lecture at Girton and Newnham Colleges, this is exactly what *A Room of One's Own* should be: a text for the women and girls who are the future of women's writing.

Woolf's diary entry reveals the drawback of her charming, unthreatening tone: adhering to the polite 'surface manner' of the Victorian drawing room leaves the reader to infer the unsaid and to correctly read through her irony, thereby risking that her more serious criticism will pass unnoticed (*MoB* 152). The very subtle interplay between Woolf's deletion of Jane Eyre's narrativisation of herself in the two paragraphs quoted in *A Room of One's Own* and its 'use of ellipses as an organizing principle to mirror the absence of women from patriarchal history, of women's writing from the canon' identified by Jane Marcus is one such casualty, only apparent to the most astute of readers.[52] In contrast, Brontë directly and unambiguously sets out women's desires and discontents in the extract from *Jane Eyre*, rejecting all blame from the beginning. Brontë's speech disrupts the 'easy reading' and allows Woolf to express her personal anger, albeit in another woman's voice: as Long argues, this act of 'ventriloquism' grants Woolf

> the best of both worlds: she is able without embarrassment to express her own anger through the voice of "a most singular and eloquent woman" (*E* 2.28) while at the same time, [ ... ] allowing herself to criticize Brontë's angry voice on literary grounds.[53]

Long's easy dismissal of Woolf's demolition of Brontë's life and work as merely literary criticism ignores its personal component: the attack on Brontë publicly severs all possible connection between Woolf and the flawed and angry woman writer. Yet in turning to Brontë to express an anger she would not voice herself, *A Room of One's Own* also preserves traces of her earlier admiration for the 'hard-pressed captain [ ... ] proudly annihilat[ing] the enemy' (*E* 2.29) – in a deformed and twisted way.

### A Victorian Everywoman

In the 1930s, the Brontës, alongside other Victorian novelists, experienced a popular revival. '[F]rom the late 1920s there was an unprecedented biodrama boom' driven by a middlebrow reading public which 'was increasingly interested in Victorian literature and culture' – a trend which the Hogarth Press followed with Woolf's *Flush* and *The Years*, among others.[54] Nicola Humble notes that '[t]he Brontës were in many ways the perfect middlebrow subject: available both for serious analysis and gossipy speculation; their works clearly of high literary status, but also intimately familiar to many middle-class women through repeated adolescent readings'. Thematically, these middlebrow readings echo Woolf's criticism of the previous decade, focusing on 'the social and geographical isolation of the family, the claustrophobia of their domestic life, and their use of literature as an escape'.[55]

Paradoxically, the peak of this Brontë revival coincides with Woolf's turn from them: her case study of Charlotte Brontë in *Three Guineas* is her last significant piece of criticism. Privately, she continued to be interested in Brontëiana, as when she skewered E. F. Benson's biography of Charlotte Brontë in a letter to Nelly Cecil in 1932. As a nephew of the Sidgwick family, who had briefly and unsuccessfully employed Brontë as a governess in 1839, Benson intended his biography to offer a correction of what he perceived as Gaskell's overly flattering portrait: his Charlotte is rigid and self-centred and fails to understand the tortured genius of her siblings Branwell and Emily.[56] Woolf's dismissal of Benson's biography suggests a certain amount of protectiveness of Brontë:

> I daresay [*Charlotte Brontë* by] E. F. Benson was all right – its only I detest the collocation (is that the word?) of that tubby ruddy fleshy little Clubman with Charlotte. Its impure. Its like cats marrying dogs – against the right order of things. Let him stick to Dodo. I cant follow the Bronte enthusiasts. A lunatic, living I think near Hatfield, has sent me a book proving that Branwell [Brontë] wrote Wuthering Heights – the work (her work that is,) she says, of years. One of Benson's points was that Charlotte had no feeling of any kind for the other sex; but was entirely decimated (is that a word?) by passion for one of those obscure old frumps – Hussey, [Ellen] Nussey – what was her name? Yet I can remember, or think I can, old George Smith preening himself – hundreds of years ago – when my mother said – oh this is millions of years ago, I may well have invented it – 'I am sure Charlotte was in love with you Mr Smith'. (*L* 5.80)

Lumping Benson with fanatical Branwell enthusiasts, Woolf dismisses out of hand his insistence that 'there is so much queer and seemingly strong evidence that [Branwell] not only knew about it [*Wuthering Heights*], but had something to do with it'.[57] Woolf's contemptuous reference to Benson's popular *Dodo* series (1893–1921), featuring 'the smoking, shooting, screaming composer of Masses, Miss Staines' as a caricature of Ethel Smyth, suggests a cause for her antipathy.[58] While Woolf was by no means always positively disposed towards either woman, she clearly resents Benson's self-aggrandisement at their expense. Thus, she is also unimpressed with Benson's queering of Brontë's relationship with Ellen Nussey. Following 'an emotional thread that for years was of vividest colour in Charlotte's life, and continued, more soberly hued, to the end of it', Benson uncovers 'one of those violent homosexual attachments which, so common are they among adolescents of either sex, must be considered normal rather than abnormal'.[59] In strong contrast to Woolf's centenary essay, which celebrated Brontë's ability to adapt to different readers' needs, she now rigidly denies her queer potential, thereby complicating Jane Lilienfeld's assertion that 'the reconstructed figure of the lesbian Brontë [encountered through Vita Sackville-West] reshaped Woolf's earlier conception of Brontë'.[60] Instead, Woolf counters Benson's suggestion that '[n]ever again did [Charlotte Brontë] give her heart to anyone, man or woman, in joy and exaltation'[61] with her own memories of the Smith family's heterosexual Brontë cult – 'ke[eping] Charlotte Brontes socks in a glass case in his drawing room' (*L* 5.96)) to deny his theories plausibility.

Resentment at men's uses of Charlotte Brontë, whether Smith's, Benson's or the Reverend Patrick Brontë's, link Woolf's impromptu analysis in her letter to Nelly Cecil with *Three Guineas*. *Three Guineas* departs from the more restrained feminism of *A Room of One's Own*: Woolf firmly and directly attributes women's suffering to an oppressive patriarchal system perpetuated by men. It therefore represents a culmination of Woolf's partial but complex identification with Brontë's anger. Thus, Lilienfeld emphasises that 'Woolf adapts not only the fearlessness of Charlotte Brontë, but one of her central images' in the fires set ablaze by the daughters of educated men.[62] Woolf's fire imagery recalls her earlier reviews with their assertion that Brontë's writing issued from 'a deep place where the fire is eternal' (*E* 2.30). However, the externalisation of these fires also mirrors Woolf's shift away from an analysis that foregrounds Brontë's personal response to one that focuses on the society around her: once again, the focus is on the woman, not the writer.

In *Three Guineas*, Woolf returns to Gaskell's parallel currents: her close reading of domestic life in Haworth Parsonage both follows and subverts traditional Brontë biography. The first edition of *The Life of Charlotte Brontë* had featured multiple sensational anecdotes of Patrick Brontë's domestic tyranny, which allegedly caused the Brontë children to live in miserable conditions even before their more famous suffering at the Clergy Daughters' School. While lack of reliable evidence compelled Gaskell to cut the majority of these anecdotes from subsequent editions,[63] stories of this 'strange eccentricity' still found their way into Leslie Stephen's entry on Charlotte Brontë for the *Dictionary of National Biography*:

> He enforced strict discipline; the children were fed on potatoes without meat to make them hardy. He burnt their boots when he thought them too smart, and for the same reason destroyed a silk gown of his wife's. He generally restrained open expression of his anger, but would relieve his feelings by firing pistols out of his back-door or destroying articles of furniture. [ . . . ] He was unsocial in his habits, loved solitary rambles over the moors, and, in consequence of some weakness of digestion, dined alone even before his wife's death and to the end of his own life.[64]

If Woolf had wanted a portrait of Patrick Brontë as a sensational villain, these Victorian sources certainly provided it. Instead, however, she limits her analysis to a superficially much more mundane subject: Patrick Brontë's refusal to sanction his daughter's marriage to his curate Arthur Nicholls.

> There is the case of the Rev. Patrick Brontë. The Rev. Arthur Nicholls was in love with his daughter Charlotte; 'What his words were,' she wrote, when Mr Nicholls proposed to her, 'you can imagine; his manner you can hardly realize nor can I forget it . . . I asked if he had spoken to Papa. He said he dared not.' Why did he dare not? He was strong and young and passionately in love; the father was old. The reason is immediately apparent. 'He [the Rev. Patrick Brontë] always disapproved of marriages, and constantly talked against them. But he more than disapproved this time; he could not bear the idea of this attachment of Mr Nicholls to his daughter. Fearing the consequences . . . she made haste to give her father a promise that, on the morrow, Mr Nicholls should have a distinct refusal.' Mr Nicholls left Haworth; Charlotte remained with her father. Her married life – it was to be a short one – was shortened still further by her father's wish. (3G 258–9)

Again, Woolf's account is based on Gaskell's biography. However, she omits part of the last sentence of the quotation to better adapt Brontë's situation to her argument: 'Fearing the consequences *of agitation to one so recently an invalid* she made haste to give her father a promise'.[65] In keeping with the anecdotes of Patrick Brontë's violent outbursts, fear of violence rather than concern for her father's health appears to drive Brontë's decision in Woolf's account.

This omission may also be driven by a strong personal identification of this situation. As Lilienfeld and Hermione Lee note, Brontë's brief married existence bears a strong resemblance to Stella Duckworth's marriage to Jack Hills, similarly disapproved of by Leslie Stephen.[66] Like Charlotte Brontë, Stella died from complications related to pregnancy early in her marriage; and Leslie Stephen's emotional manipulation of Stella resonates with Brontë's concern for her father's health, as Woolf's later analysis in 'A Sketch of the Past' suggests: 'He was jealous clearly. But in those days nothing was clear. He had his traditional pose; he was the lonely; the deserted; the unhappy old man. In fact he was possessive; hurt; a man jealous of a young man' (*MoB* 115). Stephen's behaviour matches the 'infantile fixation' with which Woolf diagnosed Patrick Brontë: by amending Gaskell's quotation Woolf therefore at once retains its personal significance while also distancing herself from the situation.

Woolf's return to Brontë as a Victorian woman and daughter maps out the limits of her protest. In strong contrast to the anger so publicly expressed in *Jane Eyre*, and noted in *A Room of One's Own*, in private Brontë dutifully accepted her father's decision and became a Victorian everywoman. Woolf traces how the overwhelming power of custom and society manage to silence even the most angry critic:

> he has nature to protect him, law to protect him; and property to protect him. Thus protected it was perfectly possible for the Rev. Patrick Brontë to cause 'acute pain' to his daughter Charlotte [ . . . ] without incurring any censure from the society in which he practised the profession of a priest of the Church of England. (*3G* 263)

Woolf's criticism of Patrick Brontë's socially sanctioned torture resembles her analysis of her own 'tyrant father – the exacting, the violent, the histrionic, the demonstrative, the self-centred, the self pitying, the deaf, the appealing, the alternately loved and hated father' (*MoB* 123), the well-liked and highly respected literary critic and biographer. Nevertheless, she follows the example of her flawed but relatable predecessor by publicly spelling out in *Three Guineas* 'the things it was impossible to say aloud' as a girl in Hyde Park Gate (*MoB* 116).

Woolf's final reference to Brontë, in a July 1938 letter to a Chinese correspondent, offers something like a rough summary of her four decades of criticism: 'The life of Charlotte Brontë will perhaps give you a feeling for the life of women writers in England in the 19th century – their difficulties and how she overcame them' (*L* 6.259). Tracing both Brontë's ordinariness as a Victorian woman, and her unique literary genius, Woolf's essays waver between distance and identification. She never quite frees herself from the critical legacies of Gaskell and Stephen, and Brontë remains representative of the flawed women writers of the nineteenth century. However, in spite of these obstacles, Woolf ultimately returns to viewing Brontë as a role model: successfully overcoming personal and societal obstacles, she achieved literary success and personal happiness without ever once losing her voice.

## Notes

1. Cora Kaplan, *Victoriana: Histories, Fictions, Criticism* (New York: Columbia University Press, 2007), p. 17.
2. Andrea Zemgulys, *Modernism and the Locations of Literary Heritage* (Cambridge: Cambridge University Press, 2008); Cora Kaplan, 'Heroines, Hysteria and History: Jane Eyre and Her Critics', in *Victoriana: Histories, Fictions, Criticism* (New York: Columbia University Press, 2007), pp. 15–36; Long; Jane Marcus, 'Daughters of Anger/Material Girls: Con/Textualizing Feminist Criticism'.
3. Jane Lilienfeld, '"The gift of a china inkpot": Violet Dickinson, Virginia Woolf, Elizabeth Gaskell, Charlotte Brontë, and the Love of Women in Writing', in *Virginia Woolf: Lesbian Readings*, ed. by Eileen Barrett and Patricia Cramer (New York: New York University Press, 1997), pp. 37–56.
4. Such as fellow Modernist May Sinclair's *The Three Brontës* (1912) and Hogarth Press publication *The Brontës* (1935) by middlebrow novelist and journalist E. M. Delafield. Although Woolf's letters discuss select new works on the Brontës (for example, by Clement Shorter and E. F. Benson), she seems to have read neither of these. See Hilary Newman for a good overview of the various Hogarth Press Brontë publications. 'The Hogarth Press, the Brontes, and the "Wuthering Heights" Authorship Debate', *Virginia Woolf Bulletin*, 52 (2016), 11–19.
5. Published 21 December 1904. Although 'The Son of Royal Langbrith' was published on 14 December, she wrote 'Haworth, November, 1904' first (*L* 1.158).
6. Nicola Watson, 'Introduction', in *Literary Tourism and Nineteenth Century Culture*, ed. by Nicola Watson (Basingstoke: Palgrave Macmillan, 2009), pp. 1–12 (p. 3).
7. Gaskell, p. 15.
8. Nicola Watson, 'Homes and Haunts', in *The Literary Tourist: Readers and Places in Romantic and Victorian Britain* (Basingstoke: Palgrave Macmillan, 2006), pp. 90–117 (p. 126).
9. Gaskell, p. 11.
10. Deirdre D'Albertis, '"Bookmaking out of the remains of the dead": Elizabeth Gaskell's The Life of Charlotte Brontë', *Victorian Studies: A Journal of the Humanities, Arts and Sciences*, 39.1 (1995), 1–31 (p. 1).
11. Zemgulys, p. 154.
12. The Brontë Society, formed in 1894, opened the museum in 1895. It did not move into its present home in the Brontë parsonage until 1928. See Lucasta Miller, *The Brontë Myth* (London: Vintage, 2001), p. 101.
13. Deborah Wynne similarly sees Woolf 'succumb[ing] to the allure of the objects on display'. Additionally, she notes that Brontë's tiny, frail body was often employed by Gaskell to counter charges of Brontë's coarseness and masculinity and assert her femininity and vulnerability. As Woolf was

considerably taller than Brontë, her surprise at these 'little' 'trifling' relics might also be a reaction to their actual material dimensions as well as Brontë's lack of physical presence. 'The "Charlotte" Cult: Writing the Literary Pilgrimage, from Gaskell to Woolf', in *Charlotte Brontë: Legacies and Afterlives* (Manchester: Manchester University Press, 2017), pp. 54; 47–48.

14. Deborah Lutz, 'The Dead Still Among Us: Victorian Secular Relics, Hair Jewelry, and Death Culture', *Victorian Literature and Culture*, 39.01 (2011), 127–42 (p. 135).
15. Zemgulys, p. 155; Amber Pouliot reaches a similar conclusion in 'Serena Partridge's "Accessories": Fabricating Uncertainty in the Brontë Parsonage Museum', *Journal of Victorian Culture*, 25.2 (2020), 279–99 (p. 283).
16. Gaskell, p. 271.
17. Linda H. Peterson, *Becoming a Woman of Letters: Myths of Authorship and Facts of the Victorian Market* (Princeton, NJ: Princeton University Press, 2009), p. 134.
18. D'Albertis, p. 9.
19. Rebecca Bowler observes a similar tendency in May Sinclair's Brontë writings, in which 'social and domestic material realities both have a pervasive and corrosive influence on genius, while the romanticized wild and *unsocialized* environment is a kind of sacred materiality to be cherished'. Pouliot, p. 282; Rebecca Bowler, 'May Sinclair and the Brontë Myth: Rewilding and Dissocializing Charlotte', *Feminist Modernist Studies*, 4.6 (2020), 1–17 (p. 2).
20. Watson, 'Homes and Haunts', p. 118.
21. 'The sisters retained their old habit, which was begun in their aunt's lifetime, of putting away their work at nine o'clock, and beginning their steady pacing up and down the sitting room. At this time, they talked over the stories they were engaged upon, and discussed their plots. Once or twice a week, each read to the others what she had written, and heard what they had to say about it'. Gaskell, p. 247.
22. Linda H. Peterson, 'Triangulation, Desire, and Discontent in "The Life of Charlotte Brontë"', *Studies in English Literature, 1500–1900*, 47.4 (2007), 901–20 (p. 905).
23. Jane Lilienfeld has noted the biographical similarities between Woolf and Brontë – their shared motherlessness and loss of family members, as well as their conventional and possessive fathers – to argue that there existed 'areas of identification with the Victorian novelist, for the imagination that saw the parsonage saw it with a view of Woolf's own life'. However, Lilienfeld's family-focused analysis obscures Brontë potential importance as a model of female authorship even at this early point in time. Lilienfeld, pp. 51–2.
24. Brosnan, p. 47.
25. Iser, p. 279.
26. Cuddy-Keane, pp. 133, 121.
27. *The Brontës: The Critical Heritage*, ed. by Miriam Allott (London: Routledge & Kegan Paul, 1974), pp. 84, 89, 101.
28. Leslie Stephen, 'Hours in a Library: No XVII – Charlotte Brontë', *The Cornhill Magazine*, 36.216 (1877), 723–39 (p. 735).
29. Stephen, 'Charlotte Bronte', p. 737.

30. Ibid.
31. Gaskell, p. 425.
32. 'An Unrequited Love? Charlotte Brontë's Letters to Constantin Heger – English and Drama Blog' <https://blogs.bl.uk/english-and-drama/2015/12/charlotte-bront%C3%ABs-letters-to-constantin-heger.html> (accessed 17 March 2021).
33. Stephen, 'Charlotte Bronte', p. 732.
34. Bowler, pp. 8, quotation on p. 9. Hilary Newman notes that by 1905, Clement Shorter's dismissal of the Brussels affair was already decidedly more cautious than in his 1896 biography. She also maps out Sinclair's continued resistance to regarding Heger as influential to Brontë's literary development even after the publication of the letters. I am very grateful to her for allowing me read her unpublished article on 'May Sinclair, Charlotte Brontë, the Critics and *The Times*'.
35. '[T]he Charlotte Brontë reliquary [in Haworth] afforded Woolf an early insight into how the personal can obtrude in both writing and reading, insight that her work of feminist criticism will explain.' Zemgulys, p. 157.
36. Pouliot, p. 284.
37. The equally famous anecdote of Emily 'studying German out of an open book, propped up before her, as she kneaded the dough; but no study, however interesting, interfered with the goodness of the bread, which was always light and excellent' offers more scope for a productive coexistence of domestic and intellectual employment: here, even Gaskell concedes that 'in their careful employment of their time, they found many an odd five minutes for reading while watching the cakes, and managed the union of the two kinds of employment better than King Alfred'. Gaskell, pp. 246, 110.
38. Miller, p. 85; Corbett, *Behind the Times: Virginia Woolf in Late-Victorian Contexts*, p. 78; see also *PA* 121.
39. Stephen, 'Charlotte Bronte', p. 729.
40. Kaplan, *Victoriana*, p. 19.
41. Gaskell, pp. 273–4; de Gay, *Virginia Woolf's Novels and the Literary Past*, p. 25.
42. Gilbert and Gubar, pp. 359–60.
43. Cora Kaplan, 'Pandora's Box: Subjectivity, Class and Sexuality in Socialist-Feminist Criticism', in *British Feminist Though: A Reader*, ed. by Terry Lovell (Oxford: Blackwell, 1990), pp. 345–66; Kaplan, 'Heroines, Hysteria and History: Jane Eyre and Her Critics', p. 19.
44. Jane Marcus, 'Daughters of Anger/Material Girls: Con/Textualizing Feminist Criticism', pp. 300, 292.
45. The manuscript version reads:
    One can say, I thought, laying the book down beside / Pride and Prejudice that the woman who wrote those two / passages has more genius than Jane Austen; but, if one / she will never get it out of her whole & entire. She / Her books will be deformed & twisted. She is / at war with herself. Her vision will be distorted. / She will be in a rage where she should be calm; / She will – [be?] – at war with herself. She will die / cramped and thwarted. (*W&F* 105)

46. Long, p. 81.
47. Stephen, 'Charlotte Bronte', p. 737.
48. Gualtieri, p. 70.
49. Cuddy-Keane, pp. 145, 146.
50. Gewirtz, pp. 11, 16.
51. Long, p. 78.
52. Jane Marcus, 'Daughters of Anger/Material Girls: Con/Textualizing Feminist Criticism', p. 299.
53. Long, pp. 90, 91.
54. Amber Regis, 'Charlotte Bronte on Stage: 1930s Biodrama and the Archive/Museum Performed', in *Charlotte Brontë: Legacies and Afterlives*, by Amber Regis and Deborah Wynne (Manchester: Manchester University Press, 2017), pp. 116–42 (p. 116); Melissa Sullivan, 'The Middlebrows of the Hogarth Press: Rose Macaulay, E. M. Delafield and Cultural Hierarchies in Interwar Britain', in *Leonard and Virginia Woolf: The Hogarth Press and Networks of Modernism*, ed. by Helen Southworth (Edinburgh: Edinburgh University Press, 2010), pp. 52–73 (pp. 67–69, quotation on p. 65). Other Hogarth publications include *The Brontës: Their Lives Recorded by Their Contemporaries* (1935) and *Ladies and Gentlemen in Victorian Fiction* (1937) by middlebrow author E. M. Delafield. Sullivan argues that Delafield's focus on Charlotte Yonge in *Ladies and Gentlemen in Victorian Fiction* (1937) puts into practice the feminist recovery of forgotten (popular) women writers that Woolf demands in *A Room of One's Own*. Likewise, Delafield's choice to present the Brontës through contemporary documents such as Charlotte's school report ('writes indifferently', quoted in Battershill, p. 130.) aligns it with the archival focus which Regis identifies in 1930s biofiction following the opening of the Parsonage Museum (but also Woolf's evidence-based approach in *Three Guineas*). Some examples of Middlebrow works that are preoccupied with the Brontës' lives or works are Stella Gibson's *Cold Comfort Farm* (1932), which can be read as a parodic take on the world of *Wuthering Heights* (but also features a self-satisfied male intellectual writing a life of Branwell Brontë), and Rachel Ferguson's *The Brontës Went to Woolworths* (1931), in which the Carne sisters both emulate the Brontës' vivid fantasy life and are visited by their ghosts. In E. M. Delafield's *The Diary of a Provincial Lady* and Elizabeth Taylor's *At Mrs Lippincote's* (1945), middle-class protagonists' knowledge of the Brontës' works and lives flags their status as intellectually engaged readers, and the appeal of reading as an escape from their mundane domestic routine.
55. Humble, *The Feminine Middlebrow Novel, 1920s to 1950s*, pp. 176–83, quotations on p. 177.
56. In keeping with this very critical stance, E. F. Benson dismisses Brontë's complaints about her employers and fails to include anecdotes about her difficulties in managing the Sidgwick children. In contrast, Claire Harman notes A. C. Benson's recollection that 'one of his cousins "certainly on one occasion threw a Bible at Miss Brontë"'. Claire Harman, *Charlotte Brontë: A Life* (London: Penguin Books, 2015), p. 117.
57. E. F. Benson, *Charlotte Brontë* (London: Longmans, Green & Co., 1932), p. 169; See Newman for a discussion of the 'Lunatic near Hatfield'.

58. 'DODO', *The Spectator Archive*, 1893 <http://archive.spectator.co.uk/article/17th-june-1893/22/dodo> (accessed 5 February 2018); Elizabeth R. Kertesz, 'Smyth, Dame Ethel Mary (1858–1944), Composer, Writer, and Suffragist', *Oxford Dictionary of National Biography* <http://www.oxforddnb.com/view/10.1093/ref:odnb/9780198614128.001.0001/odnb-9780198614128-e-36173> (accessed 5 February 2018).
59. Coming from a particularly queer family, Benson is of course highly attuned to the queer potential of their relationship. See Simon Goldhill, *A Very Queer Family Indeed: Sex, Religion and the Bensons in Victorian Britain* (Chicago: University of Chicago Press, 2016); Benson, pp. 37–8.
60. Lilienfeld, p. 49.
61. Benson, p. 43.
62. Lilienfeld, p. 54.
63. See Gaskell, pp. 469–72, notes to pp. 43 and 44, for an overview of Gaskell's deletions.
64. Leslie Stephen, 'Brontë, Charlotte', *Dictionary of National Biography Archive*, 1885 <https://doi.org/10.1093/odnb/9780192683120.013.3523>.
65. My italics. Gaskell, p. 420.
66. Lilienfeld, p. 51; Hermione Lee, *Virginia Woolf*, p. 139.

Chapter 5

# 'A gap in your library, Madam': The Lives of Professional Women

'The Victorian age, to hazard another generalisation, was the age of the professional man' (E 2.35), Woolf asserts in a 1916 essay on the Victorian biographer Samuel Butler. Given her deep immersion in late-Victorian literary networks, Woolf knew that this applied to authorship as well as more traditional professions. Leslie Stephen's career as a journalist, editor, and biographer coincided with the radical transformation of the literary market through better copyright protection, the growth of markets outside of lending libraries, and the relative profitability of journalism, which made authorship a viable career option for a growing number of writers.[1] After leaving a lectureship at Cambridge University, Stephen quickly moved from contributing miscellaneous essays and literary criticism to a variety of journals to the more lucrative position of editor of the *Cornhill Magazine*; and, having solidified his reputation as a scholar and biographer, he eventually assumed the editorship of the *Dictionary of National Biography*.

If Stephen's early career demonstrates how a versatile writer could contrive to survive as a professional journalist, this later eminent position aligns him closely with the development of a culture of literary celebrity from the 1880s onwards. Sarah Wah identifies a 'contemporary shift in public interest from a writer's work to publications that disclosed details about a favourite author's private life' as a key feature.[2] Where earlier writers had published from the anonymity of their home, authors now needed to actively manage 'the structures of feeling generated by a publicity-hungry culture': the writer had become a public professional.[3] This development included the woman writer as well as the man of letters: although inequalities in pay and prestige persisted, by the end of the century, female authorship had been normalised enough for Linda Peterson to argue that 'a duality – if, indeed, it is legitimate to reduce complexities to binaries – splits not "proper lady" from the "woman writer" (a socially gendered distinction) but the popular writer from the high-art woman of letters (economic and aesthetic distinctions)'.[4]

Although Virginia Woolf lived and wrote during a period when professional authorship was the norm, her history of women's writing largely fails to acknowledge this development. When the narrator of *Three Guineas* turns to the nineteenth century in a quest for female role models in the professions, she is disappointed: 'But there would seem to be a gap in your library, Madam. There are no lives of professional women in the nineteenth century' (*3G* 200). This gap is one of Woolf's own making. In *A Room of One's Own*, she praises Aphra Behn for making a living of writing in Restoration society, but prioritises the drawing-room existence of nineteenth-century middle-class women over a detailed examination of the financial independence the literary marketplace could offer. The nineteenth-century writers who most attracted Woolf's attention are not the newly emerging professional women of the second half of the century, but earlier, quintessentially domestic women writers. Jane Austen, working anonymously in the privacy of her own home, is the ideal of this female mode of writing, but Woolf strives to extend it to Mary Russell Mitford, Elizabeth Barrett Browning and Charlotte Brontë by focusing on their enforced domesticity rather than their social lives and literary networks. Woolf's reinterpretation benefits from the fact that none of these women easily fits the mould of later professional writers. Although Charlotte Brontë's identity was an open secret in literary circles, she continued to publish as Currer Bell even after her 'Biographical Preface' to *Wuthering Heights* and *Agnes Grey* (1850) had revealed the sisters' identities. Likewise, Elizabeth Barrett Browning's move from domestic imprisonment to virtual exile in Italy ensured that '[t]he marketplace never penetrates Barrett Browning's domestic privacy, thus enabling her to pursue a literary career in a hermetically sealed environment', as Alexis Easley argues.[5] The career of Mary Russell Mitford, the only one of these women to depend financially on her writing, more closely resembles that of later professional authors, but interpretations of her life obey the logic of early nineteenth-century female authorship: her ability to represent the 'proper lady' is central to the rural nostalgia that dominates her afterlife.

Broadly speaking, Woolf therefore enacts a Modernist break with the past by omitting late-Victorian women of letters from her female literary history. Her analyses of Austen's exemplary femininity, Brontë's failure to conform and Mitford's genteel charade of domestic bliss most strongly reflect Peterson's earlier socially gendered distinctions rather than the aesthetic and economic ones that dominate the late-Victorian period. Paradoxically, although Woolf deplores the impact of the Victorian drawing room on women's writing, she shows little interest in mid- and late-Victorian women writers who do manage to break free from its confines, instead promoting a narrative that seamlessly moves from the mid-century to Modernism. In *Behind the Times: Virginia Woolf in Late Victorian Contexts*, Mary Jean Corbett traces how Woolf actively writes late Victorians such as New Woman novelist Sarah Grand as well as late-Victorian bestseller Lucy Clifford out of the recent literary past: this 'active disavowal' is just 'one facet of Woolf's broader and deeper drive to establish relations with an earlier, "greater" Victorian generation while bypassing an intermediate and, to her mind, imperfect one'.[6] Transitional women writers such as Vernon Lee and Alice Meynell suffer a similar fate: unlike Wells, Bennett and Galsworthy, whom Woolf acknowledges as influential writers of modernity in 'Modern Fiction', they are largely ignored in her public writing and riddled with scorn in the privacy of her diary and letters. Woolf's desire to distance herself from a transitional Victorian generation therefore obscures the literary influence of almost half a century of modern authorship and writing, and targets women, more strongly associated with commercial forms of writing, more than men.[7]

This development is gradual rather that sudden. This chapter complements scholarship on Woolf's better-established disregard of late Victorians with a closer investigation of her engagement with those slightly predating them. I propose a slightly earlier date, the 1860s, as a turning point in her engagement with women writers. The idea of 1860 as a watershed moment recurs in Woolf's late writing. In *Between the Acts*, Miss La Trobe stages the Victorian age as an 1860s upper-middle-class picnic party, the epitome of 'prosperity and respectability' (*BTA* 97): a hysterically overwrought engagement between Eleanor Hardcastle and Edgar Thorold 'To convert the heathen! [ . . . ] To help our fellow men!' (*BTA* 102) lampoons empire and religion as well as an obsession with marriage and 'Home, Sweet Home' (*BTA* 103). Woolf draws on similar clichés in mapping out the divided allegiances of Hyde Park Gate:

> Father himself was a typical Victorian. George and Gerald were consenting and approving Victorians. So that we [Vanessa and Virginia] had two quarrels to wage; two fights to fight; one with them individually; and one with them socially. We were living say in 1910; they were living in 1860. (*MoB* 149–50)

While these examples target the 1860s as the epitome of Victorian society in its most conventional and objectionable form, in 'A Sketch of the Past' Woolf offers a romantic picture of gatherings of distinguished visual artists at Little Holland House. Yet in making it the context of her mother's 'education' – 'She was taught there to take such part as girls did then in the lives of distinguished men; to pour out tea; to hand them their strawberries and cream; to listen devoutly, reverently to their wisdom' (*MoB* 99) – Woolf again draws a close connection between a very narrow definition of femininity and the 1860s. Determined by family anecdotes and the Stephens' social and literary networks, it is the post-1860s Victorian world that Woolf is most desirous to leave behind, and this chapter will trace how she enacts this break through a devaluation of its women writers.

Gaps are by necessity conspicuous through an absence of material. To challenge Woolf on her lack of professional women, I therefore focus on those mid- to late-nineteenth-century professionals who do attract her attention. George Eliot, Mary Augusta Ward and Margaret Oliphant represent female professionalism in very distinctive ways. Eliot, a public intellectual, represents the 'high-art woman of letters' invoked by Peterson and served as an aspirational model for women writers like Ward and Oliphant, who failed to rise beyond the status of popular writers. Ward's role as social reformer and anti-suffragist points to another route towards female professionalisation, albeit an unpaid one; and Oliphant's prolific career as a literary critic serves as a useful reminder of the importance of non-fiction in female literary histories. All three share long and productive careers that, like Woolf's own, span journalism and fiction, and see them transformed into public figures to varying degrees. That Woolf strongly prefers the domestic amateur over these public professionals again signals a desire to distinguish herself from preceding generations. Likewise, her comparative lack of interest in discussing them in print alongside a shift towards intense debate in letters and diaries makes evident a willingness to consign them to obscurity: while the women writers of the preceding chapters were subject to revision and re-evaluation throughout serial reviews, Eliot, Ward and Oliphant instead are fixed for posterity in much shorter moments of engagement.

### 'That deluded woman': George Eliot

Unquestionably one of the most successful Victorian novelists and a woman celebrated for her intellect, George Eliot (1819–80) shows by dint of her career what a male pseudonym can do for a talented and ambitious woman. While Mary Ann Evans's early life as housekeeper and caretaker to an ageing father resembles that of a conventional Victorian daughter (albeit an agnostic one with exceptional intellectual curiosity), her move to London in the early 1850s set in motion a carefully managed literary career that ultimately saw her transformed into a sexless writer.[8] Working as reviewer and editor for John Chapman's radical *Westminster Review*, Evans quickly learned to mask her gender and '[assert] her authority in strategic and necessarily clandestine ways, most often by using Chapman's nominal editorship as her cover', as Fionnuala Dillane argues.[9] A career in fiction as 'George Eliot' therefore offered Evans an opportunity to maintain this more authoritative male persona, and guaranteed an unbiased reception from a readership unaware of her journalistic origins. It also dissociated the novelist George Eliot, the moral voice of a generation, from Evans's more controversial private life with George Henry Lewes: Rosemary Ashton suggests that Eliot's pseudonym endured after her true identity became known because it allowed readers and reviewers to circumvent the morally loaded choices between Miss Evans and Mrs Lewes.[10]

Eliot's active management of her public persona and the continued use of her pseudonym distinguish her from the earlier writers in Woolf's canon. Unlike the Brontës, whose pseudonymous existence ended when Gaskell's biography opened their private life at the parsonage to the reading public, George Eliot remained a 'name without person', as Gillian Beer notes: she lacked the authenticity of a private existence and could not be pictured at home.[11] Contemporary periodicals resolved this lack of intimate access by turning to her fiction: Dillane posits that 'Evans was made real by being turned into George Eliot the wise and witty Warwickshire inhabitant who fictionalizes her native landscape and language [ . . . ]; alternatively, she was made supra-real, as George Eliot, the intellectual and incorporeal, otherworldly moral authority'.[12] This supra-real persona supported Eliot's own efforts to 'indirectly [encourage] publicity which helped to define her position as something grander than storyteller', as Sarah Wah notes, and shaped John Cross's reverential *George Eliot's Life as Related in Her Letters and Journals* (1885). Consisting of extracts from letters and journals arranged and edited by her husband, Cross 'endeavoured to form an *autobiography* (if the term may be permitted) of George Eliot'.[13] Cross's unconventional proceeding promises direct access to Eliot's 'intimate life' through 'a narrative of day-to-day life with the play of light and shade, which only letters, written in various moods, can give, and without which no portrait can be a good likeness', but he also ensured that every letter was 'pruned of everything that seemed to me irrelevant to my purpose – of everything that I thought my wife would have wished to be omitted'.[14] Cross's life is almost aggressively literary, and offers detailed insights into Eliot's extensive reading, literary criticism, and the composition of her works, but his censorship not only stripped the letters of all signs of wit or humour, but subdued events with monumental impact on Eliot's life, such as her loss of faith and union with Lewes, and flattened her personality into utter blandness: the biography is, in Gladstone's famous words, 'not a life at all. It is a Reticence in three volumes'.[15] Cross therefore assumed 'the memorializing role conventionally reserved for great men's widows' and limited readers' access to Evans's personal life to avoid the moral quandary of her life with Lewes.[16] In spite of her earlier eminence, Eliot was caught up in a late-Victorian backlash against women writers, her loss of popularity attributed to the negative impact of Cross's biography by Rosemary Ashton and Joanne Shattock, or to a 'a male clubland taking its revenge for the long years of [her] supremacy' by Elisabeth Jay.[17]

When writing about George Eliot, Woolf had access to a wealth of biographical information. She could not, however, simply reinvent her: some of Eliot's contemporaries were still living, and without an authentic domestic environment to link public persona and woman, Woolf struggled to find a clear stance. Consequently, her lead article on Eliot's centenary, commissioned in 1919 by *Times Literary Supplement* editor Bruce Richmond (*E* 4.179), lacks the strong sense of a writer's personality that characterises much of her other criticism from this period; while its unaltered inclusion in the first *Common Reader* suggests that Woolf was not interested in revisiting Eliot once done. Although Leslie Stephen had written an 1885 *Dictionary of National Biography* entry as well as the 1902 volume on *George Eliot* for Macmillan's *English Men of Letters*, there are surprisingly few echoes of Stephen in Woolf's article. Instead, she researched Eliot meticulously and extensively: although the review was not published until November, she had already begun her preparatory reading in January.

Woolf's awareness of Eliot's comparatively close proximity to her own life shapes this enquiry from the beginning: thus, she confesses to Margaret Llewelyn Davies, that 'George Eliot fascinates me. Did your father know her? or was she too much under a cloud? Nobody called on her, so she says; and yet her virtue seems to me excessive' (*L* 2.285). Similarly, writing to Nelly Cecil, she delights in including absurd gossip gathered from old acquaintances alongside more serious biographical sources:

> I am reading through the whole of George Eliot, in order to sum her up, once and for all, upon her anniversary, which happily is still months ahead. So far, I have already made way with her life, which is a book of the greatest fascination, and I can see already that no one else has ever known her as I know her. [ . . . ] I think she is a highly feminine and attractive character – most impulsive and ill-balanced (Mrs Prothero once told me that she – George

Eliot that is – had a child by a professor in Edinburgh – she knew it for a fact – indeed the child is a well known Professor somewhere else – ) and I only wish she had lived nowadays, and so been saved all that nonsense. I mean, being so serious, and digging up fossils, and all the rest of it. Perhaps too she would have written, not exactly better, but less facetiously. It was an unfortunate thing to be the first woman of the age. But she comes very well out of it so far [ . . . ] – but I haven't begun her novels. (*L* 2.321)

Highlighting the fundamental importance of biographical research to her writing process, Woolf's letter implies a strong contradiction between Eliot's' 'highly feminine and attractive character' and her autodidactic intellectualism and keen interest in geology: the woman clearly is at odds with the writer. The damaging literary effect of Eliot's public eminence is a recurring preoccupation in Woolf's criticism, and her first impression is ambivalent despite initial enthusiasm: at best, she is hesitant to settle on one coherent and consistent image of Eliot.

This tension between radically different interpretations of the author and woman also characterises the finished article. Although 'George Eliot' is intended as a character study, Woolf fails her promise to 'sum her up, once and for all'. The essay lacks the strong sense of personality which had characterised 'Jane Austen' and 'Charlotte Brontë' and instead begins with an admission of Woolf's own ignorance:

> To read George Eliot attentively is to become aware of how little one knows about her. It is also to become aware of the credulity, not very creditable to one's insight, with which, half-consciously and partly maliciously, one had accepted the late Victorian version of a deluded woman who held phantom sway over subjects even more deluded than herself. (*E* 4.170)

Disguised as a general reference to Eliot's waning popularity, Woolf likely also reflects on her own malicious satire in the unpublished fictional review 'Memoirs of a Novelist' (1909). Miss Willatt shares Eliot's markedly 'studious habits', a period of intense religiosity inspired by a close female friendship, and a heavy but intelligent face with 'a bold nose for a woman' (*CSF* 71). In a parody of both Eliot and the title of Anny Thackeray Ritchie's collective literary biography *A Book of Sibyls* (1883), Miss Willatt gains fame and devoted admirers with popular novels on 'the soul': 'if Sibyls are only half inspired, conscious of the folly of their disciples, sorry for them, very vain of their applause and much muddled in their own brains all at once, then Miss Willatt was a Sibyl too' (*CSF* 78).

Elaine Showalter praises Woolf's article as 'a watershed in Eliot criticism, a significant rehabilitation of a major figure in the female tradition after a generation's scornful neglect'; while Shattock sees it as a first step in 'a slow process of revaluation'.[18] However, Woolf's rehabilitation is hesitant: echoes of her earlier malicious satire recur in the ambivalent and unflattering contemporary recollections of Eliot, invoked to trace how she became 'one of the butts for youth to laugh at' (*E* 4.171). Woolf depicts the cult of worship around Eliot without much sympathy: recollections of reverential afternoons at The Priory, such as Meredith's disdain for '"the errant woman" on the daïs' (*E* 4.171), recall Woolf's earlier image of Miss Willatt 'like some gorged spider at the centre of her web' (*CSF* 78). Similarly, she ironically invokes Anny Thackeray Ritchie's recollection of 'not exactly a personal friend, but a good and benevolent impulse' as a 'more intimate indoor portrait' (*E* 4.172, 171). Kaiser Loges links this hazy but benevolent mode of commemoration to Miss Willatt's comically inept biographer Miss Linsett, but Ritchie's commemoration of Eliot as an incorporeal moral influence also shows the lasting success of Eliot's own myth-making.[19] Most striking, however, is Woolf's almost exclusive use of private (if second-hand) recollections of Eliot. She draws extensively on Leslie Stephen's correspondence to assemble this collage of recollections, demonstrating the oppressiveness of recent memory: this abundance of anecdotes fixes Eliot in a posthumous performance of greatness. Noting how these anecdotes differ from other literary gossip, Woolf hints at the misogyny that may motivate Eliot's detractors:

> one feels that the recorder, even when he was in the actual presence, kept his distance and kept his head, and never read the novels in later years with the light of a vivid, or puzzling, or beautiful personality dazzling in his eyes. In fiction, where so much of personality is revealed, the absence of charm is a great lack. (*E* 4.172)

Underlying Woolf's analysis of Eliot's literary afterlife is therefore a recognition of her 'anomalous' status as a great female writer: contrasting the Victorian sage and imposing intellectual figure with 'the eccentricities and inequalities of temper which give to so many artists the endearing simplicity of children', Woolf asserts the importance of reading Eliot as a woman.

This focus on Eliot's femininity brings Woolf's own ambivalence about her public and professional persona to the forefront of the review. From her wide-ranging intellectual interests, to her relationship with Lewes and ultimately her fame, Woolf's summary of the 'singularly depressing record' of her life highlights how Eliot lived in awkward alienation from Victorian society. Caught between a very narrow domestic sphere and intellectual pursuits which in Woolf's rendering appear equally unfulfilling, this brief summary of Eliot's persistent quest for knowledge plays into stereotypes of women's unsuitability for intellectual labour when she presents, via quotations from Cross's biography, a joyless image of Eliot 'raising herself with groans and struggles from the intolerable boredom of petty provincial society' into socially isolated intellectualism (*E* 4.172). Woolf's ambivalent sympathy for this 'deep-seated and noble ambition' is made apparent in the 'strong desire that the stages of her pilgrimage might have been made, if not more easy, at least more beautiful' (*E* 4.172). Unlike the literary self-education of Elizabeth Barrett Browning and Aurora Leigh, which resonate powerfully with her own experiences, Woolf's article faintly echoes the anti-intellectualist stance of her letter to Nelly Cecil and puts her at odds with Leslie Stephen's biography, written almost twenty years earlier. Stephen had depicted the breadth of Eliot's religious and philosophical learning with much sympathy, but also emphasised how her network of friends in Coventry and London allowed intellectual exchange with likeminded people.[20]

Woolf presents Eliot's partnership with Lewes as the decisive event of her life, lapsing into a curiously conservative register:

> at the height of her powers, and in the fullness of her freedom, she made the decision which was of such profound moment to her and still matters even to us, and went to Weimar, alone with George Henry Lewes. The books which followed so soon after her union testify in the fullest manner to the great liberation which had come to her with personal happiness. (*E* 4.173)

Although surprising coming from the liberal bastion of Bloomsbury, Woolf's stance is biographically well-established. Cross had contextualised Eliot's decision through her own letter to Caroline Bray, which explained that 'We are leading no life of self-indulgence, except indeed that, being happy in each other, we find everything easy'; while Leslie Stephen's 1885 *Dictionary of National Biography* entry sympathetically emphasised that 'No legal marriage, however, could have called forth greater mutual devotion'.[21] Tracey Rosenberg notes that a similar rhetorical move is pervasive in Victorian biographies of Eliot: 'Without being so womanly as to choose a life with George Lewes over social respectability, this argument insists, the woman could never have been a writer'.[22] However, Woolf's caution and reserve in discussing Eliot's private life cannot be blamed on Bruce Richmond's editorial policy alone. Leila Brosnan argues that the *Times Literary Supplement* house style, which required 'formality and a certain degree of refinement', quickly led Woolf to develop a double-layered style which avoided direct controversy through the skilful deployment of quotation, patterns of repetition and other rhetorical devices.[23] Hence, Woolf's slightly stilted phrasing might be owed to the *TLS*, but the underlying values are deployed for a purpose. Suggesting that without Lewes, there would have been no Eliot, Woolf emphasises Eliot's 'dependen[ce] upon affection' (*E* 4.173) to feminise her, yet also points to the damage the woman did to the writer: 'she lost the power to move on equal terms unnoted among her kind; and the loss for a novelist was serious' (*E* 4.174).

Although a strong interest in the impact of women's social positions on their writing is characteristic of Woolf's thinking in the 1920s, in this respect, 'George Eliot' differs considerably from the majority of her reviews, articles and essays. In 'Women Novelists' (1918), Woolf had argued of the example of Eliot that a pseudonym could allow women 'to free their own consciousness as they wrote from the tyranny of what was expected from their sex' (*E* 2.315). Now, however, Eliot's lack of a domestic persona meant that Woolf could not approach her in her usual manner to examine her life in its domestic context. The previous chapters in this book have shown that Woolf was keenly aware of the strong symbolical potential of scenes like Jane Austen hiding her manuscripts or Charlotte Brontë peeling the potatoes: they came to represent women's inability to work uninterrupted in the middle-class household. In contrast, Eliot's environment offers no such lasting image. 'Women Novelists' and 'George Eliot' avoid any closer examination of her writing habits and the question of the Leweses' household management. This is all the more surprising as Cross's life offers at least some scope for such explorations. For instance, in one of his narrative inserts he reports of the couple's early life that

> Both she and Mr Lewes were now working very hard for what would bring immediate profit [i.e. journalism], as they had to support not only themselves but his children and their mother. They had only one sitting-room between them; and I remember, in a walk on St George's Hill, near Weybridge, in 1871, she told me that the scratching of another pen used to affect her nerves to such an extent that it nearly drove her wild.[24]

Woolf's hesitancy to tackle this aspect of Eliot's life, with its interlinking of financial family obligations, journalism and the lack of a private work space, suggests both the lasting impact of Eliot's supra-real persona as well as the enduring taboo of Mary Ann Evans's domestic life.

Eliot's ability to escape the Victorian drawing room makes her a singularity in Woolf's canon of women writers, and consequently a more formidable rival. Although in 1919 Woolf had not yet, in Alison Booth's words, 'succeeded to the title that only George Eliot had won before her, that of the Grand Old Woman of English Letters', Eliot's successful career as a journalist and novelist, as well as her cosmopolitan life within a wide literary network already resembled Woolf's own life and career much more than the private and anonymous literary existences of Jane Austen and Charlotte Brontë.[25] While Woolf frequently and forcefully laments that Austen and Brontë's lack of connections and early deaths prevented them from profiting fully from their increasing literary fame, she neglects or undermines these aspects of Eliot's career. Woolf strongly emphasises the alienating effect of Eliot's fame, which prevented her from meeting others as equals. Similarly, despite her insistence that a larger income would have changed the lives of Austen and Brontë, Woolf is reluctant to acknowledge the financial and literary ambitions shaping Eliot's career. While Stephen's biography had pragmatically acknowledged that 'there were sound utilitarian reasons for trying an experiment in the direction of the most profitable variety of literature', Woolf pursues a narrative of artistic self-improvement in which fiction is the inevitable next step to journalism, thereby resisting the inversion of traditional hierarchies between journalistic hack work, the result of artistic compromise and financial necessity, and the superior motivation of fiction.[26] This disregard of Eliot's public eminence as well as her financial success ultimately turns a potentially exemplary career into another example of female suffering in a patriarchal society.

Like Woolf's other centenary articles from this period, 'George Eliot' attempts to give a sketch of her character as seen in her fiction. Merging two of the popular images of Eliot identified by Dillane – the nostalgic inhabitant of the rural past, and a disembodied mind – Woolf envisions Eliot's writing as a mental retreat from the social isolation of the present:

> [B]asking in the light and sunshine of *Scenes of Clerical Life*, feeling the large mature mind spreading itself with a luxurious sense of freedom in the world of her 'remote past' [ . . . ] Everything to such a mind was gain. All experience filtered down through layer after layer of perception and reflection, enriching and nourishing. (*E* 4.174)

Envisioning the working of Eliot's mind as an organic process which transforms memory into generalised human experience, Woolf explicitly contrasts Eliot's interest in 'ordinary joys and sorrows' with 'the fiery egotism of Jane Eyre' (*E* 4.174). Unlike Brontë, Eliot manages to transcend the 'sense of one's own individuality, unsated and unsubdued' (*E* 4.174) that for Woolf marks and mars Brontë's writing. Noting that these early works are also the only ones which passed for a male author's work, Alison Booth hints at Woolf's potential gender bias here.[27] Yet this absolute impersonality is also the quality Woolf most praised in Austen's writing during the 1920s: struggling with the 'damned egotistical self' (*D* 2.14), she particularly noted examples of writers who left no traces of personal grievances and suffering in their work.

In her impromptu epistolary criticism, Woolf had also asserted that Eliot was 'highly feminine' and this, in combination with her well-documented unwillingness to exist within the confines of conventional Victorian womanhood, complicates Woolf's task as a critic. Arguing that Eliot's impersonality fails when it comes to her heroines, Woolf qualifies her previous praise:

> [T]here are, even in the early works, traces of that troubled spirit, that exacting and questioning and baffled presence who was George Eliot herself. [ . . . ] Those who fall foul of George Eliot do so, we incline to think, on account of her heroines; and with good reason; for there is no doubt that they bring out the worst of her, lead her into difficult places, make her self-conscious, didactic, and occasionally vulgar. (E 4.176)

Drawing a line from Dinah Morris's religious and intellectual self-determination to Maggie Tulliver, and Dorothea Brooke's less fruitful search for 'one scarcely knows what' (E 4.176), Woolf reads them as autobiographical conduits expressing their author's desire for freedom and independence: 'their story is the incomplete version of the story of George Eliot herself' (E 4.178). Woolf here anticipates early feminist criticism of Eliot, which often rejected her for her refusal to validate women's discontent with society.[28] Tracing Eliot's failure to write successfully 'from a personal standpoint' to her age as well as self-consciousness, Woolf again draws on a late-Victorian construction of Eliot: Booth notes that 'in *George Eliot*, Stephen attributes Eliot's limitations to a natural feminine diffidence and desire for respectability'.[29] Woolf charges Eliot with creating an unmanageable heroine in *The Mill on the Floss* (1860): 'before George Eliot knows what has happened she has a full-grown woman on her hands demanding what neither gipsies, nor dolls, nor St Ogg's itself is capable of giving her' (E 4.176); and complains of her 'clumsy satire' of 'good society' (E 4.177), a reminder both of Eliot's social seclusion and her comparatively humble origins that matches Woolf's less subtle criticisms of Charlotte Brontë. Contrasting Eliot's handling of dialogue with Jane Austen's 'unerring taste which chooses one sentence and compresses the heart of a scene within that', Woolf somewhat unfairly criticises 'the brewing and gathering and thickening of the cloud which will burst upon our heads at the moment of crisis in a shower of disillusionment and verbosity' (E 4.177). That 'Mrs Casaubon would have talked for an hour' where Austen's Emma relied on witty brevity illustrates difference in style, but is also another instance of Woolf's weaponisation of Austen's feminine perfection. This critical assessment of Eliot's dialogues likely draws at least partially on an anecdote from

Mary Augusta Ward's *A Writer's Recollections* (1918), which Woolf was reading in September 1919. Ward recalls meeting George Eliot at a dinner party and, her disappointment at the great novelist's silence palpable, Eliot's 'evident wish to be kind to a young girl':

> George Eliot sat down in the darkness and I beside her. Then she talked for about twenty minutes, with perfect ease and finish, without misplacing a word or dropping a sentence, and I realised at last that I was in the presence of a great writer. Not a great *talker*.[30]

Although neither used nor acknowledged by Woolf, Ward's anecdote offers a more relatable portrait than Woolf's opening paragraphs: although still drawn to eminent monologue, Eliot's friendliness towards an intellectual young girl establishes a mutual ground between them. In contrast, Woolf, herself only four years younger than the Eliot of *The Mill on the Floss*, blames her verbosity on 'an elderly dread of fatigue from the effort of emotional concentration' (*E* 4.177) and casts her predecessor as positively geriatric.

Eliot's heroines also recall the biographical strategies traced by Rosenberg. Like their creator, their excessive femininity betrays them, but is also an essential component to Eliot's literary success. Woolf echoes this interpretation in her second, more conciliatory assessment:

> The ancient consciousness of woman, charged with suffering and sensibility, and for so many ages dumb, seems in them to have brimmed and overflowed and uttered a demand for something – they scarcely know what – for something that is perhaps incompatible with the facts of human existence. (*E* 4.178).

This reading hints at a problem larger than Eliot herself: with her heroines merely a conduit for a mystical womanhood in search of its purpose, it seems entirely appropriate that 'the struggle ends, [ . . . ] in tragedy, or in a compromise that is even more melancholy' (*E* 4.178). In line with this emphatically feminine reading, Eliot becomes a figure of heroic resistance: 'she would not renounce her own inheritance – the difference of view, the difference of standard – nor accept an inappropriate reward' (*E* 4.178). Thus, in spite of having begun her leader with an unapproachably eminent literary celebrity, Woolf ends it by aligning Eliot with suffering femininity:

> Thus we behold her, a memorable figure, inordinately praised and shrinking from her fame, despondent, reserved, shuddering back into the arms of love as if there alone were satisfaction and, it might be, justification, at the same time reaching out with 'a fastidious yet hungry ambition' for all that life

could offer the free and inquiring mind and confronting her feminine aspirations with the real world of men. (*E* 4.178)

Presenting a woman who retreats from the reader into the anonymity of an unknown domestic life and ultimately the grave, Woolf's final appeal, that 'we must lay upon her grave whatever we have it in our power to bestow of laurel and rose' (*E* 4.179), remains ambiguous.

Notably, Woolf does not follow up on her own appeal with particular alacrity. Although she revisited George Eliot in two shorter articles in the 1920s, she fails to recover her: Eliot's image remains fixed and if anything, Woolf's subtle dismissal strengthened. Her centenary article was quickly followed by a short profile of Eliot for the *Daily Herald*'s 'Great Names' series in 1921. Like most articles in the series, it functions as educational advertising: the overview of Eliot's life and work (finished within a week of the original request (*E* 3.294 n1)) concludes with a recommendation of Blackwood's editions of her works. The *Daily Herald* was a radical newspaper with strong links to the labour movement and party, and in what is likely a pitch to its more socialist readership, Woolf aggressively foregrounds Eliot's humble origins. As 'the granddaughter of a carpenter' who 'made herself, by sheer determination one of the most learned women – or men – of her time' (*E* 3.293), Eliot loses some of the grandeur and tragedy that had characterised her in the *TLS* article. Likewise, Woolf cuts the extensive reflections on her flawed femininity in favour of a simpler overview of Eliot's literary career, pitching the early rural novels, based on personal experience and artistically most successful, against the flawed but more interesting 'book-learned' ones, which permanently expanded the scope of the novel: 'She was one of the first English novelists to discover that men and women think as well as feel, and the discovery was of great artistic moment' (*E* 3.294). Again, however, Woolf remains ambiguous about Eliot's longer-term relevance. Suggesting that 'it seems likely that she will come through the cloud which obscured her after the publication of her life – a dismal soliloquy – and hold her place permanently among the great English novelists' (*E* 3.294), the article undermines Eliot's position as one of the 'Great Names' of English literature as much as it nominally asserts it.

In 1926, Woolf reviewed R. Brimley Johnson's selection of *The Letters of George Eliot* for the *TLS*, which offered an opportunity to revise her previous position. A similar selection of Barrett Browning's letters (1906) had resulted in a lasting impression of her private suffering, while Austen's juvenilia and letters suggested an entirely new (and uncensored) irreverent and satirical persona. Here, however, Woolf invokes the possibility of a more intimate portrait of Eliot alongside monumental graveyard imagery that metonymically undermines it throughout the rest of the review:

> George Eliot lies flattened under the tomb that Mr Cross built over her, to all appearances completely dead. No writer of equal vitality as a writer so entirely lacks vitality as a human being. Yet when the solemnity of the tomb is violated, when her letters are broken into fragments and presented in a volume of modest size, they reflect a character full of variety and full of conflict – qualities that sort ill with the calm composure of death. (E 4.386)

Confirming the causal relationship between Cross's biography and Eliot's reputation which her centenary article had only hinted at, Woolf offers a commentary on Victorian hagiographies that anticipates the '[fig]ure [ . . . ] above life size in top-hat and frock-coat', the '[n]oble, upright, chaste, severe [ . . . ] Victorian worthies' (E 4.475, 474) of 'The New Biography' published a year later. No matter how much Woolf celebrates the insights to be gained from the letters, she invokes the possibility of a closer connection only to reject it. Pointing to Eliot's views on religion, her move from rural isolation to London literary society, and her changing stance on marriage, Woolf argues that 'nobody changed her skin more completely in the course of sixty-one years' (E 4.387). Eliot therefore emerges both as the victim of an inept biographer who failed to preserve her personality, and as an inherently contradictory and inaccessible subject which cannot easily be captured in her complexity. Indeed, Woolf implies that her 'unusual violence' of character was partially innate, thus subtly shifting blame from biographer to subject: 'there was a strain of impressionability in George Eliot which would have made her uneasy whatever her circumstances. There was something alive and emotional in her which tended to upset the outward solemnity' (E 4.387).

With a temperament that 'impeded her in many ways as a writer' (E 4.387), but expanded her sphere far beyond that of many of her contemporaries, Eliot is suited neither as a model for Woolf's own writing, nor as a candidate for reinvention. Where Woolf had previously seen her at odds with Victorian morality and femininity, she now finds her an important representative of the period itself: 'The whole of the nineteenth century seems to be mirrored in the depth of that sensitive and profound mind which lies buried, so far as the life of the body is concerned, under Mr Cross's tomb' (E 4.388). Eliot's relentless pursuit of all branches of knowledge, her desire for self-improvement, and her incontestable greatness make her an easy target for Woolf's desire for a break with the past. While she is too famous to be entirely absent from Woolf's library, her independent existence as a professional writer without an authenticated home, as well as her omnipresence on the Victorian literary scene disqualify her from the extensive rewriting and reinvention earlier writers benefited from. At the same time, the persistent and metonymical use of tombs and graves also makes clear Woolf's unwillingness to assert Eliot's continued relevance to a modern society: now safely established as a leading Modernist novelist, Woolf is only too happy to publicly bury the Victorian past.

*A Room of One's Own* does little to change this image of remote greatness. As with most of her case studies, Woolf resorts to a streamlined narrative that emphasises the wider feminist argument at the expense of Eliot's individuality. Nevertheless, Eliot's significance pales in comparison to the fundamental role that Jane Austen and Charlotte Brontë, determined by their more domestic careers, play in the development of Woolf's argument. As a public persona with relatively great personal and financial freedom, Eliot fits uneasily into the argument of *A Room of One's Own* and threatens to undermine Woolf's cause by her very existence: as Jay suggests, Eliot embodies the myth that 'because a woman had been admitted to the pantheon, gender bias had been overcome'.[31] Partly in consequence of this uneasy fit, Woolf attempts to shape Eliot's life into an example of suffering from specifically domestic restraints. From her seclusion 'in the common sitting-room of that respectable house', Eliot 'escaped after much tribulation, but only to a secluded villa in St John's Wood. And there she settled down in the shadow of the world's disapproval' (*AROO* 64). Woolf's emphasis on Eliot's isolation captures her marginalised social position in the 1850s and early 1860s, yet her subsequent fame as novelist triumphed over most contemporaries' moral concerns. The imposing figure of the sibyl holding court for her admirers is entirely absent: here, Woolf is content to echo Victorian rhetoric of fallen women to reduce Eliot to a clichéd trope. Additionally, Woolf attempts to fashion Eliot's life into an example of women's limited experience of the world: 'Had Tolstoy lived at the Priory in seclusion with a married lady "cut off from what is called the world", however edifying the moral lesson, he could scarcely, I thought, have written *War and Peace*' (*AROO* 64). Although the passage implicitly recalls some of Woolf's earlier criticism of the moral didacticism introduced through Eliot's heroines, her wider point about the limited scope of women's experience seems ill-suited to Eliot, who she had previously praised for widening the scope of the English novel with *Middlemarch*.

Woolf's reinterpretation of Eliot's career not only contradicts her own previous judgements, it also relies on a disingenuous reading of gender, genre and the literary marketplace. Lamenting the predominance of the novel as the only acceptable form of female expression, she suggests that 'the overflow of George Eliot's capacious mind should have spread itself when the creative impulse was spent upon history and biography' (*AROO* 61). Again, this presentation of Eliot is misleading: in addition to a subtle denigration of Eliot's work, Woolf ignores that as a leading intellectual, nothing was stopping Eliot from moving into new genres. By the 1860s, women such as Eliot's fellow Blackwood's author Margaret Oliphant and Mary Augusta Ward were writing biography and history, respectively, and for popular as well as scholarly audiences. Pragmatically, sales figures presented a much greater incentive for Eliot to continue writing fiction. Woolf's reluctance to fully embrace Eliot as a public intellectual and widely celebrated writer therefore points to the tension at the heart of *A Room of One's Own*. An inherent preference for the gentlemanly amateur writer of independent means is central to her argument that 'a woman must have money and a room of her own if she is to write fiction' (*AROO* 1), but fundamentally at odds with the claim that middle-class women's emergence in the literary marketplace is 'of greater importance than the Crusades or the Wars of the Roses' (*AROO* 59).[32] Woolf clearly recognises the importance of this development, but avoids a closer analysis of how women's literary careers had changed over the course of the nineteenth century. Eliot is unquestionably representative of a new type of professional, financially successful writer: without the strong association with a domestic environment that Woolf bases much her argument on, and rising to fame as a public intellectual, she differs markedly from the majority of women assembled in *A Room of One's Own*. Woolf's silence is therefore evidence of her unwillingness to confront the more recent developments in female authorship. Although she never dismissed Eliot's qualities as a writer entirely, she could not bring herself to revisit her again. Turning down an invitation to write an introduction to *Middlemarch* in 1930, she explained that 'I have written at length about George Eliot, and much though I admire her, do not feel that I can begin again on that subject' (*L* 4.178): as far as Woolf was concerned, Eliot could remain buried in Cross's tomb.

## 'The compromise': Mrs Humphry Ward

'Mrs Ward is dead; poor Mrs Humphry Ward; & it appears that she was merely a woman of straw after all – shovelled into the grave & already forgotten. The most perfunctory earth strewing even by the orthodox' (*D* 2.29). Thus Virginia Woolf noted the death of late-Victorian novelist, anti-suffragist and philanthropist Mary Augusta Ward (1851–1920).

Although their careers overlapped for fifteen years, they are rarely mentioned together. Woolf's engagement with the women writers discussed in the previous chapter took place in her published essays and reviews. In contrast, she engages with Ward mainly in the more private spaces of her diary and letters – with the exception of a posthumous review of *The Life of Mrs Humphry Ward* (1923). Ward was neither a true contemporary to Woolf, nor a predecessor in a meaningful way. Although her career as journalist, historian and novelist once again offers itself as a model for Woolf's own, Woolf vehemently rejects all that she represents: as a bestselling novelist losing her grip on her mass audience around the turn of the century, leader of the female anti-suffrage league and writer of war propaganda, Ward becomes doubly representative of late-Victorian society and the artistically compromised professional writer.

Ward represents another manifestation of the female professional lives that Woolf could have drawn on in *Three Guineas*. Belonging to Julia Stephen's generation, Ward, too, was 'born into a large connection' (*MoB* 79): she was the granddaughter of Dr Thomas Arnold, legendary headmaster of Rugby, and niece of Matthew Arnold. Due to her father's erratic career, she spent her childhood at boarding schools before joining the rest of her family in Oxford, where Thomas Arnold for a while pursued the university career which Leslie Stephen had renounced (although Arnold's wavering between Catholicism and the Church of England lacks the finality of Stephen's agnosticism). Ward's deep immersion in the intellectual environment of Oxford proved a lasting influence on her life: she gained privileged access to the Bodleian library to research early Spanish history and (like Woolf) studied Greek and Latin, but also worked to increase women's access to education through the Lectures for Women Committee, and ultimately the establishment of Somerville Hall.[33] In 1881, her husband left Oxford to join the staff of *The Times*, and the couple took up residence in Bloomsbury to become working journalists: Ward contributed reviews to a range of journals including the clerical *Guardian* of Woolf's early career and undertook the 'sheer, hard, brain-stretching work' of writing scholarly articles for the *Dictionary of Christian Biography* as well as translations and reviews from French, until her second novel *Robert Elsmere* (1888), a 'drama of religious faith and doubt', launched her into literary fame.[34] Ward combined a literary career as 'a "serious" novelist of ideas'[35] with social activism, sponsoring and organising philanthropic working-class settlements in London, which included pioneering classes for children with disabilities and after-school playgroups for the children of working mothers. Her career began to decline after the turn of the century: her increasingly bad health, the financial drain of her country estate, and the financial irresponsibility of her husband and son all impacted the quality and quantity of her work; while her decision to head the Women's Anti-Suffrage Association in 1908 led to a loss of popularity and alienation from family, friends and other reformers.[36] During the First World War, Ward became a writer of war propaganda at the invitation of Theodore Roosevelt, and was made a Commander of the Most Excellent Order of the British Empire in 1919, but she never recovered her previous popularity and spent the last year of her life virtually bankrupt and severely ill. Unlike other popular writers from the same period, she is still awaiting critical recovery – at least partially due to her reputation as a conservative anti-suffragist and war propagandist, which tend to overshadow her sustained commitment to social reform and earlier literary reputation.

Although many of Woolf's references to Ward's fiction mock her preference for aristocratic characters and settings, the Wards moved in similar circles to the Stephens. Their acquaintance likely began in the 1880s: the anonymously published *Echoes of the Eighties: Leaves from the Diary of a Victorian Lady*, plausibly attributed to Ward by John Cooper, contains several mentions of Leslie Stephen and his wife ('who looked very beautiful in what appeared to be an Indian table cover, which however she wore as a shawl').[37] Janet Penrose Trevelyan recalls 'Leslie Stephen, who wrote to her often, especially after his wife's death and came at intervals to Grosvenor Place for a long *tête-à-tête*, sitting on the sofa beside Mrs. Ward, his ear-trumpet between them',[38] and Ward is part of the social scene captured in Woolf's early diary (*PA* 18, 47, 102). With Leslie Stephen's death, this changes: Ward, symbolic of the oppressive Victorian world of Hyde Park Gate, is eagerly left behind. Thus, in 1904, Woolf and her siblings 'travelled [to Venice] with the Humphrey [*sic*] Wards who, happily, have disappeared' (*L* 1.137); while in 1905, she notes of her Morley College work that 'Mrs. H. Ward, curiously, wrote to suggest Passmore Edwards work to N. & me, but I have a valid excuse!' (*PA* 220).[39] After a chance meeting at a 'vast melancholy party' in 1911, Woolf reported to Vanessa that

> I was glad to find that they are as vapid and commonplace as we used to find them, so that we [were] right to hate them. The old passion to fly before them overcame me. Imagine [ . . . ] Mrs Humphrey [*sic*] Ward shrilling. (*L* 1.468)

In addition to this personal antipathy, Ward becomes an easy target for quips about literary corruption and bad taste: a string of mocking references runs through Woolf's private and public writing, as when she wishes that 'Providence were a better judge of literature and then we should be spared Humphrey [*sic*] Wards, or she might publish them in Paradise' (*L* 1.71) in a letter to Violet Dickinson, or comments in her diary that the birth announcement 'His Perfect Gift' would make 'a good title for an Academy picture, or a Mrs Ward novel' (*D* 1.57). Slightly more restrained in print, she draws on Ward's undoubted Victorian eminence to criticise the nostalgic golden chariots on the cover of Constance Hill's *Maria Edgeworth and Her Circle* (1909): 'we should think it strange if the future biographer of "Mrs Humphry Ward and her circle" illustrated his meaning by a hansom cab' (*E* 1.315), a reference which nonetheless aligns Ward with relics from the past, suitable for treatment by incompetent lady biographers.

It is unclear how much of Ward's fiction Woolf ever reviewed: a review of Ward's novel *Fenwick's Career* in the *Guardian* (May 1906) is listed as a 'doubtful attribution' in the first volume of Woolf's *Essays*, but there are good reasons for accepting it as her work. From her letters, it is clear that Woolf wrote a review of the novel in April 1906 which she may have submitted to the *Guardian* after its rejection from the *Speaker*: 'I sent my H[umphry] Ward to the Speaker, but I see they have a review already, longer and even more vindictive than mine. They call her a snob, and a sentimentalist, with no knowledge of art, or humanity' (*L* 1.219).

*Fenwick's Career*, loosely based on the painter George Romney's desertion of his wife for his muse and art, marks a 'distinct decline in the quality of her writing'.[40] Unsurprisingly, neither the extant *Guardian* review nor the unknown *Speaker* review is particularly positive; additionally, the politely ambivalent tone stylistically matches contemporary reviews by Woolf even if it doesn't share phrases with her reading notes (*E* 1.376 n1). The focus on Ward's streamlined writing process, implicitly contrasted with the novel's topic of artistic inspiration and passion, is plausible given Woolf's dislike of Ward's writing and follows the slant of her private comments. Ward is presented as a skilled craftsman assembling a bestseller, and her characters, morally sanitised to make them more palatable, are 'cogs to make the story move or padding to round it off'. Likewise, the reviewer's praise of the skilful plot construction sounds decidedly hollow:

> It goes without saying that these disjointed bones we have roughly sketched are put each in its proper place, that the skeleton is completed and clothed with consummate literary skill. Here, as elsewhere, there is no slipshod work, no fine writing; the pen is a servant, never for one instant allowed either to shirk or to domineer, and, further, it is the servant of a remarkably fine, acute, and observant mind. (*E* 1.375)

In a review of a novel concerned with 'art and the artistic temperament' (*E* 1.374), Ward's firm control over her pen suggests a single-minded dedication to the demands of the market as well as a lack of artistic imagination and inspiration. Likewise, the way the skeletal imagery of the quotation works to undercut the ambivalent praise – hinting that the novel resembles Frankenstein's Monster in the way it is constructed from disparate ideas torturously brought to life – matches the double-layered writing style identified by Brosnan; and the remarkable mind resonates with Woolf's later, equally double-edged praise of Eliot and Oliphant. While the review lacks the outright condemnation of Woolf's reading notes, 'a flimsy book held together by the spun web of words' (*E* 1.376 n1), its focus on Ward's mechanical production and complete submission to audience expectations and money also recur in Woolf's private reflections on Ward's life.

With growing maturity as a writer, Woolf also pits her own approach to fiction against Ward's. Her takedown of *Eltham House* (1915) 'by that old mangy hack' in a letter to Nelly Cecil emphasises Ward's out-datedness and popular appeal:

> It seems to me the writing of a woman who has been accidentally locked in to the housekeeper's room of Longleat say for the past 20 years; and has done nothing but absorb family portraits and family plate. [ . . . ] its a vile book, and after gulping it down, I felt morally debased. My nurse however, is absorbed by it. (*L* 2.68).

John Sutherland suggests that 'by 1918, vilification of Mrs Humphry Ward had reached the level of a minor art form'.[41] Dr Arnold and his public school system was one of the Victorian institutions debunked in Lytton Strachey's *Eminent Victorians* (1918), and Woolf maliciously records that Ward 'was raging publicly against the defamation of her grandfather' (*L* 2.281).[42] Ward's downfall appears inextricably connected to Woolf's own literary ascendance, as when she writes triumphantly to Vanessa Bell in March 1919: 'It is rather fun about the Athenaeum, as every one is to write what they like, and Mrs Ward is to be exposed, and in time they hope to print imaginative prose by me' (*L* 2.341). Woolf's confident claim to the future of fiction echoes the way in which her *TLS* review decisively entombs Eliot in her grave. However, this mockery is shot through with a fascination with and recognition of the issues that shaped Ward's career. In 1917, learning of the Wards' 'near bankruptcy 4 years ago' enables Woolf to reconcile 'her charm & wit & character all marked as a woman, full of knowledge & humour' with her novels: 'she rescued the whole lot by driving her pen day & night' (*D* 1.62). This commitment gives a purpose to the mechanical production observed in the *Guardian* review, but Ward's increasing loss of control over both her fiction and her finances is also refractured by the familiar imagery: beneath the established hierarchy of Ward's mastery of her servant pen also lurk the much less settled one of master and monster. Similarly, although Woolf's first reaction to the Representation of the People Act 1918 is glee that 'the great lady at Stocks must be feeling uncomfortable', this is followed by an acute analysis of a highly intelligent and ambitious woman in search of a wider sphere:

> I am malicious enough to suppose that if by some process of selection she alone could represent Belgravia in the House of Lords, the change would not seem so devastating. Imagine her neatly accoutred in black trousers (so my imagination sees her) upon the bench at the Hague Conference! (D 1.207)

The same uneasy fascination dominates Woolf's ruminations on Ward's *A Writer's Recollections* (1918) in a lengthy diary entry in September 1919. Evidence both of her wide-ranging reading of all forms of life writing and an obsessive interest in Ward, Woolf's entry speculates on success and public recognition: 'private "reflection" might serve as her mode of steeling herself against reviews and sales figures yet to come, which would deem *Night and Day* an aesthetic and/or commercial success and/or failure', as Corbett observes.[43] Woolf had read the memoir a year earlier and declared it 'a masterpiece without rival' to Vanessa (L 2.307); in a letter to Ka Arnold-Foster she announced that '[i]n its way it seems to me only comparable with Hamlet – for the insight it gives one into the recesses of the human heart. And what a heart!' (L 2.309) Woolf's flippant remarks target the volume's superficiality and reticence on personal matters. Ward's memoir makes the most of her literary connections and descent, capitalising on 'the Doctor', the Arnold family's links (however tenuous) to Charlotte Brontë, Wordsworth and Arthur Clough, and the figure of Matthew Arnold himself. Ward herself doesn't enter the narrative until chapter 6: although she retrospectively emphasises her embeddedness in this intellectual network, her silence on her childhood and teenage years hints at a displaced colonial child's isolation from the Arnold family. Ward's narrative, presented as a series of anecdotes of famous friends and acquaintances, steers away from personal introspection and offers instead a summary of the high points of her career. Judiciously stopping with the turn of the century, only the epilogue alludes to the eighteen years and sixteen novels, two plays, three memoirs and two works of war propaganda; 'perhaps signaling her sense that the turn of the century put a period to her wavering claim to posterity'.[44] Nevertheless, there are occasional moments of sincerity that pierce through the haze: Ward's love of learning ('The great Library, in particular, became to me a living and inspiring presence'), as well as her recollection of the 'feeling of sheer amazement at the range and power of human thought and at such a date in history which a leisurely and careful reading of that play [Aeschylus' *Agamemnon*] awakened in me' offer occasional glimpses at a much more sympathetic female scholar who would not be out of place as one of Woolf's case studies in *Three Guineas*.⁴⁵ Likewise, Ward recollects

> one summer afternoon, in particular, when as I was in a hansom driving idly westward towards Hyde Park Gate, thinking of a hundred things at once, this consciousness of *intensification*, of a heightened meaning in everything – the broad street, the crowd of moving figures and carriages, the houses looking down upon it – seized upon me with a rush. 'Yes – it is good – the mere living!'⁴⁶

This moment of heightened experience suggests Ward's potential for a shared modernity that links her with succeeding generations of Modernist writers, if only tenuously.

Although Woolf's reflections are private, she frames her second encounter with Ward's *Recollections* highly effectively. Encountering the volume in Lewes public library, 'full of old ghosts; books half way to decomposition', Woolf subtly assigns Ward to a distant and irrelevant past. The library's boardless books are covered in brown paper, 'as much alike outwardly as charity schoolchildren' (*D* 1.300), but haphazardly arranged: Ward's memoir is surrounded by eighteenth-century travel narratives, fictional sermons by nineteenth-century reformers and late-Victorian yachting romances (*D* 1.300 n8). Yet Woolf finds herself compulsively reading the memoir: 'I could not resist Mrs Ward, & I stand in her unconscionably long hours, as if she were a bath of tepid water that one lacks the courage to leave'. Woolf's initial ambivalent sympathy for Ward's short-lived brush with fame – 'No one has had a deeper draught of it. The poor woman, now conscious of a little chill, brings out her old praises & hangs them out of her front windows' – quickly turns into scorn for the advertising spectacle occasioned by *Marcella*, published at the height of Ward's popularity in 1894. Her strong distaste for this public display combines the gendered unease which Woolf exhibited towards Eliot's eminence in the contemporary 'George Eliot' review with a rejection of Ward's brand of popular writing:

> And indeed these poor old grandees, solicited I suppose by presentation copies & the rest, do seem to have perjured themselves cheerfully, though I can see them winking. My point is however, that all this blare & pomp has no effect on the sensitive reader, as I claim to be. Perhaps the winks are too evident. The enormous sales, the American editions, the rumble & reverberation – Piccadilly placarded with posters 'Marcella out!' – seem like the drum & cymbals of a country fair. No, nothing of this counts – She herself, setting out to write an intimate account of feelings & thoughts, gives nothing but

bills of fare & pass books. At what point did she cease thinking? Long Long ago, I should say; & then came to believe implicitly in the mummery: names of the great serve as an umbrella covering vacancy. (D 1.300)

In setting herself and by extension her competing aesthetics against this unwilling and unthinking consumption, which also characterises her own reading of Ward, Woolf resorts to familiar binaries. Thus, Andreas Huyssen argues that '[t]he lure of mass culture, after all, has been described as the threat of losing oneself in dreams and delusions and of merely consuming rather than producing'.[47] Yet although Ward remembers the publication of *Marcella* as 'the happiest date in my literary life' – 'The book, for all the hard work that had gone to it, had none the less been a pleasure to write' – she recollects this media spectacle as 'a thing which never happened to me before or since'.[48] Woolf therefore singles out an unrepresentative moment to undermine both Ward's early fiction and motivations: as Corbett notes, 'Woolf discounts the testimonials from the three "great" men [Walter Pater, Henry James, George Meredith] – not incidentally, three of her favourite late-Victorian writers – by doubting their sincerity, attributing their positive comments to "presentation copies & the rest"'.[49]

Woolf's diary entry charts a moment of literary resolve: setting her own vision against Ward's fame, she asserts 'What would it profit me to gain the approval of the whole world and lose that single voice?' (D 1.299). However, her diary entry also stages Ward as a private figure in the household of literature: 'all tea table talk to admonish the young [ . . . ] What a portrait of the Servants Hall; with Mrs. H. W. for housekeeper, & Uncle Matt. the master' (D 1.300).[50] Woolf's tea-table talk recalls her later analysis of her own Victorian 'tea-table training' and its foundation on 'restraint, sympathy, unselfishness – all civilized qualities' (*MoB* 152) closely associated with the social life of Hyde Park Gate: 'Victorian society began to exert its pressure at about half past four. [ . . . ] we must be tidied and in our places, [Vanessa] at the tea table, I on the sofa, for Mrs Green was coming; or Mrs Humphrey [sic] Ward' (*MoB* 151). Julia Stephen had considered Ward (alongside social reformers Octavia Hill and Florence Nightingale) a model of exemplary femininity for her daughters to emulate.[51] Yet Woolf's strong rejection of Ward's antiquated morality, political conservatism and the strongly gendered 'game of Victorian society' (*MoB* 152) certainly suggest that, as Sutherland argues, '[s]corn for what Mrs Humphry Ward represented was formative in Virginia Woolf's evolution'.[52] More poignantly, while Julia Stephen's early death meant that Woolf's memories of her were frozen in time, Mary Augusta Ward offered one possible answer to the question of what a woman of her generation 'would have looked like now in a room full of other people' (*MoB* 107).

In this clash of generations, Woolf ultimately gets the last word. Yet like the 'drum & cymbals of a country fair' that advertised her novels, Ward's funeral was a public spectacle, and belies Woolf's attempt to pre-emptively banish her into obscurity. Anne Olivier Bell notes of Woolf's diary entry on Ward's death (quoted at the beginning of this section) that Ward 'had a tremendous send-off, with condolences from Royalty and the eminent, a Times leader, a two-column obituary, and a country funeral at Aldbury', while the Dean of St Paul's 'ventured his opinion that she was "perhaps the greatest Englishwoman of our time"' (*D* 2.29 n7). However, like Eliot, who remains buried in her Victorian tomb, Ward posthumously depends on Woolf's goodwill: a review of her biography offers Woolf the opportunity to publicly assess the truth of this claim. 'The Compromise' (*Nation & Athenaeum*, 1923) tackles Ward's complex legacy head on: 'None of the great Victorian reputations has sunk lower than that of Mrs Humphry Ward' (*E* 3.380). Although the review lacks the acerbity of Woolf's private comments and instead strikes an elegiac note in mourning Ward's wasted potential, Woolf's stated intention of 'hand[ing] on the dilemma to our readers' (*E* 3.381) is at odds with her evident desire to banish her fiction to the dustheaps of literature:

> Her novels, already strangely out of date, hang in the lumber room of letters like the mantles of our aunts, and produce in us the same desire that they do to smash the window and let in the air, to light the fire and pile the rubbish on top. [ . . . ] there is a quality, perhaps a lack of quality, about the novels of Mrs Ward which makes it improbable that, however much they fade, they will ever become picturesque. (*E* 3.380)

Woolf's allusion to suffragettes' tactics in the opening lines of the article serves as a tacit reminder that Ward was firmly on the wrong side of political progress. However, although *The Life of Mrs Humphry Ward* outwardly conforms to a tradition of respectful family biography, Janet Penrose Trevelyan strikes a successful balance between reticence and disclosure. Thus, her volume sheds more light on Ward's early years and her quasi-abandonment at a series of boarding schools by her family and offers some insight into 'how she was always at work, writing articles or reviewing books to eke out the family income' in spite of bad health and frequent illness.[53] Trevelyan traces how Ward's idealistic goal for an intellectual community of Christians quickly transformed into the Passmore Edwards Settlement and its innovative and much needed programmes for working class children: yet the schools for children with physical disabilities, holiday programmes, and after-school play centres also required fundraising and committee-work on an enormous scale that left less and less time for serious thought and writing. Lest the narrative become too celebratory, she also notes little quirks, like her mother's lack of patience for 'bores' and the niceties of London social etiquette: 'she would sorrowfully declare that the motto of the Ward family ought to be: "Never went and never wrote"'.[54]

Woolf credits Trevelyan with presenting Ward's life from 'a different angle': the biography 'so permeates us with the sense of the presence of a human being that by the time we have finished it we are more disposed to ask questions than pass judgement' (*E* 3.381). The review therefore presents a surprisingly conciliatory view and continues Woolf's earlier speculations about Ward's motivations and character. She presents Ward's early career at Oxford with sympathy, but 'why' becomes the dominant note for the rest of her life: why social climbing, why children's play centres, why write 'at breathless speed novels which filial piety calls autumnal, but the critic unfortunately must call bad'? Trevelyan offers one answer when she observes that it was her mother's 'fundamental instinct to work herself to the bone and then to share her good times with others less fortunate, and since this process made away with her earnings she would work herself to the bone again'.[55] This echoes Woolf's description of Mrs Ramsay (and Julia Stephen) 'giving, giving, giving' (*TL* 163): Ward merely enacted this model of female philanthropy on a much larger and more public scale than that of Julia Stephen's domestic self-sacrifice. Woolf admits to another, the lack of established careers for women of Ward's generation, when she observes that

> It is impossible to remain a schoolgirl in the Bodleian for ever, and, once you breast the complicated currents of modern life at their strongest, there is little time to ask questions, and none to answer them. One thing merges in another; one thing leads to another. (*E* 3.382)

In Woolf's hands, Ward's reformist activism inevitably but seamlessly leads her to her unwilling involvement with the Anti-Suffrage League, then war propaganda. Implicitly, this foregrounds the 'subjection to and complicity with the patriarchal colonial arrangements on which the empire depended at home and abroad', which Corbett traces in Woolf's engagement with 'Pattledom' and Julia Stephen's philanthropy.[56] Ward's affinity with the patriarchal institutions Woolf would later denounce in *Three Guineas* provides a political context for her aggressive whys, but also transforms Ward's life into a cautionary tale against women's public engagement, emphasising the loss of control caused by the 'rising needs and ambitions' of the schoolgirl in the Bodleian.⁵⁷ Tellingly, Woolf's proposed alternative to this betrayal of Ward's youthful love for literature and learning is a 'hard life of unremunerative toil' culminating in a standard work of Spanish history (*E* 3.381): in its reliance on self-abnegation and suppressed ambition, this is a falling back on the ideal of a domestic literary career in obscurity.

Although the review is nominally open-ended, Woolf's decision to judge Ward by her betrayal of her early ideals makes her own position clear: 'Mrs Ward was beloved, famous, and prosperous in the highest degree. And if to achieve all this implies some compromise, still – but here we reach the dilemma which we intend to pass on to our readers' (*E* 3.383). Superficially, Woolf's rhetorical strategy in 'The Compromise' may conform to a dialogic impersonality that encourages her readers' unprejudiced judgement, as Katerina Koutsantoni finds of the *Common Reader*, yet her personal position remained unchanged.⁵⁸ The typescript version of 'Professions for Women', Woolf's Speech to the London Society for Women's Service, once again pits her own nascent career against Ward's waning one: the young writer's editor

> replied that Mrs Ward had just written her fifty sixth masterpiece and that it would not matter one straw to her or anybody else if an uneducated and probably incompetent young woman said what she thought of it. Hence I became a reviewer. (*P* xxix)

As late as 1933, Woolf was crudely joking that 'they cant [*sic*] say of Hugh [Walpole] and Virginia that they're Mrs Ward's miscarriages: we are our own begetters anyhow' (*L* 5.264), emphatically discounting Ward as a potential role model for her own career.

## 'Enslaving her intellectual liberty': Margaret Oliphant

As the title of this chapter notes, the narrator of *Three Guineas* encounters 'a gap in [her] library': '[t]here are no lives of professional women in the nineteenth century' (*3G* 200). Woolf's engagement with George Eliot and Mary Augusta Ward demonstrates that this absence is largely hyperbolical and deliberate. Even more notable, among the copious case studies in *Three Guineas* is included the autobiography of one of the most prominent women of letters of the nineteenth century, Margaret Oliphant Wilson Oliphant (1828–97). With a career that spanned the second half of the nineteenth century, Oliphant is undeniably a professional writer: she was an important contributor to *Blackwood's Edinburgh Magazine* for almost fifty years and an extremely prolific writer of novels, short stories and biographies for the popular market. Drawing on Woolf's stance in 'The Compromise', this section stands under the heading of another why. Why, in *Three Guineas*, does Woolf turn to Victorian woman of letters Margaret Oliphant, rather than propagandist and anti-suffragist Mary Augusta Ward, to illustrate women writers' compromises, and a failure to 'protect culture and intellectual liberty' (*3G* 216)?

As with Eliot and Ward, Oliphant's reputation suffered in the twentieth century. Elisabeth Jay notes that 'swiftly changing literary preoccupations of the end of the century made Margaret Oliphant a convenient symbol for the outdated female romancers of domestic fiction who had too often been prepared to sacrifice artistic integrity to financial need'.[59] This makes Woolf's sudden recovery of Oliphant all the more puzzling: had she written about her in her early career, like Ward, or ignored her altogether, her earlier popularity and subsequent disappearance would offer a convenient explanation. Instead, Woolf breaks forty years of silence only to summarily dismiss Oliphant's literary career: illustrating the dilemma of the professional woman of letters by accusing her of intellectual prostitution for the sake of feeding her children, this sudden recovery of a popular writer of the previous century illustrates both that such acts need not be beneficial or feminist, and that the scarcity of professional women writers in Woolf's fictional library is a deliberate choice.

While Woolf's analysis of Ward's compromise had focused on the artistic costs of her ambitious social climbing and far-ranging philanthropic schemes, she uses Oliphant to demonstrate a more fundamental failure of 'disinterested' criticism through the necessity of earning her own and her children's living. Woolf turns to Oliphant to demonstrate the futility of asking those 'daughters of educated men who have to earn their livings by reading and writing' for support: 'we can spare ourselves the trouble of addressing our appeal to them, for they will no more be able to protect disinterested culture and intellectual liberty than she was' (*3G* 217).

> [Mrs Oliphant] was an educated man's daughter who earned her living by reading and writing. She wrote books of all kinds. Novels, biographies, histories, handbooks of Florence and Rome, reviews, newspaper articles innumerable came from her pen. With the proceeds she earned her living and educated her children. But how far did she protect culture and intellectual liberty? That you can judge for yourself [ . . . ] When you have done, examine the state of your own mind, and ask yourself whether that reading has led you to respect disinterested culture and intellectual liberty. Has it not on the contrary smeared your mind and dejected your imagination, and led you to

deplore the fact that Mrs Oliphant sold her brain, her very admirable brain, prostituted her culture and enslaved her intellectual liberty in order that she might earn her living and educate her children? (3G 216–17)

This attack on Oliphant follows the rhetoric of Woolf's engagement with Ward: complimenting her intelligence while dismissing virtually every other aspect of her working life, she suggests that Oliphant's oeuvre corrupts its readers' minds, morality, and English culture itself.

By questioning the very possibility of writing disinterestedly for pay, Woolf offers an extreme interpretation of Arnold's edict of 'a free play of the mind on all subjects which it touches [ . . . ] steadily refusing to lend itself to any of those ulterior, political, practical considerations about ideas'.[60] Positing Oliphant's criticism as implicit collusion with patriarchal society and Oliphant herself as incapable of preventing the rise of fascism echoes the inevitability of Ward's transformation from social reformer to leader of the Anti-Suffrage League and war propagandist. Additionally, it serves to position the narrator herself as the right kind of writer. In her analysis of Woolf's 1939 pamphlet 'Reviewing', Gualtieri notes that

> the thorny question of the relationship between writing and market demands is solved by confining the reviewer to the role of little more than a skilled worker, an automaton in fact whose job could just as easily be performed by a machine. This [ . . . ] manages to preserve the critic in a situation of integrity, and independence from literary journalism.[61]

*Three Guineas* suggests a similar separation between Oliphant's incessant production as a reviewer, and Woolf's own integrity as a critic, financially independent and outside the control of an editor. Yet paradoxically, it is the absence of 'ulterior, political, practical considerations' that ultimately condemns Oliphant, but not Woolf the feminist cultural critic. As McNees notes, in spite of Woolf's intense preoccupation with the Arnoldian critic in some of her self-reflective essays on literary criticism, '*A Room of One's Own* (1929) and *Three Guineas* (1938) position her in a more adversarial role [ . . . ] Woolf's principal departure from Arnold's critique lies, particularly in *Three Guineas*, in her condemnation of society as patriarchal and thus hostile to professional women'.[62]

As before, this rhetorical manoeuvre has its place within the internal logic of the essay, but it is also a gesture that distances Woolf from a potential predecessor. As a novelist *and* influential literary critic, Oliphant commanded a public platform which Woolf's earlier domestic amateur writers had lacked. Oliphant's sustained commitment to both forms of writing also separates her from writers like George Eliot, who saw journalism as an apprenticeship for her more prestigious fiction. Joanne Shattock notes that it was Oliphant's prolific journalism and consequent public omnipresence, not her novels, which drew forth criticism like Henry James's complaint that 'no woman had ever, for half a century, had her personal "say" so publicly and irresponsibly'. She argues that

> [Oliphant's] reviewing was phenomenal in its bulk and considerable in its impact. In her writing life of over forty years there were few of her contemporaries, male or female, not to mention writers of the past whose work did not come under her scrutiny. In this she was the precursor of [ . . . ] Virginia Woolf and Alice Meynell, two early modernist women writers for whom journalism was a persistent strand throughout their writing lives.[63]

Woolf's claim that Oliphant 'prostituted her culture and enslaved her intellectual liberty' thus undermines the institutional weight attached to her position as the official critical voice of *Blackwood's*. Her characterisation of the 'inconceivable licence of the profession of letters', unregulated and with relatively low barriers of entry:

> Books, pens and paper are so cheap, reading and writing have been, since the eighteenth century at least, so universally taught in our class, that it was impossible for any body of men to corner the necessary knowledge or refuse admittance. (3G 214–15)

plays down the obstacles faced by women of letters as well as the strategies they devised to circumvent them. As female journalists in a male-dominated environment, Oliphant, Woolf and countless others shared the experience of competing with university-educated men and developing quietly subversive strategies for writing under an editor's radar. Decades of writing for *Blackwood's Edinburgh Magazine* honed Oliphant's skills in assuming, but also subtly undermining, a male point of view in her reviews and essays, and Woolf likewise learned to cultivate a 'surface manner' while writing for the *Times Literary Supplement*: a suave, polite, 'side-long' approach which allowed her to 'slip in things that would be inaudible if one marched straight up and spoke out loud' (*MoB* 152). Dismissing the possibility of protest and intellectual challenge to occur in ordinary journalism for common readers, Woolf pessimistically appears to discount much of her own as well as Oliphant's oeuvre.

Intriguingly, this discussion of Oliphant is one of the few places in which the American and British editions of *Three Guineas* differ; and these editorial changes obscure the extent to which Woolf manipulates Oliphant's career in her brief overview. Emily Blair's reading of this passage hinges on the three dots which come to represent the futility of Oliphant's career in the American edition of *Three Guineas*: 'judge for yourself by reading first a few of her novels . . . conclude by sousing yourself in the innumerable faded articles, reviews, sketches of one kind or another which she contributed to literary papers'.[64] However, the British version gives a list of works instead. This allows a more detailed analysis of how Woolf's highly eclectic selection of works both undermines Oliphant's reputation and highlights the themes she appears to consider representative of Oliphant's life:

> judge for yourself by reading first a few of her novels: *The Duke's Daughter, Diana Trelawny, Harry Joscelyn*, say; continue with the lives of Sheridan and Cervantes; go on to the *Makers of Florence and Rome*; conclude by sousing yourself in the innumerable faded articles, reviews, sketches of one kind or another which she contributed to literary papers. (*3G* 216–17)

This selection of works excludes the first three decades of Oliphant's career and all of her best novels, at the expense of later work from the 1880s and 1890s. Arguably, the variety and quantity, as well as the differing quality of Oliphant's writings makes it difficult to declare any one work characteristic of her style, but virtually all Victorian and modern assessments of Oliphant's career single out the *Chronicles of Carlingford* (mainly 1860s) and her supernatural *Stories of the Seen and Unseen* (from 1880 onwards) as her best work. Thus, Richard Garnett's 1901 *Dictionary of National Biography* entry praises both of these series as well as later novels like *Hester* and *The Ladies Lindores* (both 1883). That Woolf must have read the *DNB* entry is evident from her footnote, which quotes Garnett's article to prove that Oliphant 'lived in perpetual embarrassment' (*3G* 307 n7), but omits his more measured assessment that

> Her great gifts – invention, humour, pathos, the power of bringing persons and scenes vividly before the eye – could hardly have been augmented by any amount of study, and no study could have given her the incommunicable something that stamps the great author.[65]

Likewise, Blair points to another source of positive Oliphant criticism available to Woolf. Brimley Johnson's *The Women Novelists* (1918), which she had reviewed for the *Times Literary Supplement* (albeit with a focus on the early nineteenth century), also includes an entry on Oliphant which singles out *The Chronicles of Carlingford* for 'approach[ing] genius' and praises her as the first female 'all-round practical journalist, [ . . . ] handling history and biography like a person of culture'.[66] While a bias towards Oliphant's later work might be explained by the greater likeliness of Woolf's having encountered it, the complete exclusion of all of her best works must be deliberate; as is the selective use of this source material.

Woolf's random selection from Oliphant's oeuvre of over 100 works, likely unfamiliar to many of her contemporary readers, underscores her claims about Oliphant's lack of literary legacy. The selection appears to be dictated by a desire to emphasise how financial pressure and market-orientation shaped Oliphant's non-fiction. The lives of Cervantes (1880) and Sheridan (1883) (for *Blackwood's* 'Foreign Classics for English Readers', of which she was the editor, and Macmillan's *English Men of Letters*, respectively) are part of Oliphant's contribution to the masses of educational literature with popular appeal published during the period: Leslie Stephen wrote multiple volumes for Macmillan's *English Men of Letters* around the same time. Collecting readable critical biographies for popular readers, these series were not designed to present new scholarship or advance literary criticism; and although Oliphant's works were generally well received, they were also composed very quickly, as noted in the *Spectator* review of *Cervantes*: 'She is a little too unfalteringly eulogistic, perhaps, and her work bears occasional signs of hurry; but she sees the true value of things, and does not easily lend herself to vain inquiries'.[67] Likewise, the beautifully bound and illustrated coffee-table volumes *Makers of Florence: Dante, Giotto, Savonarola and Their City* (1876) and *The Makers of Modern Rome* (1895) demonstrate Oliphant's keen awareness of a growing demand for travel literature: Jay commends 'Mrs Oliphant's power to recognise the demands of the market and transform these into a vehicle for her own talents' in condensing history through anecdote and linking disparate material with confident commentary.[68]

George Levine asserts that 'whatever their overall merits', any and all of Oliphant's novels will contain 'sequences as strong as any one might find in the work of canonical Victorian novelists':

> in the end what makes her work a distinctive and important addition to the achievement of the Victorian novel is a tough-minded confrontation with the felt life of ordinary middle-class people (almost always women) with moral conventions and with novelistic representations of the virtues of the bourgeois family.[69]

Consequently, Oliphant's works occupy a paradoxical place in *Three Guineas*: superficially chosen as evidence of a mercenary corruption of literature and culture, the novels and guide books nevertheless offer their own analysis of women's disadvantaged position in society that subtly supports Woolf's argument. *The Makers of Modern Rome* offers a historical precursor to Woolf's Outsiders Society in Oliphant's eloquent commentary on women's position in early Christian society. Explaining female saints' withdrawal into exile as a result of their marginalised social position, Oliphant points to

> the struggle with the authorities of her family for the training of a son, for the marriage of a daughter, from which a woman might shrink with a sense of impotence, knowing the prestige of the noble guardian against whom she would have to contend, and all the forces of family pride, of tradition and use and wont, that would be arrayed against her.[70]

However, this subtle dialogue, in which the analysis of patriarchal family dynamics underpinning Oliphant's works questions Woolf's sweeping dismissal of their value, is lost to any but the most committed readers of Oliphant's work. Instead, Woolf amplifies Oliphant's own pre-emptive dismissal of the value of her popular history, written by 'a mind a little exercised in the aspects of humanity, but not trained in the ways of learning', and ignores the potential for subversiveness to exist quietly, even in mass-market volumes.

*The Duke's Daughter* (1890), *Diana Trelawny* (written 1877, published 1892) and *Harry Joscelyn* (1881) all participate in late-Victorian debates of marriage and female independence, situating Oliphant as doubly outdated: first by the thematic overlap with New Women writing which Woolf in her early career rejects as 'behind the times' in its sexual mores, and second, and even more so, because Oliphant's reluctance to assert women's rights without significant qualifications weakens her support of female agency: her heroines suffer meekly and their virtues reform oppressive fathers and husbands.[71] Nevertheless, her close readings of the dynamics of the Victorian home match Woolf's own analysis. Oliphant's depictions of despotic fathers and their compulsive need to control their daughters' lives speak to the pervasiveness of the infantile fixation diagnosed by Woolf. Thus, *The Duke's Daughter* (1890) departs from 'the code of female self-sacrifice she had so long preached [ . . . to] explore what might be considered sufficient cause to justify female rebellion'.[72] Yet the novel's melodramatic plot hinges on Lady Jane's socially unacceptable 'half-married' status after her clandestine wedding is interrupted by her controlling father; and when a servant accidentally releases her from his imprisonment, she begs her father's forgiveness for her secret marriage before forgiving him for her imprisonment, suggesting that Oliphant found it hard to let go entirely of angelic suffering and female self-sacrifice. *Harry Joscelyn* (1881) likewise begins with a household suffering under the rule of a despotic and irascible father. Oliphant traces how Ralph Joscelyn's misogynist contempt for women allows his son to blame his failures, the consequence of egotism and entitlement, on the women in his life. Again, however, Oliphant undercuts her analysis by making the youngest daughter an agent of moral reform, suggesting that true female virtue will overcome even the worst oppression. Yet ultimately, the novel also demonstrates her unparalleled skill for endings which 'cast a shadow back over the novel as a whole and raise unsettling questions about the reader's expectation of fiction and life'.[73] '[Mrs Joscelyn] saw her children now and then, and they were all happy, and in no need of her. What could any woman desire more?':[74] a poignant questioning of maternal self-sacrifice that, as Jay observes, 'raised the ghost of many Victorian women's fears'.[75] Although Oliphant does not mount a full critique of the virtues she preached, the novel shows her self-awareness as well as her capacity to evaluate her ideological position critically from multiple perspectives; while her examination of male tyranny again echoes Woolf's many biographical case studies.

*Diana Trelawny* (written in 1877, published in 1892) is perhaps the most puzzling in this list: like the others, it cannot be counted among Oliphant's best work by any stretch of the imagination, yet its uncompromised scepticism towards marriage demonstrates that she was capable of a sustained critical examination of Victorian ideology. The novel sympathises with Diana, a former governess turned country squire, who values her independence too much to marry; while Oliphant's depiction of the accidental engagement and only moderately unhappy marriage between Diana's conventional protégée Sophy and Diana's own suitor draws attention to marriage's lack of meaning in a society where it is the universal expectation for women, notwithstanding their inclinations. At most, the novel's publication history offers an example of the ubiquity and low aesthetic and financial value of Oliphant's work: Blackwood's misplaced the manuscript for thirteen years after submission and only published the novel after it was accidentally rediscovered.[76]

If Woolf's selection of Oliphant's works is biased, then what of her facts? In her summary of Oliphant's life, Woolf draws on 'an illuminating and indeed moving piece of work, the autobiography of Mrs Oliphant, which is full of facts' (3G 216). As Woolf should know, life writing is rarely so simple: her emphasis on the factual veracity of her reading obscures the extent of her own bias, but also misrepresents the character of the *Autobiography and Letters of Mrs Oliphant* (1899). The *Autobiography* is neither a straightforward text nor a reliable interpretation of Oliphant's life and, like John Cross's biography of George Eliot, hindered Woolf's understanding as much as it helped: like the novels, it occupies an ambivalent status as material witnesses to Oliphant's failure as well as a subtle intertext to Woolf's argument. Like Woolf's own 'A Sketch of the Past', Oliphant's autobiography was experimental and fragmented as well as incomplete at the time of her death, offering none of the temporal and structural certainties of a more conventional Life. Written over the course of four decades, the manuscript chronicles Oliphant's life as well as the deaths of her husband, daughter and two sons.[77] It follows a circular narrative of grief and recovery interspersed with reflections on the conflicting demands of professional and family life: Oliphant's awareness of the 'multitude of competing meanings' available for interpreting the events of her life makes the *Autobiography* 'at times seem like a deconstructionist's paradise'.[78]

Although the *Autobiography* was begun as a private family memoir, the death of the majority of this audience led Oliphant to redesign it as a public memoir and posthumous insurance policy. Consequently, her cousin and editor Annie Coghill rearranged the manuscript, making the *Autobiography* as much Coghill's interpretation of her cousin's life as it is Oliphant's own. Jay represents the prevalent critical attitude when she argues that 'the reshaping of her autobiography by her literary executors contrived to transform this passionate, witty, wryly self-aware, and immensely energetic author into a model of quietly suffering Victorian femininity'.[79] Coghill also relies heavily on Oliphant's correspondence with three generations of Blackwoods to cover the years and events left out in the original manuscript. As business correspondence (in spite of their longstanding friendship), these letters present Oliphant mainly as a literary manager, pragmatically pitching articles, novels and non-fiction likely to sell, and asking for loans and advances. This emphasis on Oliphant's artistic and literal self-sacrifice for her children – 'I have worked a hole into my right forefinger', she recorded at one point[80] – as well as her absolute devotion to her sons, therefore resonates strongly with Woolf's analysis in *Three Guineas*.

The *Autobiography* offers passages that seem to confirm Woolf's assertion 'that Mrs Oliphant sold her brain, her very admirable brain, prostituted her culture and enslaved her intellectual liberty in order that she might earn her living and educate her children' (*3G* 216). Thus, Oliphant reflects that:

> I remember that I said to myself, having then perhaps a little stirring of ambition, that I must make up my mind to think no more of that, and that to bring up the boys for the service of God was better than to write a fine novel [ . . . ] It seemed rather a fine thing to make that resolution (though in reality I had no choice); but now I think that if I had taken the other way, which seemed the less noble, it might have been better for all of us. I might have done better work. I should in all probability have earned nearly as much for half the production had I done less.[81]

In this account, motherhood and writing, as well as domestic and public life, are inextricably connected: financial necessity dictates artistic choices, and Oliphant undercuts her own speculations about a more satisfying compromise by emphasising her lack of choice. In a twist on *Three Guineas*' 'Arthur's Education Fund', Oliphant sacrificed her own career to send her sons to Eton and Oxford, putting her faith in the university system whose shortcomings Woolf condemns in *Three Guineas*. However, this straightforward reading is not allowed to stand: Oliphant questions the nobility, as well as usefulness, of such female self-sacrifice and dismisses her speculations out of hand: 'What casuists we are on our own behalf! This is altogether self-defence'.[82]

This is not the only challenge to a more streamlined narrative of Oliphant's intellectual prostitution for the sake of her children. Ruminating on the interconnections of gender, professionalism and motherhood, Oliphant pits her own career against that of George Eliot, the main contemporary representative of serious and disinterested fiction:

> I have been tempted to begin writing by George Eliot's life – with that curious kind of self-compassion which one cannot get clear of. I wonder if I am a little envious of her? I always avoid considering formally what my own mind is worth. [ . . . ] I have written because it gave me pleasure, because it came natural to me, because it was like talking or breathing, besides the big fact that it was necessary for me to work for my children. That, however, was not the first motive, so that when I laugh inquiries off and say that it is my trade, I do it only by way of eluding the question, which I have neither time nor wish to enter into.[83]

Although fascinated by the fame and material conditions of her rival *Blackwood's* author, 'kept [ . . . ] in a mental greenhouse and taken care of', Oliphant rejects Eliot's success as unnatural and unfeminine and firmly separates Mary Ann Evans from it: 'I think she must have been a dull woman with a great genius distinct from herself, something like the gift of the old prophets, which they sometimes exercised with only a dim perception of what it meant'.[84] Oliphant's account of her own writing practices in contrast explicitly aligns herself with a female tradition of domestic drawing room writing:

> My study, all the study I have ever attained to, is the second little drawing-room where all the (feminine) life of the house goes on [ . . . ] Miss Austen, I believe, wrote in the same way, and very much for the same reason [ . . . ] My mother, I believe, would have felt her pride and rapture much checked, almost humiliated, if she had conceived that I stood in need of any artificial aids of that or any other description. That would at once have made the work unnatural to her eyes, and also to mine.[85]

This ideal of female authorship, domesticated, organic, and requiring no 'artificial aids', recalls Woolf's analysis of historical women's writing in 'Women and Fiction'. Praising 'its divine spontaneity, like that of the blackbird's song or the thrush's. It was untaught; it was from the heart', Woolf also argues that this unconscious mode of writing can lack artistry and sophistication: 'chattering and garrulous – mere talk spilt over paper and left to dry in pools and blots' (E 5.34). Viewed in these terms, the self-indulgence of the *Autobiography*, written in bursts of grief and despair after the deaths of successive family members, condemns Oliphant's writing as surely as any financial compromises: despite its subtle resonances with her own argument, Woolf dismisses Oliphant's work because of its lack of conscious artistry. A recognition of how her self-presentation impacted her status as writer also runs through the *Autobiography*: unlike George Eliot, who 'took herself with tremendous seriousness [ . . . ] and was always on duty' Oliphant's 'carelessness in asserting my claim with everyone is very much against me'.[86] This is ultimately also the case for the *Autobiography*. With Oliphant's self-deprecating ruminations placed at the beginning of the published work, the text pre-emptively undercuts the value of her work: it helped denigrate her reputation and made it easy for Woolf to craft a narrative that reduces Oliphant's significance to her maternal sacrifices.

Given that Woolf needed to manipulate Oliphant's life and works to fit into the argumentative structure of *Three Guineas*, I want to return to my earlier question: what makes Woolf decide on Margaret Oliphant as the prime candidate for 'intellectual prostitution', particularly if her writing life also offers evidence of the subtle subversion practised by professional women writers? Oliphant fits more neatly into Woolf's selection of predominantly nineteenth-century lives than Ward's epoch-spanning life might have done; additionally, the *Autobiography* itself undermines her posthumous reputation. Woolf perhaps also preferred a writer without close living relatives or descendants to avoid the backlash that a public lambasting of Ward, related to Huxleys and Trevelyans, might have caused. However, Oliphant's presence in *Three Guineas* is also another indicator of the Victorian legacies in Woolf's thinking: in setting up Oliphant as the epitome of intellectual prostitution, she draws extensively on Leslie Stephen's essay on 'Southey's Letters' (originally published in *The National Review* in 1899, republished in *Studies of a Biographer* in 1902). Like Woolf, Stephen illustrates the man of letters' dilemma by using Oliphant's then recent *Autobiography*:

> The problem which presents itself to the professional man of letters might be illustrated by that most pathetic autobiography of Mrs. Oliphant which

has, I think, been rather harshly judged. Mrs. Oliphant thought (and, as I believe, with some justice) that, if freed from pecuniary pressure, she could have rivalled some more successful authors, and possibly have written a novel fit to stand on the same shelf with *Adam Bede*. She resigned her chance of such fame because she wished to send her sons to Eton. It is, of course, clear enough that, if she had sent them to some humbler school, she might have come nearer to combining the two aims, and have kept her family without sacrificing her talents to over-production. But, granting the force of the dilemma, I confess that I honour rather than blame the choice. I take it to be better for a parent to do his (or her) parental duty than to sacrifice the duty to art or the demands of posterity.[87]

Although Stephen presents Southey as just as prolific and commercially compromised, it is Oliphant who is judged and condemned for her incessant literary production: making a woman the scapegoat for men of letters' compromises, the essay casts popular fiction as inherently female, inferior and compromised.[88] Stephen's criticism presents a blueprint for Woolf: she repeats his rhetorical movement, briefly invoking Oliphant only to condemn her, and like him reduces the *Autobiography* to its emotional impact, with Stephen's 'most pathetic autobiography' finding its match in Woolf's 'indeed moving piece of work'. Both suggest that Oliphant's career, free from financial pressures, would have taken a different path, and emphasise the duties that motherhood added. Although Woolf omits the jibe against Oliphant's social aspirations, it resonates with her critique of the 'great patriarchal machine' (*MoB* 155) through which Oliphant unsuccessfully tried to launch her son's careers.

Oliphant's life is only one of the vast number of case studies that supports Woolf's analysis in *Three Guineas*, but Woolf's impact on her afterlife is significant. Although Woolf continues her revision of Stephen's criticism by embedding it within the feminist analysis of *Three Guineas*, she also prominently reduces Oliphant to a reductive but memorable anecdote that continued to influence subsequent biographers and critics, as noted by Elizabeth Langland.[89] This is even more notable as Woolf was faced with two almost diametrically opposed sources when choosing how to approach Oliphant: Leslie Stephen's brief dismissal in 'Southey's Letters' competes with Anny Thackeray Ritchie's recollection of literary mentorship and mutual appreciation. Stephen's private reflections on Oliphant are sparse, but his record of her death in the *Mausoleum Book* reveals his pity for her futile maternal sacrifices: 'Now both boys are dead and before their death had given her much trouble. She was, they said, glad to die, and I don't wonder: but she was a brave good woman and kind to us'.[90] This strongly gendered perspective resonates with Oliphant's own references to Stephen in her private writing.

Thus, Stephen becomes the embodiment of the social and professional privileges of the Victorian man of letters when she pointedly notes to Macmillan partner George Craik that

> [t]he only way such kind thoughts could come to practical benefit would be to find me something like an editorship where there would be a steady income without perpetual strain, such as his friends have found more than once for Leslie Stephen, but then he is a man.[91]

Similarly, Jay speculates that a sudden increase of remarrying widowers in Oliphant's late-1870s fiction may be reflective of her extensive discussions with Anny Thackeray Ritchie about Stephen's second marriage, noting that '[i]n a gossipy letter she wrote of him, to John Blackwood, "He appeared the most heartbroken of bereaved husbands two years ago, as well as the most melancholy of men – he is just now on the eve of a second marriage"'.[92] Oliphant's unwilling fascination with Stephen is even more apparent in the unedited manuscript version of the *Autobiography*, which dissects his personality in great detail to come to the conclusion that 'the man has a great deal of charm. He is a cantankerous person and has not a good word for anybody, yet he has a fascination which is more effective than any amount of goodness'.[93] In the published version, this is reduced to an acknowledgement of Stephen's masculine powers as editor and mountaineer, kindly taking Oliphant's sons on walking tours and accepting work for the *Cornhill Magazine*.[94]

Woolf's perpetuation of Leslie Stephen's view of Oliphant thus paradoxically puts a male narrative of female compromise at the centre of *Three Guineas*' radical feminism. Woolf ignores an alternative literary history offered by Anny Thackeray Ritchie, whose lifelong friendship with Oliphant offers an example of mutual literary appreciation and informal female mentorship based on a shared appreciation of domestic realist fiction.[95] Unlike Stephen and Woolf, Ritchie assigned Oliphant a firm place in the history of women's writing. Her collection of female literary biography, the *Book of Sibyls* (1883), is dedicated 'To Mrs Oliphant: My little record would not seem to me in any way complete without your name, dear Sibyl of our own'. Ritchie also resists the devaluation of her friend's career and groups Oliphant with firmly canonical authors like George Eliot and Charlotte Brontë as one of the 'torchbearers of the early Victorian days' in her *Discourse on Modern Sibyls* (1912), which emphasises the specifically female form of Oliphant's professionalism: '[h]er work was never-ceasing, but it scarcely seemed to interfere with her hospitable life among her friends'.[96] Ritchie's essay points to a different course Woolf's literary history could have taken, centred around a mutually supportive network of women writers who, as Woolf noted of Eliot, 'would not renounce [their] own inheritance – the difference of view, the difference of standard' (*E* 4.178) and worked within the confines of gendered double standards to reach their own definition of professional authorship and artistic success. Yet by rejecting Ritchie's Victorian sibyls, George Eliot and Margaret Oliphant, as well as the more ambivalent example of Mary Augusta Ward, Woolf distances herself from these professionals and creates a gap in her library. This vividly illustrates the problems that can prevent women from thinking back through their mothers: by reducing Eliot and Oliphant to martyrs to their gender and by dismissing Ward entirely, Woolf obscures the presence of female literary professionals in the nineteenth century and undermines their achievements. Her engagement with these writers also shows how she deliberately shaped her female canon to assert her difference by rejecting both popular writing and overtly Victorian constructs of femininity. Biography, which had allowed experimentation and recovery in her engagement with earlier writers, now serves as a tool for keeping these writers at bay as, caught in a moment of uncertain canonicity, Woolf shapes their afterlives to conform to her own conception of professional writing.

## Notes

1. Graham Law maps these changes and their impact on the author in 'The Professionalization of Authorship', in *The Nineteenth-Century Novel 1820–1880*, The Oxford History of the Novel in English, vol. III (Oxford: Oxford University Press, 2012), 37–55 (pp. 37, 45).
2. Sarah Wah, '"The most churlish of celebrities": George Eliot, John Cross and the Question of High Status', *Journal of Victorian Culture*, 15.3 (2010), 370–87 (p. 371).
3. Kyriaki Hadjiafxendi, 'Negotiating Fame: Mid-Victorian Women Writers and the Romantic Myth of the Gentlemanly Reviewer', in *Crafting the Woman Professional in the Long Nineteenth Century*, ed. by Kyriaki Hadjiafxendi and Patricia Zakreski (Proquest Ebook Central / Taylor and Francis, 2016), pp. 187–205 (p. 190). Pdf accessed 8 August 2017.
4. Linda H. Peterson, *Becoming a Woman of Letters: Myths of Authorship and Facts of the Victorian Market* (Princeton, NJ: Princeton University Press, 2009), p. 11.
5. Alexis Easley, *Literary Celebrity, Gender and Victorian Authorship, 1850–1914* (Newark: University of Delaware Press, 2011), p. 61.
6. Corbett, 'Ashamed of the inkpot', para. 6; see also *Behind the Times: Virginia* Woolf *in Late-Victorian Contexts*.
7. Mary Jean Corbett is the authority on Woolf in late-Victorian contexts; but Sarah Parker offered a detailed analysis of Woolf's desire to distance

herself from a potentially influential predecessor in her keynote 'Who's Afraid of Alice Meynell?' for the Midlands Modernist Network conference 'Transitions: Bridging the Victorian–Modernist Divide' at the University of Birmingham (2018).

8. Various critics have charted this process: Dillane details Eliot's efforts to obscure her journalistic origins; Wah analyses Eliot's engagement with celebrity culture; and Price discusses Eliot's highly effective publication strategies. See Fionnuala Dillane, *Before George Eliot: Marian Evans and the Periodical Press* (Cambridge: Cambridge University Press, 2013); Wah; Leah Price, 'George Eliot and the Production of Consumers', *NOVEL: A Forum on Fiction*, 30 (1997), 145–69.

9. Fionnuala Dillane, '"The character of editress": Marian Evans at the Westminster Review, 1851–54', *Tulsa Studies in Women's Literature*, 30.2 (2013), 269–90 (p. 271).

10. Rosemary Ashton, 'Evans, Marian', *Oxford Dictionary of National Biography* <http://www.oxforddnb.com/view/article/6794?docPos=1> (accessed 26 April 2017).

11. Gillian Beer, quoted in Dillane, *Before George Eliot: Marian Evans and the Periodical Press*, p. 17.

12. Dillane, *Before George Eliot: Marian Evans and the Periodical Press*, pp. 145–6.

13. George Eliot, *George Eliot's Life as Related in Her Letters and Journals*, ed. by John Cross, 3 vols (Edinburgh and London: William Blackwood and Sons, 1885), vol. I, p. v.

14. See Harris for a closer analysis of this editorial proceeding. Eliot, I, p. vi; Margaret Harris, 'J. W. Cross Defends G. H. Lewes', *George Eliot Review: Journal of the George Eliot Fellowship*, 40 (2009), 28–37.

15. Quoted in Harris, p. 28 and Shattock, 'Jane Austen and George Eliot', p. 16.

16. Price, p. 156.

17. Ashton suggests that 'by the 1890s George Eliot was being described as a heavy, humourless writer' because of Cross's censorship of her life and letters, where Jay sees pure misogyny. Ashton; Elisabeth Jay, 'Mrs. Oliphant: The Hero as Woman of Letters, or Autobiography, a Gendered Genre', *Caliban*, 31 (1994), 85–95 (p. 87); Shattock, 'Jane Austen and George Eliot', p. 10.

18. Elaine Showalter, 'The Greening of Sister George', *Nineteenth-Century Fiction*, 35.3 (1980), 292–311 (p. 292); Shattock, 'Jane Austen and George Eliot', pp. 17–18.

19. Mary Kaiser Loges, 'Inventing Victorians: Virginia Woolf's "Memoirs of a Novelist"', *The Victorian Newsletter*, 73 (1988), 1–2 (p. 2); Anny Thackeray Ritchie, *A Discourse on Modern Sibyls*, Pamphlet No. 24 (London: The English Association, 1913), p. 4.

20. Shattock praises it as an 'intellectual biography' as well as the first critical biography of George Eliot. 'Jane Austen and George Eliot', p. 17; Leslie Stephen, *George Eliot*, English Men of Letters (London: Macmillan & Co., 1902), pp. 21–38.

21. Eliot, I, p. 265; Leslie Stephen, 'Cross, Mary Ann', *Dictionary of National Biography Archive*, 1888 <https://doi.org/10.1093/odnb/9780192683120.013.6794>.

22. Tracey S. Rosenberg, 'The Awkward Blot: George Eliot's Reception and The Ideal Woman Writer', *Nineteenth-Century Gender Studies*, 3.1 (2007), para. 9.
23. Brosnan, p. 64.
24. Eliot, I, p. 312.
25. Alison Booth, *Greatness Engendered: George Eliot and Virginia Woolf*, Reading Women Writing (Ithaca, NY: Cornell University Press, 1992), p. 1.
26. Stephen, *George Eliot*, p. 52.
27. Booth, *Greatness Engendered: George Eliot and Virginia Woolf*, p. 56.
28. Rosenberg, para. 14.
29. Booth, *Greatness Engendered: George Eliot and Virginia Woolf*, p. 54.
30. Ward is eager to ensure that her readers know that this is a compliment of sorts: 'Impossible for her to talk her books, or evolve her books from conversation, like Madame de Stael. She was too self-conscious, too desperately reflective, too rich in second-thoughts for that. But in tete-a-tete, and with time to choose her words, she could in monologue, with just enough stimulus from a companion to keep it going produce on a listener exactly the impression of some of her best work'. Mrs Humphry Ward, *A Writer's Recollections*, 3rd edn (London: W. Collins Sons & Co Ltd, 1919), p. 108.
31. Jay, 'Mrs. Oliphant', p. 87.
32. Gualtieri similarly observes that 'On the one hand, there is her awareness of the importance of the professionalisation of women's writing as an instrument of emancipation. On the other, there is her suspicion, as a writer and a reader, of the institutionalisation of literature and of the professional critic as a figure that symbolises a restriction rather than a widening of access and, consequently, a weakening of literature's universal appeal'. Gualtieri, p. 69.
33. John Sutherland, 'A Girl in the Bodleian: Mary Ward's Room of Her Own', *Victorian Literature and Culture*, 16 (1988), 169–80.
34. John Sutherland, 'Ward [Née Arnold], Mary Augusta [Known as Mrs Humphry Ward]', *Oxford Dictionary of National Biography* <http://www.oxforddnb.com/view/article/36736?docPos=1> (accessed 19 May 2017); John Sutherland, *Mrs Humphry Ward: Eminent Victorian, Pre-Eminent Edwardian* (Oxford: Oxford University Press, 1991), pp. 124–31; Ward, p. 163.
35. Corbett, *Behind the Times: Virginia Woolf in Late-Victorian Contexts*, p. 135.
36. John Sutherland, 'Ward [Née Arnold], Mary Augusta [Known as Mrs Humphry Ward]'; Sutherland, *Mrs Humphry Ward: Eminent Victorian, Pre-Eminent Edwardian*.
37. John Cooper, 'Oscar Wilde's Cello Coat', *Oscar Wilde in America :: Blog*, 2018 <https://oscarwildeinamerica.blog/2018/01/04/oscar-wildes-cello-coat> (accessed 28 February 2018); *Echoes of the 'Eighties: Leaves from the Diary of a Victorian Lady*, ed. by Wilfred Partington (London: Eveleigh Nash Company, 1921), p. 160.
38. Janet Penrose Trevelyan, *The Life of Mrs Humphry Ward* (London: Constable and Company Ltd, 1923), p. 189; see also Ward, p. 317.
39. Leslie Stephen was Vice-President of Ward's Bloomsbury settlement, making this suggestion less curious than Woolf implies here. S. P. Rosenbaum,

*Edwardian Bloomsbury: The Early Literary History of the Bloomsbury Group*, vol. II (New York: St Martin's Press, 1994), p. 152.
40. Sutherland, 'Ward'.
41. John Sutherland, *Mrs Humphry Ward: Eminent Victorian, Pre-Eminent Edwardian*, p. 201.
42. Ward's *A Writer's Recollections* even features a footnote, inserted at the last minute, condemning this 'foolish essay'. Ward, p. 8n.
43. Corbett, *Behind the Times: Virginia Woolf in Late-Victorian Contexts*, p. 134.
44. Corbett, *Behind the Times: Virginia Woolf in Late-Victorian Contexts*, p. 135.
45. Ward, pp. 109, 345.
46. Ward, p. 197.
47. Andreas Huyssen, *After the Great Divide: Modernism, Mass Culture, Postmodernism* (Bloomington: Indiana University Press, 1986), p. 55.
48. Ward, p. 301.
49. Presentation copies like the one of *Helbeck of Bannisdale* still in Woolf's library today: 'For Leslie Stephen, with whom I had only lately made warm and close friends, I had a copy bound, without the final chapter, that the book might not, by its tragic close, depress one who had known so much sorrow.' Ward, p. 317; Corbett, *Behind the Times: Virginia Woolf in Late-Victorian Contexts*, p. 133.
50. See also Corbett, *Behind the Times: Virginia Woolf in Late-Victorian Contexts*, p. 133.
51. Jane Garnett, 'Stephen [Née Jackson], Julia Prinsep (1846–1895), Celebrated Beauty and Philanthropist', *Oxford Dictionary of National Biography* <http://www.oxforddnb.com/view/10.1093/ref:odnb/9780198614128.001.0001/odnb-9780198614128-e-46943> (accessed 14 March 2018).
52. John Sutherland, *Mrs Humphry Ward: Eminent Victorian, Pre-Eminent Edwardian*, p. 201.
53. Trevelyan, pp. 23, 26.
54. Trevelyan, p. 192.
55. Trevelyan, p. 37.
56. Corbett, *Behind the Times: Virginia Woolf in Late-Victorian Contexts*, p. 152.
57. Ward, p. 102. This echo of *A Writer's Recollections* suggests that Woolf might have reread the autobiography a third time in her quest for an answer.
58. Koutsantoni, *Virginia Woolf's Common Reader*, pp. 101–22; 149–60; 'The Impersonal Strategy'.
59. Elisabeth Jay, 'Oliphant, Margaret Oliphant Wilson', *Oxford Dictionary of National Biography* <http://www.oxforddnb.com/view/article/20712?docPos=1> (accessed 18 May 2017).
60. Matthew Arnold, 'The Function of Criticism at the Present Time', in *The Function of Criticism at the Present Time and An Essay on Style* (New York: Macmillan & Co., 1895), pp. 3–86 (p. 39).
61. Gualtieri, p. 65.
62. Corbett also addresses Oliphant and disinterestedness in the context of Woolf's treatment of Josephine Butler's (even more disinterested, because charitable) work against the Contagious Diseases Acts, but pays less

attention to the tension inherent in Woolf's position. McNees argues for Arnold as an influential model of criticism for Woolf's purely literary criticism, but points to the limited usefulness of this model for her feminist criticism. Corbett, *Behind the Times: Virginia Woolf in Late-Victorian Contexts*, pp. 106–8; Eleanor McNees, 'The Stephen Inheritance: Virginia Woolf and the Burden of the Arnoldian Critic', *The Cambridge Quarterly*, 44.2 (2015), 119–45 (p. 133).

63. Joanne Shattock, 'Work for Women: Margaret Oliphant's Journalism', in *Nineteenth-Century Media and the Construction of Identities*, ed. by Laurel Brake, Bill Bell and David Finkelstein (New York: Palgrave, 2000), pp. 165–77 (pp. 167, 168).
64. Blair, p. 127.
65. Richard Garnett, 'Oliphant, Margaret Oliphant', *Dictionary of National Biography*, 1901 <https://doi.org/10.1093/odnb/9780192683120.013.20712>.
66. Blair, p. 112; R. Brimley (Reginald Brimley) Johnson, *The Women Novelists* (London: W. Collins, 1918), p. 191 <http://archive.org/details/womennovelists00johnrich> (accessed 17 November 2021).
67. 'Mrs. Oliphant's Cervantes', *The Spectator Archive*, 1880 <http://archive.spectator.co.uk/article/20th-november-1880/20/mrs-oliphants-cervantes> (accessed 10 September 2017).
68. Elisabeth Jay, *Mrs Oliphant: 'A Fiction to Herself'. A Literary Life* (Oxford: Clarendon Press, 1995), p. 255.
69. George Levine, 'Reading Margaret Oliphant', *Journal of Victorian Culture*, 19.2 (2014), 232–46 (pp. 232, 236) <https://doi.org/10.1080/13555502.2014.919081>.
70. Margaret Oliphant, *The Makers of Modern Rome; in Four Books* (London: Macmillan, 1895), p. 8 <http://archive.org/details/makersofmodernro00olip> (accessed 17 November 2021).
71. Corbett, *Behind the Times: Virginia Woolf in Late-Victorian Contexts*, pp. 67–105.
72. Jay, *A Fiction to Herself*, p. 119.
73. Jay, *A Fiction to Herself*, p. 6.
74. Margaret Oliphant, *Harry Joscelyn*, vol, III (London: Hurst and Blackett, 1881), p. 312.
75. Jay, *A Fiction to Herself*, p. 131.
76. Jay, *A Fiction to Herself*, p. 271.
77. Frank Oliphant died of tuberculosis in Italy in 1859 – unexpectedly to his wife, who, despite the fact she was the family's main breadwinner, was not informed of his terminal diagnosis; leaving her alone in Italy, in debt and with three little children. Two of Oliphant's five children, born between 1853 and 1859, died as infants, her only surviving daughter Maggie died in Rome in 1864. Her brother's bankruptcy in the early 1870s left her caring for his son Frank and two of his daughters. Frank Wilson died in 1879; Oliphant's own sons, Cyril and Cecco (Francis), died in 1890 and 1894 respectively, without ever having achieved financial independence. Her nieces Margaret (Madge) and Janet (Denny) survived her, the former by some months, the latter lived until 1954.
78. Jay, *A Fiction to Herself*, p. 3.
79. Jay, 'Oliphant, Margaret Oliphant Wilson'.

80. Margaret Oliphant, *The Autobiography and Letters of Mrs. M. O. W. Oliphant*, ed. by Annie Coghill (New York: Dodd, Mead and Company, 1899), p. 427.
81. Oliphant, *Autobiography and Letters*, p. 6.
82. Oliphant, *Autobiography and Letters*, p. 7.
83. Oliphant, *Autobiography and Letters*, p. 4.
84. Oliphant, *Autobiography and Letters*, pp. 5; 7.
85. Oliphant, *Autobiography and Letters*, p. 24.
86. Oliphant, *Autobiography and Letters*, pp. 7; 5.
87. Leslie Stephen, 'Southey's Letters', in *Studies of a Biographer*, vol. IV (London: Duckworth & Co., 1902), pp. 45–85 (p. 48) <http://archive.org/details/studiesabiograp03stepgoog> (accessed 17 November 2021).
88. Stephen, 'Southey's Letters', p. 50.
89. Elizabeth Langland, 'The Receptions of Charlotte Bronte, Charles Dickens, George Eliot, and Thomas Hardy', in *A Companion to The Victorian Novel*, ed. by Patrick Brantlinger and William B. Thesing (Oxford: Blackwell Publishing, 2002), pp. 387–405 (pp. 402–3).
90. Stephen, *Sir Leslie Stephen's Mausoleum Book*, pp. 103–4.
91. Jay, *A Fiction to Herself*, p. 249.
92. Jay, *A Fiction to Herself*, p. 125.
93. Margaret Oliphant, *The Autobiography of Margaret Oliphant*, ed. by Elisabeth Jay (Ormskirk: Broadview, 2002), p. 199.
94. See also Blair's discussion of Oliphant's palpable resentment in her review of Stephen's *The Playground of Europe* (1871): Stephen takes on an 'almost metonymic function, 'he represents the wide sphere of male activities that she cannot enjoy merely because she is a woman. Blair, p. 118; Oliphant, *Autobiography*, p. 198.
95. See Oliphant's review of Ritchie's first novel: Margaret Oliphant, 'Novels.', *Blackwood's Edinburgh Magazine*, 94.574 (1863), 168–83 (pp. 171, 178).
96. Anny Thackeray Ritchie, *A Book of Sibyls* (London: Smith Elder & Co., 1883); Ritchie, *A Discourse on Modern Sibyls*, p. 9.

# Chapter 6

# Writing Virginia Woolf: Autobiographical Fragments

Throughout this book, I have tried to shed new light on Virginia Woolf's engagement with nineteenth-century women writers, tracing how the tropes and narratives surrounding the domestic amateur writer constitute a lasting Victorian legacy in Woolf's articles and reviews. Woolf's view of her predecessors as fundamentally flawed writers, the victims of an oppressive patriarchal society, emerges clearly in the collective biography of her non-fiction; as does the importance of biography for the rise and fall of literary reputations. Speculative personas for Austen, Brontë, Mitford and others emerge clearly under Woolf's analytical pen: her interest in character and scene-making results in vivid, if not always strictly factual, sketches. However, the writing of biography is a mutually constitutive process. Woolf uses women writer's lives for experimental life writing and situates herself against them to demarcate her own sphere of work, her artistry, literary integrity and innovation as a challenger of the egotism of Charlotte Brontë, a critic of the intellectual prostitution of Ward and Oliphant, and a descendant of a proto-Modernist Jane Austen. A logical conclusion to this study of Woolf's engagement with her predecessors' literary lives is to ask how her representation of her own writing life compares: did female biography change on or about December 1910?

In 'A Sketch of the Past' Woolf posits that memoirs fail most frequently because '[t]hey leave out the person to whom things happened' (*MoB* 79). The same cannot be said of Woolf studies: Woolf's works are frequently read with an eye on her life, social networks, activities as a publisher, her involvement with feminist and activist causes, education, Christianity, her romantic relationships, or medical experiences. Woolf scholars by and large defy Barthes's concept of the death of the author to explore the myriad ways her life and literature intersect and inform each other. Textually, this endeavour draws on a wide and amorphous body of materials that, like the reviews and articles I analysed, blur the boundaries between fiction and biography and offer intriguing but often contradictory portraits of the many different selves of 'the person to whom things happened'. The female narrators of *A Room of One's Own*, *Three Guineas*, and 'Professions for Women' offer a tantalisingly autobiografictional glimpse into the lives of professional women writers in the twentieth century; Woolf's autobiographical sketches and memoir fragments shed light on her childhood and formative years; and her diary and letters provide copious snapshots of the daily minutiae of her life and as such, perhaps, come closest to offering factual evidence.

Ella Ophir notes that 'among [Woolf's diary's] many purposes and facets is the intention, explicit and sustained, to create a detailed record of the past for the future': 'Old Virginia often appears in the diary as a kind of historiographical Superego, judging, chiding, and demanding of her wayward younger self the proper materials from which to compose a proper memoir'.[1] This 'proper' memoir was never completed: Virginia Woolf's autobiographical oeuvre is fragmented and stems from a variety of periods and impulses. Although she began two memoirs and wrote a few autobiographical sketches, none of these give an account of her whole life: in spite of their disparate origins and forms, they share a broad temporal focus on the marriage of Leslie and Julia Stephen and Virginia's childhood and formative years in a Victorian household up to and including her step-sister Stella's death. Written at either end of her literary career, 'Reminiscences' (1907) and 'A Sketch of the Past' (1938 onwards) are private narratives that centre on Leslie and Julia Stephen as the key to understanding family life in Hyde Park Gate amid an ongoing negotiation with Victorian legacies. In contrast, the Bloomsbury memoir club papers '22 Hyde Park Gate' (1920/1) and 'Old Bloomsbury' (1921/2) address – and seek to impress – an audience of close friends:[2] although they offer the only sustained account of Woolf's life and her social emancipation following her father's death, they tell us nothing about her literary life.

Collectively, Woolf's memoir fragments are therefore almost entirely silent on her life as a writer. Reflections on writing – as a woman, as a Modernist, even as a means of generating an income, can be found in other places: scattered about her diary, in *A Room of One's Own* and *Three Guineas*, and through speculative biographical readings of the material remnants of her life, such as Leslie Hankins's close reading of 'the Saga of Virginia Woolf's standing desk' or Jane de Gay's exploration of domestic sacred (writing) spaces at Monk's House.[3] Yet Woolf's failure to account for her life as a writer is striking considering how much importance she attached to female biography, particularly as a corrective to male historiography: if there is a gap in the library of professional women's lives, Woolf never closes it by adding her own volume.

Some of this silence may be circumstantial: had Woolf lived longer, she might well have produced a lucid commentary combining female authorship and autobiography. Yet gaps, silences and the unspeakable define the fragments collected in *Moments of Being*, from Lytton Strachey's iconoclastic identification of 'Semen' on Vanessa Bell's dress, breaking down 'all barriers of reticence and reserve' (*MoB* 56), the clichéd and obfuscating phraseology of 'Reminiscences', to the silence surrounding Vanessa and Virginia's ambitions even in 'A Sketch of the Past'. Gaps also determine the chronology of these fragments: only the Memoir club paper 'Am I a Snob?', and the contemporary platform of 'A Sketch of the Past', set in 1939–40, manage to move beyond the tight grip of the Victorian period. Focusing on the two memoir fragments, 'Reminiscences' and 'A Sketch of the Past', this coda explores Woolf's search for a mode of narration that allows her to square ambition and authorship with an inheritance of femininity; and places her sketches in the context of the Stephen family memoirs.

## 'Sincere but conventional': 'Reminiscences'

In 'A Sketch of the Past', Woolf recalls that

> while we [Vanessa and Virginia] looked into the future, we were completely under the power of the past. Explorers and revolutionists, as we both were by nature, we lived under the sway of a society that was about fifty years too old for us. (*MoB* 149)

This is nowhere clearer than in the memoir fragment 'Reminiscences', nominally a biography of Vanessa Bell begun in 1907 and abandoned a year later, making it one of a series of exercises in biographical writing from this period (*MoB* 167). Woolf looks back to the life of Hyde Park Gate to look to the future of Vanessa Bell's unborn child, Julian, the addressee of the fragment. But although 'Reminiscences' was written a year after the feminist interventions of 'Phyllis and Rosamond' and 'The Journal of Mistress Joan Martyn', both of which emphasise the importance of feminist historiography through fictional (auto)biography, and contemporaneously with 'Friendship's Gallery', her exuberant metabiographical life of Violet Dickinson, the fragment reverts almost seamlessly to the cautiously hagiographic style of her 'Recollections of Sir Leslie Stephen', written for Maitland's biography (1906). 'Reminiscences' earnestly participates in the long tradition of Stephen family biography, stretching from her great-grandfather James Stephen II (1758–1832) via Leslie Stephen's book-length letter to his wife's children, *The Mausoleum Book*, to Woolf's own memoir: 'her writings take their place in an almost organic tradition spanning more than a century of British intellectual and literary history', Christopher Dahl observes.[4]

Perhaps because of the weight of this legacy, Woolf stays well away from stylistic experiments in life writing, modelling her work instead on the *Mausoleum Book*. Jeanne Schulkind suggests that in the fragment, 'no meaningful distinction can be made between biography (of Vanessa) and autobiography' (*MoB* 168); while Dahl notes the structural and stylistic similarities between 'Reminiscences' and Leslie Stephen's *Mausoleum Book*. Both consist of 'a series of portraits held together by the first-person voice of their author, whose relation to the various figures portrayed is the real focus of the work'.[5] However, even more central than the relation between author and family is that between Julia Stephen and her husband and children. The ambitions of both Stephen girls are erased almost completely from the narrative; instead, the four chapters of 'Reminiscences' are shaped by the loss of a succession of mother figures – Julia Stephen, Stella Duckworth and Vanessa Stephen. Grappling with Julia's apparently flawless embodiment of Victorian femininity, Woolf at once elevates her to mythical status and concedes the flattening effect of her eulogy:

> Written words of a person who is dead or still alive tend most unfortunately to drape themselves in smooth folds annulling all evidence of life. You will find not in what I say, or again in those sincere but conventional phrases in the life of your grandfather, or in the noble lamentations with which he fills the pages of his autobiography, any semblance of a woman whom you can love. (*MoB* 8)

Although 'Reminiscences' shares its focal point and, by its own author's admission, its defects, with other Stephen family memoirs, it deviates from their perspective. Most importantly, Woolf offers a female perspective on life in Hyde Park Gate through a detailed staging of various types of mothering and emotional labour. From the first paragraph of the memoir, Woolf foreshadows Vanessa's future maternal excellence by depicting her care (as the eldest Stephen girl) for her younger siblings. This strictly gendered division of labour also informs her depiction of Julia's delight in

> transact[ing] all those trifling businesses which, as women feel instinctively, are somehow derogatory to the dignity which they like to discover in clever men. [. . .] But she never belittled her own works, thinking them, if properly discharged, of equal, though other, importance with her husband's. (*MoB* 9)

Over the course of four chapters, this celebration of female labour in the vein of Victorian anti-feminists gives way to a more critical assessment of the repeated sacrifices of female labour and lives to Leslie Stephen and his family. Woolf's brief reference in chapter 2 to Stella's 'peculiar position' (*MoB* 14) as intimate confidante to a Carlylean man of letters upholds the previously established division of female service to male genius. However, Vanessa's 'coming into this inheritance, with all its complications' in chapter 4 begins a process of articulation of and reflection on the sacrifices behind this inheritance of femininity: 'so many demands were made on her; it was, in a sense, so easy to be what was expected, with such models before her, but also it was so hard to be herself' (*MoB* 25–6). Woolf's shift to 'we' instead of 'I' obscures her role in placing demands on Vanessa, but also works to create a sense of a united female resistance against male tyranny:[6]

> We remembered how he had tasked Stella's strength, embittered her few months of joy [ . . . ] there were signs at once which woke us to a sort of frenzy, that he was quite prepared to take Vanessa for his next victim. [ . . . ] We made him the type of all we hated in our lives; he was the tyrant of inconceivable selfishness, who had replaced the beauty and merriment of the dead with ugliness and gloom. We were bitter, harsh, and to a great extent, unjust; but even now it seems to me that there was some truth in our complaint. (*MoB* 27)

Although Woolf begins with a rather restrained presentation of her parents' marriage as 'a triumphant life, consistently aiming at high things' (*MoB* 6), 'Reminiscences' ends by establishing, possibly for the first time, a narrative of Vanessa and Virginia united against male tyranny, which is further increased by biting portraits of George and Gerald. This foundational narrative will be refracted in Woolf's writing throughout the rest of her career, emerging in Cam's anger in *To The Lighthouse*, in Rose Pargiter's rebellion, in Woolf's diagnosis of 'infantile fixation' in *Three Guineas*, before being presented once more, now fortified with Freudian insights, in 'A Sketch of the Past'. 'Reminiscences' can therefore be read as an origin narrative for much of Woolf's later autobiographical and autobiografictional writing: it establishes a base narrative and key characters, which Woolf will return to and re-examine from different perspectives, but without moving much beyond the parameters established here.

Some of the boundaries set in 'Reminiscences' are chronological, others are gendered. As in much of Woolf's private writing of the period, women and domesticity dominate its perspective. Vanessa and Virginia exist as daughters first and foremost, cut off from all non-domestic relationships and isolated within the family group at Hyde Park Gate.[7] This hyperfocus on the female family members excludes even Adrian and Thoby, who graduate from high-chairs to masculine invisibility. Although Woolf introduces Vanessa's 'passion for art' (*MoB* 2) as a key characteristic only matched by her absolute respect for the truth, female ambition and success remain largely unspeakable:

> She drew indeed under the care of a Mr Cook, but talk of art, talk of her own gifts and loves, was unknown to her. What did she think then? For with her long fingers grouping, and her eye considering, she surely painted many pictures without a canvas. Once I saw her scrawl on a black door a great maze of lines, with white chalk. 'When I am a famous painter – ' she began, and then turned shy and rubbed it out in her capable way. And when she won the prize at her drawing school, she hardly knew, so shy was she, at the recognition of a secret, how to tell me, in order that I might repeat the news at home. 'They've given me the thing – I don't know why.' 'What thing?' 'O they say I've won it – the book – the prize you know.' She was awkward as a long-legged colt. (*MoB* 2–3)

The gaps and omissions in Vanessa's report, her awkward modesty and shyness, as well as her unpainted pictures align her with the women writers whose biographies Woolf would write over the course of the next four decades: like Austen and other early nineteenth century writers, her artistic process remains impenetrable even to close observers and family members, all evidence of creative work easily erased.

However, even this brief gesture to Vanessa's talent is superseded by Julia Stephen's death: 'her natural development, in which the artistic gift so sensitive and yet so vigorous, would have asserted itself, was checked' (*MoB* 4). From this point onwards, Vanessa's interests and schooling disappear from the narrative. This makes Woolf's approach even more drastic than that of Leslie Stephen in the *Mausoleum Book*, who contritely records in 1900 that

> Nessa – I am ashamed to say that I forgot to note this – got into the academy school last summer and has been working there steadily since our return to town. She sent the drawing for the academy to a competition at her old studio, where it got the medal.[8]

Stephen's entry confirms that Vanessa's winning of the medal postdates Julia's death: although it points to the minor importance of female education at Hyde Park Gate, it also confirms the narrative impossibility of moving past Julia Stephen's death, opening up the possibility that the development checked may have been Virginia's as much as Vanessa's.

Vanessa's unpainted pictures join the missing works of women's literary history as collateral damage of the Victorian home:

> the future was always too near and too much of a question for any sedate self expression. All these activities, too, charged the air with personal emotions and urged even children, and certainly 'the eldest', to develop one side prematurely. To help, to do something was desirable, not to obtrude diffident wishes, irrelevant and possibly expensive. (*MoB* 3)

Woolf's narrative obeys this injunction: private tragedy disrupts and ultimately displaces the tentative exploration of their future ambitions, exemplifying how completely Victorian family life and gendered expectations swallowed them up. Likewise, Woolf's own ambitions remain unarticulated in this account of her early life: only the memoir itself embodies her attempt to become the family writer and thus appropriate the position previously and prominently held by Leslie Stephen.

### 'A very subtle work on the proper writing of lives': 'A Sketch of the Past'

In a 1908 letter to Clive Bell, Virginia Woolf reflected on 'Reminiscences':

> I ask myself why write it at all? seeing I never shall recapture what you have, by your side this minute. I should like to write a very subtle work on the proper writing of lives. What it is that you can write – and what writing is. (*L* 1.25)

'Memoirs of a Novelist', written a year later, takes up this impulse, as does *Orlando* and her later essays on life writing. However, no work responds to it as completely as 'A Sketch of the Past', written at the end of her life and career: like 'Reminiscences', it is not a writer's life in a narrow sense, but it is a deeply self-reflective literary memoir. Again, Woolf engages with Leslie Stephen's *Mausoleum Book*; however, at this point in her writing life, these similarities are subtly thematic rather than structural and methodological: 'Sketch' takes up Stephen's anxieties about professional authorship and life writing to subtly assert her mastery of her profession, interweaving her literary skills with the very fabric of her life.

'A Sketch of the Past' signals Woolf's deep immersion in autobiographical traditions by beginning with a well-established trope of the genre, her audience's request for her memoir:

> Two days ago – Sunday 16th April 1939 to be precise – Nessa said that if I did not start writing my memoirs I should soon be too old. I should be eighty-five,

and should have forgotten – witness the unhappy case of Lady Strachey. As it happens that I am sick of writing Roger's life, perhaps I will spend two or three mornings making a sketch. (*MoB* 78)

Four days earlier, Woolf had informed Ethel Smyth that they had only just recovered from influenza, and that, '[w]hen woken by aeroplanes at night I read Ethel Smyth – Gleams of Memory' (*L* 5.326). Two weeks earlier, the Bloomsbury Memoir Club had met for '[a] rather scattered meeting', causing her to reflect that 'I felt I was bearing up the panoply of life & wd be glad to let it sink. I said to myself, Remember, this is the description of age coming' (*D* 5.212). The preceding diary entries record her frustration with her biography of Roger Fry and chronicle the deaths of Yeats, Jack Hills, and 'the last of the LL. Davies brothers'. The inevitability of another war looms large. 'Sketch' is thus born from a sense of things ending: while 'Reminiscences' had addressed the unborn Julian Bell, Woolf noted two months earlier that 'Franco was recognised. And Julian killed for this' (*D* 5.206).

In its mood and retrospective gaze, 'A Sketch of the Past' closely resembles the *Mausoleum Book*, whose 'narrative eventually degenerated into a "series of obituary notices"', as Trev Broughton observes.[9] Yet where Stephen addressed the next generation; Woolf, more hesitant to pass down family history, invokes her sister rather than her nephew and niece: Virginia Hyman notes that 'Woolf's autobiographical materials [ . . . ] become [ . . . ] a late, if not final, chapter in the Stephen history'.[10] Vanessa's prompt strengthens the links with the Stephen family tradition, but it is difficult to substantiate: on Thursday, 13 April, five days before she allegedly began writing, Woolf noted in her diary that she had already 'finished my first 40 pages – childhood &c – well under the week; but then they were largely autobiography [ . . . ] Charleston to tea today' (*D* 5.214). Apocryphal or not, it captures the desolation of Woolf's diary entries, threatening both the old age and slow decline of Lady Strachey and senseless destruction through the absence of Julian, Woolf's original addressee. However, the allusion to Lady Strachey and her very brief 'Some Recollections of a Long Life' also leaves open the ultimate audience for this memoir: is this private reflection, or a public narrative?

These questions echo the opening paragraph of the *Mausoleum Book*. In 'a bewildering mixture of pellucid simplicity and extreme, hairsplitting prevarication',[11] Stephen vacillates between emphasising his letter's accidental but inevitable professional finish, uncertainty regarding his public afterlife, and enjoining his children to the strictest confidentiality:

> I am so much of a professional author that I fear that what I am about to say may have the appearance of being meant for a book rather than for a letter.

> That, however, will be accidental if it happens – at any rate it will be unintentional. I am writing to you personally, my beloved children [ . . . ] and I want simply to talk to you about your mother. What I shall say is therefore absolutely confidential between you and me. [ . . . ] I will not say positively that I forbid you to make any use of this when I am dead. Indeed it might possibly be worth while for somebody to look through what I have written and make some use of it [ . . . ] I mean further to write in such a way as to put out of the question any larger use of it than I have indicated, even after my death. Having said so much, I leave the whole matter to you.[12]

Stephen, as Broughton pithily notes, 'ties himself in mesmerizing knots in the attempt [to talk to his children about their mother]. He quibbles over his own motives [ . . . ]; he veers from reasoned hope to resignation; he exhorts and cajoles' and ultimately volunteers Frederic Maitland as his preferred biographer in a discreet footnote.[13] Although 'Sketch' was written through the 'innumerable doubts, of myself as biographer: of the possibility of doing it at all' (*D* 5.207) caused by Roger Fry's biography, Woolf's opening pages respond to such professional and posthumous anxieties in a more subtle and subversive manner:

> There are several difficulties. In the first place, the enormous number of things I can remember; in the second, the number of different ways in which memoirs can be written. As a great memoir reader, I know many different ways. But if I begin to go through them and to analyse them and their merits and faults, the mornings – I cannot take more than two or three at most – will be gone. So without stopping to choose my way, in the sure and certain knowledge that it will find itself – or if not it will not matter – I begin: the first memory. (*MoB* 78)

Where Stephen anxiously asserts his professionalism, Woolf calmly performs it. Here and in the following pages, she ignores all the external markers of professional authorship – her novels, her journalism, her ownership of the Hogarth Press – that dominate Stephen's opening page and his subsequent account of his career and focuses instead on a performance of writing. This elision of professionalism recalls the narrator's strategy in 'Professions for Women', which, Gualtieri notes, 'stresses her status as an *amatrice*': in 'Sketch', 'professional expertise, though, is seen as a potential threat to the very status of the memoirs as a provisional, unfinished piece of writing that functions as a digression from work'.[14] Woolf's self-assessment as a 'great memoir reader' rather than a skilled biographer emphasises the fluidity of the genre: comprising 'many different ways' of presenting a life, its heterogeneity puts anything as fixed as Stephen's easily recognisable veneer of professionalism and the consequent publishability of his book out of the question.

'A Sketch of the Past' is, as Phyllis McCord notes, about 'the process of composition of a memoir, or of any narrative about the past, and its conclusion seems to be the extreme difficulty or even the futility of any attempt to render a life in narrative'.[15] Diving straight into the perceiving mind of 'the person to whom things happened', Woolf offers a subtle riposte to Stephen's more factual approach, which avoids 'narratives of inward events', references his published biographies to fill the gaps in his narrative, and takes a certain satisfaction in knowing that 'no adequate history of my life can ever be written' because he has no intention to share 'some struggles through which I had to pass'.[16] Superficially, Stephen's disavowal of truthfulness, explicitly breaking the autobiographical pact, is therefore at odds with Woolf's transparency in seeking to lay bare 'the person to whom things happened'. But 'A Sketch of the Past' is deceptive in its apparent truthfulness.[17] Woolf's evocative account of her first memories alerts us to the fictionality of all biography by reshaping her recollection of her mother's dress in a train coming from St Ives: 'But it is more convenient artistically to suppose that we were going to St Ives, for that will lead to my other memory, which also seems to be my first memory, and in fact it is the most important of all my memories' (*MoB* 78). Taken together, these twin memories – Julia Stephen, and a liminal moment of pure bliss listening to the sea behind the yellow blinds of Talland House nursery – introduce two key motives of 'Sketch', and drive its interrogation of Victorian femininity (often in the guise of Julia Stephen), and the moments of being that shape Woolf's writing. These flourishes of writerly bravado, expertly combining insights into the process of autobiographical writing with glimpses at the person behind the writing, take up Stephen's notes and make them Woolf's own, setting a display of literary skills and composition against his forthright assertion of professional authorship.

Yet this impressionistic approach to selfhood also leaves Virginia the person curiously undefined, as a range of critics have noted.[18] Like the *Mausoleum Book*, it is '[b]oth an invitation to and a refusal of biography'.[19] 'A Sketch of the Past' offers little in the way of those gossipy insights into her own personality that Woolf celebrates in essays like 'Indiscretions': instead, Virginia Woolf is most often 'a passive observer rather than an actor in her own life. In fact, she is usually only an "understood" presence, the filter through which Stella or Leslie or Julia passes to the secondary filter, Woolf the autobiographer', Gail Griffin notes.[20] Rather than a stylistic feature, Woolf treats this absence of her everyday life, the 'moments of non-being', as a shortcoming of the memoir:

> although it was a good day [yesterday] the goodness was embedded in a kind of nondescript cotton wool. This is always so. A great part of every day is not

lived consciously. [ . . . ] The real novelist can somehow convey both sorts of being. I think Jane Austen can; and Trollope; perhaps Thackeray and Dickens and Tolstoy. [ . . . ] But I will leave the literary side alone for the moment. (*MoB* 84)

But 'leav[ing] the literary side alone' is what Woolf cannot do: her foregrounding of the experience of writing helps and hinders in equal parts in getting to know her, as when she reflects that 'I do not know how far I differ from other people. That is another memoir writer's difficulty. [ . . . ] Owing partly to the fact that I was never at school, never competed in any way with children of my own age, I have never been able to compare my gifts and defects with other people's' (*MoB* 79). Any reader looking for outright descriptions of ordinary aspects of Woolf's existence, be it the colour of her eyes, her talents and (composition) habits, or even favourite foods, will be disappointed.

Yet Woolf's previous brief sketch of her background does subtly flag how much she deviates from the norm. Her rhetorical skills and family background come together to assert that writing was her biological and social destiny:

> Who was I then? Adeline Virginia Stephen, the second daughter of Leslie and Julia Prinsep Stephen, born on 25th January 1882, descended from a great many people, some famous, others obscure; born into a large connection, born not of rich parents, but of well-to-do parents, born into a very communicative, literate, letter writing, visiting, articulate, late nineteenth century world; so that I could if I liked to take the trouble, write a great deal here not only about my mother and father but about uncles and aunts, cousins and friends. (*MoB* 79)

Adeline Virginia Stephen was not only born into a large connection, but into a highly literary one. Woolf therefore hints that the nineteenth-century world that shaped her early life is that of Victorian men and women of letters: even those of her relatives who were not professional writers frequently published memoirs, devotional or instructional literature. In the *Mausoleum Book*, Stephen defensively notes 'that in these years (1865 and succeeding years) I had the opportunity of knowing most of the literary people of mark', offering a deeper glimpse into this world: Broughton summarises that '[a]n old boys' network is liminally present in the *Mausoleum Book*' through Stephen's account of his career.[21] 'Sketch' echoes this setting of the social scene: although Woolf omits the introductory list of most reputable connections that Leslie Stephen gives his audience of sons and daughters, she similarly establishes that 'I could if I liked to take the trouble'.

Woolf's introduction, parodically echoing a superficial way of writing lives that she mocked from sketches like 'Memoirs of a Novelist' onwards, points not to a professional network of choice, but to a social and familial heritage. Although 'Sketch' lacks Leslie Stephen's explicit moment of '[resolve] to take up literature as a profession', Woolf turns her profession into a genetic destiny by positioning herself firmly inside a 'very communicative, literate, letter writing' family.[22] Leslie Stephen had recorded her godfather's James Russell Lowell's hope 'that Virginia might be a true "sample of heredity"' in the *Mausoleum Book*.[23] Likewise, the Victorian eugenicist Francis Galton included the Stephen family in his work on *Hereditary Genius*: although he felt unable to adequately define literary genius and distinguish it from mere popularity, he concluded that 'we may rest satisfied that an analysis of kinsfolk shows literary genius to be fully as hereditary as any other kind of ability we have hitherto discussed'. Leslie Stephen is a latecomer to the family fame in this account ('a well-known contributor to periodical literature'), and Galton cautions that '[t]he proportion of eminent grandsons is small' (the possibility of eminent granddaughters is clearly too miniscule to mention).[24] Nevertheless, literature quietly joins the 'streak of the puritan, of the Clapham Sect' (*MoB* 81) and the bodily 'instincts already acquired by thousands of ancestresses in the past' (*MoB* 82) as Woolf's inheritance. Socially and genetically, 'A Sketch of the Past' subtly asserts Woolf's central position in British literary culture.

This broader family heritage complements the more introspective exploration of her personal motivation for writing. Woolf posits writing as an innate and organic response to moments of being, of 'sudden violent shock' (*MoB* 84):

> And so I go on to suppose that the shock-receiving capacity is what makes me a writer. I hazard the explanation that a shock is at once in my case followed by the desire to explain it. I feel that I have had a blow; but it is not, as I thought as a child, simply a blow from an enemy hidden behind the cotton wool of daily life; it is or will become a revelation of some order; it is a token of some real thing behind appearances; and I make it real by putting it into words. [ . . . ] Perhaps this is the strongest pleasure known to me. It is the rapture I get when in writing I seem to be discovering what belongs to what; making a scene come right; making a character come together. (*MoB* 85)

Because writing allows her to 'put the severed parts together' and make sense of the world, Woolf can conclude that 'by writing I am doing what is far more necessary than anything else' (*MoB* 86): her philosophy of 'the pattern hid behind the cotton wool' and the recognition that 'there is no Shakespeare, there is no Beethoven; certainly and emphatically there is no God; we are the words; we are the music; we are the thing itself' (*MoB* 85) at once elevates writing to a mystical status and does away with the concept of (male) literary genius that haunts Leslie Stephen's (and Galton's) account of literature. Writing as a fundamental, innate response to (the trauma of) being alive, Woolf actually comes closest to aligning herself with female modes of writing: this approach echoes the organic fusion of living and writing that Margaret Oliphant describes in her *Autobiography*, as well as Woolf's own assessment of historic women's writing as something that happened 'as instinctively as a thrush sings' (*N&D* 29), 'untaught; [ . . . ] from the heart' (*E* 5.34). Yet by universalising her experience, Woolf also inscribes herself into a humanist canon: 'All artists I suppose feel something like this. It is one of the obscure elements in life that has never been much discussed. It is left out in almost all biographies and autobiographies, even of artists' (*MoB* 86).

'A Sketch of the Past' subverts Victorian narratives of male genius on many levels: Woolf responds to the masculine narrative of professional authorship and self-doubt in the *Mausoleum Book* by appropriating the Stephen family legacy of literary genius and redefining writing as an innate artistic response. Her display of literary skill and critical expertise in constructing and shaping the narrative of 'A Sketch of the Past' affirms her claim to professional competence and even literary genius without stating it outright. However, Woolf's memoir also shares some aspects with her engagement with women writers' lives: most strikingly, the intense focus on her internal life and the desire to explain character and life through a detailed examination of Hyde Park Gate mirrors the sociological approach of her later feminist writing and turns her life into another case study of Victorian patriarchy's long hold. Griffin observes that

> Rather than conscientiously unravel the tangled lines of her personality, she habitually turns outwards [ . . . ]. The myth [of childhood oppression and hard-won liberation], and the autobiographical approach it engenders, depend upon the interpenetration of Virginia and her environment, especially her family.[25]

Woolf's focus on herself as a daughter first and foremost demonstrates how strong the hold of Victorian biography remains: like Vanessa Bell's suppressed ambitions in 'Reminiscences', her own goals and desires are only allowed to emerge fragmented and distorted amid reflections on the oppression of her home; while her narrative is so individualised that it lacks the wider applicability of the autobiografiction of *A Room of One's Own* or 'Professions for Women'. Nevertheless, her analysis of

Stephen's 'violent outbursts' gains an additional edge by her deconstruction of his affectation of the 'man of genius':

> It was part of the convention that after these outbursts, the man of genius became 'touchingly apologetic'; but he took it for granted that his wife or sister would accept his apology, that he was exempt, because of his genius, from the laws of good society. But was he a man of genius? No; that was not alas quite the case. (*MoB* 118)

Woolf's calm assessment of her father's literary career posthumously confirms Stephen's anxieties while asserting the strictures and oppressions of the Victorian home, but it maintains a resolute silence on her private desires and literary ambitions: was she a woman of genius?

Where does that leave narratives of female professionalism? As in 'Reminiscences', there are glimpses of Woolf's later life in her description of those moments when 'Victorian society did not exert any special pressure upon us. Vanessa [ . . . ] made those minute pencil drawings of Greek statues [ . . . ] or painted [ . . . ]. I read and wrote' (*MoB* 150–1). Yet these moments of creative fulfilment are spent living 'in the world which we still inhabit', outside the remit of the Victorian world of 'A Sketch of the Past'. How to move between these worlds?

If, as the narrator of 'Professions for Women' suggests, '[k]illing the Angel in the House was part of the occupation of a woman writer' (*E* 6.481) one reason for Woolf's narrative reluctance might be her unwillingness to commit to killing Julia Stephen. 'The tragedy of her death [ . . . ] was that it made her unreal' (*MoB* 105), and writing of Julia Stephen is one way of countering that: 'writing is often seen by Woolf both as an antidote to and a substitute for the act of remembering itself'.[26] As Hermione Lee observes, '[t]his repetitive, inconclusive return to the mother's death is at the heart of this remarkable adventure in life-writing, where the past can never be solved or tidied away, the subject can never be finished with'.[27] And although Woolf admits the temporal incongruity of Julia and Stella's self-sacrificing femininity ('They do not blend with the world of the living at all' (*MoB* 107)), she hesitates to enquire more deeply into the liberation that her mother's death meant in practical terms. There are hints at such a drastically different perspective when she recollects that

> my mother's death unveiled and intensified; made me suddenly develop perceptions, as if a burning glass had been laid over what was shaded and dormant. [ . . . ] I had a feeling of transparency in words when they cease to be words and become so intensified that one seems to experience them; to foretell them as if they developed what one is already feeling. [ . . . ] It matches what I have sometimes felt when I write. (*MoB* 103)

These moments of heightened perception appear as artistically important as Woolf's earlier exploration of the 'moments of being', yet this section ends rather differently, mourning the loss of her mother as a sanctioned outlet for literary ambition:

> How excited I used to be when the 'Hyde Park Gate News' was laid on her plate on Monday morning, and she liked something I had written! Never shall I forget my extremity of pleasure – it was like being a violin and being played upon – when I found that she had sent a story of mine to Madge Symonds. (*MoB* 105)[28]

The nostalgia for Julia Stephen's iconic femininity and all that it stands for emerges most strongly in 'the Victorian manner' passed down by her: beautiful, 'for it is founded upon restraint, sympathy, unselfishness – all civilized qualities' (*MoB* 152) it is a legacy of femininity so fundamental as to be inescapable. Thus, Albright concludes that '"A Sketch of the Past" is less the story of the formulation of one's self than the story of an attempt to escape from the self conventionally forced upon young women'.[29] Albright is not wrong, although he underestimates how a certain amount of nostalgia for this conventional self and its links to Julia Stephen pervades the narrative. While the gravitational pull of her death disrupts alternative narrative directions (the eventual liberty of Gordon Square, a new artistic intensity, adventures in journalism following Leslie Stephen's death), the 'surface manner' learned 'partly from memory: and mother' (*MoB* 152) also pervades much of the engagement with professional authorship of 'Sketch'. Woolf's autobiographical fragments 'slip in things that would be inaudible if one marched straight up and spoke out loud', and take a covert approach to asserting her professionalism. That they are successful is undeniable, but they also demonstrate the fundamental grip of Victorian femininity on Woolf's life writing. Would Woolf have finished her 'Sketch of the Past' had she lived longer? The manuscript, compelling as it is, shows the hold that the nineteenth century continued to exert on her autobiographical writing, but also her immense creativity in circumventing such challenges.

### Notes

1. Ella Ophir, '"Writing the history of my own times": Virginia Woolf and the Diary', in *Virginia Woolf and Heritage* (Clemson, SC: Clemson University Press/Liverpool University Press, 2017), pp. 196–201 (pp. 196, 198).
2. S. P. Rosenbaum, *The Bloomsbury Group Memoir Club*, ed. by James M. Haule (Basingstoke: Palgrave Macmillan, 2014), p. 6; Lee, Hermione,

'Introduction', in *Moments of Being: Autobiographical Writings*, by Virginia Woolf, ed. by Jeanne Schulkind (London: Pimlico, 2002), p. xii.
3. Leslie Hankins, 'Heritage Hoarding: Artifacts, Archives, and Ambiguity, or, the Saga of Virginia Woolf's Standing Desk', in *Virginia Woolf and Heritage*, ed. by Tom Breckin, Anne Reus and Jane de Gay (Clemson, SC: Clemson University Press/Liverpool University Press, 2017); Jane de Gay, *Virginia Woolf and Christian Culture* (Edinburgh: Edinburgh University Press, 2018), pp. 143–64.
4. Christopher Dahl, 'Virginia Woolf's "Moments of Being" and Autobiographical Tradition in the Stephen Family', *Journal of Modern Literature*, 10.2 (1983), 175–96 (p. 177).
5. Dahl also notes their shared rhetorical figure of defining character though simile; Stephen characterising Minnie through Anny, and Woolf Stella through Julia. Dahl, p. 181.
6. This shift away from the individuality suggested by a narratorial 'I' also resonates with LuAnn McCracken's reading of 'Reminiscences': she finds that 'what is actually contained in Woolf's first memoir [is] the literal absence of an individualized identity or an identity of her own. '"The synthesis of my being": Autobiography and the Reproduction of Identity in Virginia Woolf', *Tulsa Studies in Women's Literature*, 9.1 (1990), 58–78 (p. 63).
7. In contrast, Vanessa Bell recollects the (entertainingly disastrous) piano, singing and dancing classes they attended, as well as a brief interlude of being taught by an ordinary governess when Leslie and Julia were abroad. Vanessa Bell, *Sketches in Pen and Ink*, ed. by Lia Giachero (London: Pimlico, 1998), pp. 60–1.
8. Stephen, *Sir Leslie Stephen's Mausoleum Book*, p. 110.
9. Trev Lynn Broughton, *Men of Letters, Writing Lives: Masculinity and Literary Auto/Biography in the Late Victorian Period* (London: Routledge, 1999), p. 4.
10. Virginia Hyman, 'Reflections in the Looking-Glass: Leslie Stephen and Virginia Woolf', *Journal of Modern Literature*, 10.2 (1983), 197–216 (p. 198).
11. Broughton, p. 5.
12. Stephen, *Sir Leslie Stephen's Mausoleum Book*, pp. 3–4.
13. Broughton, p. 5.
14. Gualtieri, pp. 75; 97.
15. Phyllis Frus McCord, '"Little corks that mark a sunken net": Virginia Woolf's "Sketch of the Past" as a Fictional Memoir', *Modern Language Studies*, 16.3 (1986), 247–54 (p. 249).
16. Stephen, *Sir Leslie Stephen's Mausoleum Book*, p. 4.
17. Hannah Sullivan notes that 'The manuscript evidence shows clearly that the current text of "A Sketch" is the result of several revisionary passes, and that the diary frame is a constructed fiction rather than a sincere reporting of writing time. [ . . . ] Woolf reconstructs draft material to make an artistic whole. Because "A Sketch" is not a diary about the past but a kind of second-order diary – a diary about the process of remembering the past'. 'Autobiography and the Problem of Finish', *Biography*, 34.2 (2011), 298–325 (p. 311).

18. Daniel Albright observes that 'in this great autobiographical project one often feels that something is missing, and that the missing thing is Virginia Woolf. It is as if this vast self-attentiveness existed as much for camouflage and deception as for revelation. [ . . . ] It is a kind of autobiography which seems, in mysterious ways, to exclude the author'. LuAnn McCracken observes that the 'connection between Woolf's real-life experience and her imaginary creation becomes the focus of attention, not Woolf herself: curiously, her "self" drops from consideration'. Daniel Albright, 'Virginia Woolf as Autobiographer', *The Kenyon Review*, 6.4 (1984), 1–17 (p. 2); McCracken, p. 59.
19. Broughton, p. 6.
20. Gail Griffin, 'Braving the Mirror: Virginia Woolf as Autobiographer', *Biography*, 4.2 (1981), 108–18 (p. 112).
21. Stephen, *Sir Leslie Stephen's Mausoleum Book*, p. 8; Broughton, p. 13.
22. Stephen, *Sir Leslie Stephen's Mausoleum Book*, p. 6.
23. Stephen, *Sir Leslie Stephen's Mausoleum Book*, p. 81.
24. Francis Galton, *Hereditary Genius: An Inquiry into Its Laws and Consequences* (London: Macmillan & Co., 1892), pp. 171, 185, 171.
25. Griffin, p. 109.
26. Gualtieri, p. 104.
27. Lee notes that Woolf describes Julia Stephen's death 'three times in her diaries, three times in these memoirs, always slightly differently'; in addition to the fictional deaths of mothers in *The Voyage Out, To The Lighthouse*, and *The Years*, p. xv. Woolf herself also addresses her unwillingness to progress with her narrative: 'Why do I shirk the task, not so very hard to a professional – have I not conveyed Roger from one end of life to the other – like myself, of wafting this boy [Thoby] to my bed sitting room at Hyde Park Gate? It is because I want to go on thinking about St Ives' (*MoB* 140). Woolf focuses on her desire to avoid the misery of 1897–1904, but these are the years she partially covers after all – it is the period after (including Thoby's death) that 'Sketch' avoids.
28. Bell recounts the same anecdote, but also allows a glimpse at later and larger ambitions: 'it must have been a good deal later that she sent a short story to Tit Bits, keeping it a deadly secret from all but myself'. Bell, pp. 64, 65.
29. Albright, p. 11.

# Bibliography

Albright, Daniel, 'Virginia Woolf as Autobiographer', *The Kenyon Review*, 6.4 (1984), 1–17
Allott, Miriam, ed., *The Brontës: The Critical Heritage* (London: Routledge & Kegan Paul, 1974)
'An Unrequited Love? Charlotte Brontë's Letters to Constantin Heger – English and Drama Blog' <https://blogs.bl.uk/english-and-drama/2015/12/charlotte-bront%C3%ABs-letters-to-constantin-heger.html> (accessed 17 March 2021)
Arnold, Matthew, 'The Function of Criticism at the Present Time', in *The Function of Criticism at the Present Time and An Essay on Style* (New York: Macmillan & Co., 1895), pp. 3–86
Ashton, Rosemary, 'Evans, Marian', *Oxford Dictionary of National Biography* <http://www.oxforddnb.com/view/article/6794?docPos=1> (accessed 26 April 2017)
Atkinson, Juliette, *Victorian Biography Reconsidered: A Study of Nineteenth-Century 'Hidden' Lives* (Oxford: Oxford University Press, 2010)
Auerbach, Emily, *Searching for Jane Austen* (Madison: University of Wisconsin Press, 2004)
Auerbach, Emily, 'Searching for Jane Austen: Restoring the "Fleas" and "Bad Breath"', *Persuasions: The Jane Austen Journal*, 27 (2005), 31–8
Austen, Henry, 'Biographical Notice of the Author', in *A Memoir of Jane Austen and Other Family Recollections*, ed. by Kathryn Sutherland (Oxford: Oxford University Press, 2008), pp. 135–41
Austen, Jane, and Edward Hugessen Knatchbull-Hugessen Brabourne, *Letters of Jane Austen. Edited, with an Introduction and Critical Remarks* (London R. Bentley, 1884) <http://archive.org/details/lettersofjaneaus01austuoft> (accessed 27 September 2021)
Austen-Leigh, James Edward, *A Memoir of Jane Austen and Other Family Recollections*, ed. by Kathryn Sutherland (Oxford: Oxford University Press, 2008)
Austen-Leigh, Mary Augusta, *Personal Aspects of Jane Austen* (London: John Murray, 1920)
Backscheider, Paula R., 'Haywood [Née Fowler], Eliza (1693?–1756), Author and Actress', *Oxford Dictionary of National Biography* <https://doi.org/10.1093/ref:odnb/12798>

Bank of England, '£10 Note', 2020 <http://www.bankofengland.co.uk/banknotes/polymer-10-pound-note> (accessed 6 July 2020]
Barrett Browning, Elizabeth, '779. EBB to Mary Russell Mitford', *The Brownings' Correspondence: An Online Edition* <https://www.brownings correspondence.com/correspondence/884/?rsId=204445&returnPage=1> (accessed 10 September 2020)
Battershill, Claire, *Modernist Lives: Biography and Autobiography at Leonard and Virginia Woolf's Hogarth Press* (London: Bloomsbury Academic, 2018)
Bell, Vanessa, *Sketches in Pen and Ink*, ed. by Lia Giachero (London: Pimlico, 1998)
Benson, E. F., *Charlotte Brontë* (London: Longmans, Green & Co, 1932)
Binckes, Faith, and Carey Snyder, eds., *Women, Periodicals and Print Culture in Britain, 1890s–1920s: The Modernist Period* (Edinburgh: Edinburgh University Press, 2019)
Black, Naomi, *Virginia Woolf as Feminist* (Ithaca, NY: Cornell University Press, 2018)
Blair, Emily, *Virginia Woolf and the Nineteenth-Century Domestic Novel* (Albany: State University of New York Press, 2007)
Blouch, Christine, 'Eliza Haywood and the Romance of Obscurity', *Studies in English Literature, 1500–1900*, 31.3 (1991), 535–52
Booth, Alison, *Greatness Engendered: George Eliot and Virginia Woolf*, Reading Women Writing series (Ithaca, NY: Cornell University Press, 1992)
Booth, Alison, *Homes and Haunts: Touring Writers' Shrines and Countries* (Oxford: Oxford University Press, 2016)
Booth, Alison, *How to Make It as a Woman: Collective Biographical History from Victoria to the Present* (Chicago: University of Chicago Press, 2004)
Booth, Alison, 'Revisiting the Homes and Haunts of Mary Russell Mitford', *Nineteenth-Century Contexts*, 30.1 (2008), 39–65
Bourdieu, Pierre, *The Field of Cultural Production: Essays on Art and Literature*, ed. by Randal Johnson (New York: Columbia University Press, 1993)
Bowler, Rebecca, 'May Sinclair and the Brontë Myth: Rewilding and Dissocializing Charlotte', *Feminist Modernist Studies*, 4.6 (2020), 1–17
Briggs, Julia, *Reading Virginia Woolf* (Edinburgh: Edinburgh University Press, 2006)
Briggs, Julia, *Virginia Woolf: An Inner Life* (London: Penguin Books, 2006)
Brosnan, Leila, *Reading Virginia Woolf's Essays and Journalism: Breaking the Surface of Silence* (Edinburgh: Edinburgh University Press, 1999)
Broughton, Trev Lynn, *Men of Letters, Writing Lives: Masculinity and Literary Auto/Biography in the Late Victorian Period* (London: Routledge, 1999)
Caughie, Pamela L., 'Flush and the Literary Canon: Oh Where Oh Where Has That Little Dog Gone?', *Tulsa Studies in Women's Literature*, 10.1 (1991), 47–66
Chaney, Christine, 'The "Prophet-Poet's Book"', *Studies in English Literature, 1500–1900*, 48.4 (2008), 791–9
Clarke, Stuart N., 'Introduction', in *The Essays of Virginia Woolf, 1929–1932* (London: The Hogarth Press, 2009), pp. ix–xxi
Cooper, John, 'Oscar Wilde's Cello Coat', *Oscar Wilde in America :: Blog*, 2018 <https://oscarwildeinamerica.blog/2018/01/04/oscar-wildes-cello-coat/> (accessed 28 February 2018)

Corbett, Mary Jean, '"Ashamed of the inkpot": Virginia Woolf, Lucy Clifford, and the Literary Marketplace', *Nineteenth Century Gender Studies*, 11.3 (2015) <http://www.ncgsjournal.com/issue113/corbett.html> (accessed 6 April 2017]

Corbett, Mary Jean, 'Behind the Times? Virginia Woolf and the Third Generation', *Twentieth Century Literature*, 60.1 (2014), 27–58

Corbett, Mary Jean, *Behind the Times: Virginia Woolf in Late-Victorian Contexts* (Ithaca, NY and London: Cornell University Press, 2020)

Cordner, Sheila, 'Radical Education in Aurora Leigh', *Victorian Review*, 40.1 (2015), 233–49 <https://doi.org/10.1353/vcr.2014.0005>

Crossland, Rachel, 'Virginia Stephen's Books on the Table: The Cornhill Magazine Reviews'. Paper presented at 'Virginia Woolf and the World of Books', 27th Annual International Conference on Virginia Woolf, University of Reading, 29 June–2 July 2017

Cuddy-Keane, Melba, *Virginia Woolf, the Intellectual and the Public Sphere* (Cambridge: Cambridge University Press, 2003)

Dahl, Christopher, 'Virginia Woolf's "Moments of Being" and Autobiographical Tradition in the Stephen Family', *Journal of Modern Literature*, 10.2 (1983), 175–96

D'Albertis, Deirdre, '"Bookmaking out of the remains of the dead": Elizabeth Gaskell's The Life of Charlotte Brontë', *Victorian Studies: A Journal of the Humanities, Arts and Sciences*, 39.1 (1995), 1–31

de Gay, Jane, *Virginia Woolf and Christian Culture* (Edinburgh: Edinburgh University Press, 2018)

de Gay, Jane, *Virginia Woolf's Novels and the Literary Past* (Edinburgh: Edinburgh University Press, 2006)

Dell, Marion, *Virginia Woolf's Influential Forebears: Julia Margaret Cameron, Anny Thackeray Ritchie and Julia Prinsep Stephen* (Basingstoke: Palgrave Macmillan, 2015)

Dillane, Fionnuala, *Before George Eliot: Marian Evans and the Periodical Press* (Cambridge: Cambridge University Press, 2013)

Dillane, Fionnuala, '"The character of editress": Marian Evans at the Westminster Review, 1851–54', *Tulsa Studies in Women's Literature*, 30.2 (2013), 269–90

'DODO', *The Spectator Archive*, 1893 <http://archive.spectator.co.uk/article/17th-june-1893/22/dodo> (accessed 5 February 2018)

Easley, Alexis, *Literary Celebrity, Gender and Victorian Authorship, 1850–1914* (Newark: University of Delaware Press, 2011)

Eliot, George, *George Eliot's Life as Related in Her Letters and Journals*, vol. I, ed. by John Cross, 3 vols (Edinburgh and London: William Blackwood and Sons, 1885)

Ellis, Steve, *Virginia Woolf and the Victorians* (Cambridge: Cambridge University Press, 2007)

'E. M. Forster on the Letters of Jane Austen – Then and Now, 1932', *TLS* online <https://www.the-tls.co.uk/articles/public/e-m-forster-jane-austen> (accessed 8 March 2018)

Fernald, Anne, *Virginia Woolf: Feminism and the Reader* (Basingstoke: Palgrave Macmillan, 2006)

Forster, E. M., 'Miss Austen and Jane Austen', *Times Literary Supplement* (10 November 1932), 821

Fox, Susan Hudson, 'Woolf's Austen/Boston Tea Party: The Revolt against Literary Empire in Night and Day', in *Virginia Woolf: Emerging Perspectives*, ed. by Mark Hussey, Vara Neverow and Jane Lilienfeld (New York: Pace University Press, 1994), pp. 259–65

Freedgood, Elaine, 'What Objects Know: Circulation, Omniscience and the Comedy of Dispossession in Victorian It-Narratives', *Journal of Victorian Culture*, 15.1 (2010), 83–100

Fuller, Miriam Rheingold, '"Let me go, Mr. Thorpe; Isabella, do not hold me!": Northanger Abbey and the Domestic Gothic', *Persuasions: The Jane Austen Journal*, 32 (2010), 90–104

Galton, Francis, *Hereditary Genius: An Inquiry into Its Laws and Consequences* (London: Macmillan & Co., 1892)

Garnett, Jane, 'Stephen [Née Jackson], Julia Prinsep (1846–1895), Celebrated Beauty and Philanthropist', *Oxford Dictionary of National Biography* <http://www.oxforddnb.com/view/10.1093/ref:odnb/9780198614128.001.0001/odnb-9780198614128-e-46943> (accessed 14 March 2018)

Garnett, Richard, 'Oliphant, Margaret Oliphant', *Dictionary of National Biography*, 1901 <https://doi.org/10.1093/odnb/9780192683120.013.20712>

Garrett, Martin, 'Mitford, Mary Russell', *Oxford Dictionary of National Biography* <http://www.oxforddnb.com/view/article/18859> (accessed 1 February 2017]

Garrity, Jane, 'Selling Culture to the "Civilized": Bloomsbury, British Vogue, and the Marketing of National Identity', *Modernism/Modernity*, 6.2 (1999), 29–58 <https://doi.org/10.1353/mod.1999.0016>

Garrity, Jane, 'Virginia Woolf, Intellectual Harlotry, and 1920s British Vogue', in *Virginia Woolf in the Age of Mechanical Reproduction*, ed. by Pamela L. Caughie (New York and London: Garland, 2000), pp. 185–218

Gaskell, Elizabeth, *The Life of Charlotte Bronte* (Oxford: Oxford University Press, 2009)

Gewirtz, Isaac, '"With anger and emphasis": The Proof Copy of A Room of One's Own', *Woolf Studies Annual*, 17 (2011), 1–76

Gilbert, Sandra M., and Susan Gubar, *The Madwoman in the Attic: The Woman Writer and the Nineteenth-Century Literary Imagination*, 2nd edn (New Haven, CT and London: Yale University Press, 2000)

Goldhill, Simon, *A Very Queer Family Indeed: Sex, Religion and the Bensons in Victorian Britain* (Chicago: University of Chicago Press, 2016) <https://press.uchicago.edu/ucp/books/book/chicago/V/bo24550846.html> (accessed 6 October 2021)

Goldman, Jane, '"Ce Chien est à moi": Virginia Woolf and the Signifying Dog', *Woolf Studies Annual*, 13 (2007), 49–86

Goldman, Jane, 'Desmond MacCarthy, Life and Letters (1928–35), and Bloomsbury Modernism', in *The Oxford Critical and Cultural History of Modernist Magazines, Volume I: Britain and Ireland 1880–1955*, ed. by Peter Brooker and Andrew Thacker (Oxford: Oxford University Press, 2009), 428–52

Goldman, Jane, *The Cambridge Introduction to Virginia Woolf* (Cambridge: Cambridge University Press, 2006)
Goldman, Mark, *The Reader's Art: Virginia Woolf as Literary Critic* (The Hague: Mouton, 1976)
Griffin, Gail, 'Braving the Mirror: Virginia Woolf as Autobiographer', *Biography*, 4.2 (1981), 108–18
Gualtieri, Elena, *Virginia Woolf's Essays: Sketching the Past* (Basingstoke: Palgrave Macmillan, 2000)
Hadjiafxendi, Kyriaki, 'Negotiating Fame: Mid-Victorian Women Writers and the Romantic Myth of the Gentlemanly Reviewer', in *Crafting the Woman Professional in the Long Nineteenth Century*, ed. by Kyriaki Hadjiafxendi and Patricia Zakreski (Proquest Ebook Central / Taylor and Francis, 2016), pp. 187–205. Pdf accessed 8 August 2017
Halsey, Katie, '"Tell me of some booklings: Mary Russell Mitford's Female Literary Networks', *Women's Writing*, 18.1 (2011), 121–36
Hammill, Faye, *Women, Celebrity, and Literary Culture between the Wars* (Texas: University of Texas Press, 2007)
Hankins, Leslie, 'Heritage Hoarding: Artifacts, Archives, and Ambiguity, or, the Saga of Virginia Woolf's Standing Desk', in *Virginia Woolf and Heritage*, ed. by Jane de Gay, Tom Breckin and Anne Reus (Clemson, SC: Clemson University Press/Liverpool University Press, 2017)
Harman, Claire, *Charlotte Brontë: A Life* (London: Penguin Books, 2015)
Harman, Claire, *Fanny Burney: A Biography* (London: Harper Collins Publisher, 2000)
Harris, Margaret, 'J. W. Cross Defends G. H. Lewes', *George Eliot Review: Journal of the George Eliot Fellowship*, 40 (2009), 28–37
Herman, David, 'Modernist Life Writing and Nonhuman Lives: Ecologies of Experience in Virginia Woolf's Flush', *MFS Modern Fiction Studies*, 59.3 (2013), 547–68
Hill, Constance, *Mary Russell Mitford and Her Surroundings* (London: John Lane, The Bodley Head, 1920)
Hill, Katherine C., 'Virginia Woolf and Leslie Stephen: History and Literary Revolution', *PMLA*, 96.3 (1981), 351–62
Humble, Nicola, 'Sitting Forward or Sitting Back: Highbrow v. Middlebrow Reading', *Modernist Cultures*, 6.1 (2011), 41–59
Humble, Nicola, 'The Feminine Middlebrow Novel', in *The History of British Women's Writing, 1920–1945: Volume Eight*, ed. by Maroula Joannou, The History of British Women's Writing series (London: Palgrave Macmillan, 2013), pp. 97–111 <https://doi.org/10.1057/9781137292179_6>
Humble, Nicola, *The Feminine Middlebrow Novel, 1920s to 1950s: Class, Domesticity, and Bohemianism* (Oxford and New York: Oxford University Press, 2001)
Huyssen, Andreas, *After the Great Divide: Modernism, Mass Culture, Postmodernism* (Bloomington: Indiana University Press, 1986)
Hyman, Virginia, 'Reflections in the Looking-Glass: Leslie Stephen and Virginia Woolf', *Journal of Modern Literature*, 10.2 (1983), 197–216
Iser, Wolfgang, 'The Reading Process: A Phenomenological Approach', *New Literary History*, 3.2 (1972), 279–99

Jaillant, Lise, *Cheap Modernism: Expanding Markets, Publishers' Series and the Avant-Garde* (Edinburgh: Edinburgh University Press, 2017)

Jay, Elisabeth, *Mrs Oliphant: 'A Fiction to Herself'. A Literary Life* (Oxford: Clarendon Press, 1995)

Jay, Elisabeth, 'Mrs. Oliphant: The Hero as Woman of Letters, or Autobiography, a Gendered Genre', *Caliban*, 31 (1994), 85–95

Jay, Elisabeth, 'Oliphant, Margaret Oliphant Wilson', *Oxford Dictionary of National Biography* <http://www.oxforddnb.com/view/article/20712?docPos=1> (accessed 18 May 2017)

Johnson, R. Brimley (Reginald Brimley), *The Women Novelists* (London: W. Collins, 1918) <http://archive.org/details/womennovelists00johnrich> (accessed 17 November 2021)

Jones, Clara, *Virginia Woolf: Ambivalent Activist* (Edinburgh: Edinburgh University Press, 2015)

Kaiser Loges, Mary, 'Inventing Victorians: Virginia Woolf's "Memoirs of a Novelist"', *The Victorian Newsletter*, 73 (1988), 1–2

Kaplan, Cora, 'Heroines, Hysteria and History: Jane Eyre and Her Critics', in *Victoriana: Histories, Fictions, Criticism* (New York: Columbia University Press, 2007), pp. 15–36

Kaplan, Cora, 'Pandora's Box: Subjectivity, Class and Sexuality in Socialist-Feminist Criticism', in *British Feminist Though: A Reader*, ed. by Terry Lovell (Oxford: Blackwell, 1990), pp. 345–66

Kaplan, Cora, *Victoriana: Histories, Fictions, Criticism* (New York: Columbia University Press, 2007)

Kertesz, Elizabeth R., 'Smyth, Dame Ethel Mary (1858–1944), Composer, Writer, and Suffragist', *Oxford Dictionary of National Biography* <http://www.oxforddnb.com/view/10.1093/ref:odnb/9780198614128.001.0001/odnb-9780198614128-e-36173> (accessed 5 February 2018)

Kirkham, Margaret, 'The Austen Portraits and the Received Biography', in *Jane Austen: New Perspectives*, Women & Literature series (New York and London: Holmes & Meier, 1983), pp. 29–38

Kore-Schröder, Lena, 'Who's Afraid of Rosamond Merridew?: Reading Medieval History in "The Journal of Mistress Joan Martyn"', *Journal of the Short Story in English*, 50 (2008) <http://jsse.revues.org/719> (accessed 12 January 2015)

Koutsantoni, Katerina, 'The Impersonal Strategy: Re-Visiting Virginia Woolf's Position in The Common Reader Essays', *Women: A Cultural Review*, 20.2 (2009), 157–71 <https://doi.org/10.1080/09574040903000829>

Koutsantoni, Katerina, *Virginia Woolf's Common Reader* (Farnham: Ashgate, 2009)

Langland, Elizabeth, 'The Receptions of Charlotte Bronte, Charles Dickens, George Eliot, and Thomas Hardy', in *A Companion to The Victorian Novel*, ed. by Patrick Brantlinger and William B. Thesing (Oxford: Blackwell Publishing, 2002), pp. 387–405

Law, Graham, 'The Professionalization of Authorship', in *The Nineteenth-Century Novel 1820–1880*, vol. III, The Oxford History of the Novel in English series (Oxford: Oxford University Press, 2012), 37–55

Le Faye, Deirdre, 'Introduction', in *Selected Letters*, by Jane Austen (Oxford: Oxford University Press, 2004), pp. ix–xxxv

Leavis, Q.D., *Fiction and the Reading Public* (London: Chatto & Windus, 1939)
Lee, Elizabeth, 'Mitford, Mary Russell', *Dictionary of National Biography Archive*, 1894 <https://doi.org/10.1093/odnb/9780192683120.013.18859>
Lee, Hermione, 'Introduction', in *Moments of Being: Autobiographical Writings*, by Virginia Woolf, ed. by Jeanne Schulkind (London: Pimlico, 2002)
Lee, Hermione, 'Jane Austen Faints', in *Virginia Woolf's Nose: Essays on Biography*
Lee, Hermione, *Virginia Woolf* (London: Vintage, 1997)
Lee, Hermione, *Virginia Woolf's Nose: Essays on Biography* (Princeton, NJ: Princeton University Press, 2005)
Lee, Judith, '"Without Hate, without Bitterness, without Fear, without Protest, without Preaching": Virginia Woolf Reads Jane Austen', *Persuasions: Journal of the Jane Austen Society of North America*, 12 (1990), 111–16
Levine, George, 'Reading Margaret Oliphant', *Journal of Victorian Culture*, 19.2 (2014), 232–46 <https://doi.org/10.1080/13555502.2014.919081>
Lewis, Thomas S. W., 'Combining "the advantages of fact and fiction": Virginia Woolf's Biographies of Vita Sackville-West, Flush and Roger Fry', in *Virginia Woolf: Centennial Essays* (Troy, NY: The Whitston Publishing Company, 1983), pp. 295–324
Lilienfeld, Jane, '"The gift of a china inkpot": Violet Dickinson, Virginia Woolf, Elizabeth Gaskell, Charlotte Brontë, and the Love of Women in Writing', in *Virginia Woolf: Lesbian Readings*, ed. by Eileen Barrett and Patricia Cramer (New York: New York University Press, 1997), pp. 37–56
Long, Jean, 'The Awkward Break: Woolf's Reading of Brontë and Austen in A Room of One's Own', *Woolf Studies Annual*, 3 (1997), 76–94
Lutz, Deborah, 'The Dead Still Among Us: Victorian Secular Relics, Hair Jewelry, and Death Culture', *Victorian Literature and Culture*, 39.01 (2011), 127–42
Lynch, Deidre, 'Homes and Haunts: Austen's and Mitford's English Idylls', *PMLA*, 115.5 (2000), 1103–8
MacKay, Carol Hanbery, 'Emerging Selves: The Autobiographical Impulse in Elizabeth Barrett Browning, Anne Thackeray Ritchie, and Annie Wood Besant', in *A History of English Autobiography*, ed. by Adam Smyth (Cambridge: Cambridge University Press, 2016), pp. 207–20
Maggio, Paula, 'Digging for Buried Treasure: Theories about Weather and Fiction in Virginia Woolf's Essays', *Virginia Woolf Miscellany*, 78 (2010), 23–26
Maitland, Frederic, *The Life and Letters of Leslie Stephen* (London: Duckworth & Co., 1908)
Mansfield, Katherine, 'A Ship Comes into the Harbour', *The Athenaeum*, 21 November 1919, p. 1227
Marcus, Jane, *Art and Anger: Reading Like A Woman* (Columbus: Ohio State University Press, 1988)
Marcus, Jane, 'Daughters of Anger/Material Girls: Con/Textualizing Feminist Criticism', *Women's Studies: An Interdisciplinary Journal*, 15 (1988), 281–308
Marcus, Laura, 'The Newness of the "New Biography": Biographical Theory and Practice in the Early Twentieth Century', in *Mapping Lives: The Uses of Biography*, ed. by William St Clair and Peter France, British Academy Centenary Monographs series (Oxford: Oxford University Press, 2004), pp. 193–218

Martin, Linda, 'Elegy and the Unknowable Mind in Jacob's Room', *Studies in the Novel*, 47.2 (2015), 176–92

McCord, Phyllis Frus, '"Little corks that mark a sunken net": Virginia Woolf's "Sketch of the Past" as a Fictional Memoir', *Modern Language Studies*, 16.3 (1986), 247–54

McCracken, LuAnn, '"The synthesis of my being": Autobiography and the Reproduction of Identity in Virginia Woolf', *Tulsa Studies in Women's Literature*, 9.1 (1990), 58–78

McNees, Eleanor, 'The Stephen Inheritance: Virginia Woolf and the Burden of the Arnoldian Critic', *The Cambridge Quarterly*, 44.2 (2015), 119–45

McNeillie, Andrew, 'Introduction', in *The Essays of Virginia Woolf : Volume 4 (1925–1928)* (London: Harcourt, 1994), pp. xi–xxiii

McNeillie, Andrew, 'Introduction', in *The Essays of Virginia Woolf : Volume 1 (1904–1912)* (London: Harcourt, 1994), pp. xi–xxiii

McSweeney, Kelly, 'Introduction', in *Aurora Leigh*, by Elizabeth Barrett Browning (Oxford: Oxford University Press, 1993), pp. ix–xxxv

Miller, Lucasta, *The Brontë Myth* (London: Vintage, 2001)

Mitford, Mary Russell, *Our Village; By Miss Mitford; With an Introduction by Anne Thackeray Ritchie; and One Hundred Illustrations by Hugh Thomson*, ed. by Anny Thackeray Ritchie (London: Macmillan and Co., 1893)

Moi, Toril, 'Appropriating Bourdieu: Feminist Theory and Pierre Bourdieu's Sociology of Culture', *New Literary History*, 22.4 (1991), 1017–49 <https://doi.org/10.2307/469077>

Monk, Ray, 'Life without Theory: Biography as an Exemplar of Philosophical Understanding', *Poetics Today*, 28.3 (2007), 527–70

Monk, Ray, 'This Fictitious Life: Virginia Woolf on Biography, Reality, and Character', *Philosophy and Literature*, 31.1 (2007), 1–40 <https://doi.org/10.1353/phl.2007.0015>

Mooneyham White, Laura, and Carmen Smith, 'Discerning Voice through Austen Said: Free Indirect Discourse, Coding, and Interpretive (Un)Certainty', *Persuasions: The Jane Austen Journal On-Line*, 37.1 (2016) <http://www.jasna.org/publications/persuasions-online/vol37no1/white-smith/> (accessed 8 March 2018)

Morris, Pam, *Jane Austen, Virginia Woolf and Worldly Realism* (Edinburgh: Edinburgh University Press, 2017)

Morrison, Kevin A., 'Elizabeth Barrett Browning's Dog Days', *Tulsa Studies in Women's Literature*, 30.1 (2012), 93–115

Morrison, Kevin A., 'Foregrounding Nationalism: Mary Russell Mitford's Our Village and the Effects of Publication Context', *European Romantic Review*, 19.3 (2008), 275–87

'Mrs. Oliphant's Cervantes', *The Spectator Archive*, 1880 <http://archive.spectator.co.uk/article/20th-november-1880/20/mrs-oliphants-cervantes> (accessed 10 September 2017)

Murray, Douglas, '"She could not repent her resistance": Northanger Abbey and the #MeToo Movement', *Nineteenth Century Gender Studies*, 16.2 (2020) <https://www.ncgsjournal.com/issue162/murray.html> (accessed 19 November 2021)

Newman, Hilary, 'The Hogarth Press, the Brontes, and the "Wuthering Heights" Authorship Debate', *Virginia Woolf Bulletin*, 52 (2016), 11–19

Novak, Julia, 'The Notable Woman in Fiction: The Afterlives of Elizabeth Barrett Browning', *A/b: Auto/Biography Studies*, 1 (2016), 83–107

Oliphant, Margaret, *Harry Joscelyn*, vol. III (London: Hurst and Blackett, 1881)

Oliphant, Margaret, 'Novels.', *Blackwood's Edinburgh Magazine*, 94.574 (1863), 168–83

Oliphant, Margaret, *The Autobiography and Letters of Mrs. M.O.W. Oliphant*, ed. by Annie Coghill (New York: Dodd, Mead and Company, 1899)

Oliphant, Margaret, *The Autobiography of Margaret Oliphant*, ed. by Elisabeth Jay (Ormskirk: Broadview, 2002)

Oliphant, Margaret, *The Makers of Modern Rome; in Four Books* (London: Macmillan, 1895) <http://archive.org/details/makersofmodernro00olip> (accessed 17 November 2021)

O'Malley, Rose, 'Sororal Generations: Fanny Price's Sister Strategy', *Nineteenth Century Gender Studies*, 14.3 (2018) <http://ncgsjournal.com/issue143/omalley.html> (accessed 12 November 2021)

Onslow, Barbara, *Women of the Press in Nineteenth-Century Britain* (Basingstoke: Palgrave Macmillan, 2000)

Ophir, Ella, '"Writing the history of my own times": Virginia Woolf and the Diary', in *Virginia Woolf and Heritage*, ed. by Jane de Gay, Tom Breckin and Anne Reus (Clemson, SC: Clemson University Press/Liverpool University Press, 2017), pp. 196–201

Partington, Wilfred, ed., *Echoes of the 'Eighties: Leaves from the Diary of a Victorian Lady* (London: Eveleigh Nash Company, 1921)

Payn, James, *Some Literary Recollections* (London: Smith Elder & Co., 1884)

Peterson, Linda H, *Becoming a Woman of Letters: Myths of Authorship and Facts of the Victorian Market* (Princeton, NJ: Princeton University Press, 2009)

Peterson, Linda H., 'Triangulation, Desire, and Discontent in "The Life of Charlotte Brontë"', *Studies in English Literature, 1500–1900*, 47.4 (2007), 901–20

Pouliot, Amber, 'Serena Partridge's "Accessories": Fabricating Uncertainty in the Brontë Parsonage Museum', *Journal of Victorian Culture*, 25.2 (2020), 279–99

Price, Leah, 'George Eliot and the Production of Consumers', *NOVEL: A Forum on Fiction*, 30 (1997), 145–69

Raven, James, 'The Oxford Dictionary of National Biography: Dictionary or Encyclopaedia?', *The Historical Journal*, 50.4 (2007), 991–1006

Regis, Amber, 'Charlotte Bronte on Stage: 1930s Biodrama and the Archive/Museum Performed', in *Charlotte Brontë: Legacies and Afterlives*, by Amber Regis and Deborah Wynne (Manchester: Manchester University Press, 2017), pp. 116–42

Reynier, Christine, 'The Impure Art of Biography: Virginia Woolf's Flush', in *Mapping the Self: Space, Identity, Discourse in British Auto/Biography* (Saint-Etienne: Publications de l'Université de Saint-Etienne, 2003), pp. 187–202

Richardson, Rebecca, 'Dramatizing Intimacy: Confessions and Free Indirect Discourse in Sense and Sensibility', *ELH*, 81.1 (2014), 225–44

Ritchie, Anny Thackeray, *A Book of Sibyls* (London: Smith Elder & Co., 1883)

Ritchie, Anny Thackeray, *A Discourse on Modern Sibyls*, Pamphlet No. 24 (The English Association, 1913)

Ritchie, Anny Thackeray, 'Introduction', in *Our Village; By Miss Mitford; With an Introduction by Anne Thackeray Ritchie; and One Hundred Illustrations by Hugh Thomson*, by Mary Russell Mitford (London: Macmillan and Co., 1893)

Rosenbaum, S. P., *Edwardian Bloomsbury: The Early Literary History of the Bloomsbury Group* (New York: St Martin's Press, 1994), II

Rosenbaum, S. P., *The Bloomsbury Group Memoir Club*, ed. by James M. Haule (Basingstoke: Palgrave Macmillan, 2014)

Rosenberg, Tracey S., 'The Awkward Blot: George Eliot's Reception and The Ideal Woman Writer', *Nineteenth-Century Gender Studies*, 3.1 (2007)

Rosner, Victoria, *Modernism and the Architecture of Private Life*, Gender and Culture series (New York: Columbia University Press, 2005)

Sanders, Valerie, *Eve's Renegades: Victorian Anti-Feminist Women Novelists* (Basingstoke: Macmillan, 1996)

Sattaur, Jennifer, 'Thinking Objectively: An Overview of "Thing Theory" in Victorian Studies', *Victorian Literature and Culture*, 40.1 (2012), 347–57

Saunders, Max, *Self-Impression: Life-Writing, Autobiografiction, and the Forms of Modern Literature* (Oxford: Oxford University Press, 2010)

Scholes, Robert, and Clifford Wulfman, *Modernism in the Magazines: An Introduction* (New Haven, CT: Yale University Press, 2010)

Scott, Bonnie Kime, *In the Hollow of the Wave: Virginia Woolf and Modernist Uses of Nature* (Charlottesville: University of Virginia Press, 2012)

Shattock, Joanne, 'Jane Austen and George Eliot: Afterlives and Letters', *George Eliot Review: Journal of the George Eliot Fellowship*, 34 (2003), 7–20

Shattock, Joanne, 'Work for Women: Margaret Oliphant's Journalism', in *Nineteenth-Century Media and the Construction of Identities*, ed. by Laurel Brake, Bill Bell and David Finkelstein (New York: Palgrave, 2000), pp. 165–77

Showalter, Elaine, *A Literature of Their Own: British Women Novelists from Bronte to Lessing* (Princeton, NJ: Princeton University Press, 1977)

Showalter, Elaine, 'The Greening of Sister George', *Nineteenth-Century Fiction*, 35.3 (1980), 292–311

Silver, Brenda R., 'What's Woolf Got to Do with It?: Or, the Perils of Popularity', *MFS Modern Fiction Studies*, 38.1 (2009), 20–60

Simcox, Edith, 'George Eliot', *The Nineteenth Century: A Monthly Review*, May 1881, 778–801

Simpson, Kathryn, 'Persuading Rachel: Woolf and Austen's "Little voyage of discovery"', in *Virginia Woolf and Heritage*, ed. by Jane de Gay, Tom Breckin and Anne Reus (Clemson, SC: Clemson University Press/Liverpool University Press, 2017), pp. 141–7

Smart, Nick, '"Never see Rachel again": Virginia Woolf and the End of Domestic Fiction', in *Voyages Out, Voyages Home: Selected Papers from the Eleventh Annual Conference On Virginia Woolf*, ed. by Jane de Gay and Marion Dell (Clemson, SC: Clemson University Digital Press, 2010), pp. 62–9

Smith, Catherine F., 'Histories of a House', *Virginia Woolf Miscellany*, 18 (1982), 2

Smith, Craig, 'Across the Widest Gulf: Nonhuman Subjectivity in Virginia Woolf's "Flush"', *Twentieth Century Literature*, 48.3 (2002), 348–61

Snaith, Anna, '"My poor private voice": Virginia Woolf and Auto/Biography', in *Representing Lives: Women and Autobiography*, ed. by Alison Donnell and Pauline Polkey (Basingstoke: Macmillan, 2000), pp. 96–104
Snaith, Anna, 'Of Fanciers, Footnotes, and Fascism: Virginia Woolf's Flush', *MFS Modern Fiction Studies*, 48.3 (2002), 614–36 <https://doi.org/10.1353/mfs.2002.0070>
Snaith, Anna, *Virginia Woolf: Public and Private Negotiations* (New York: St Martin's Press, 2000)
Squier, Susan M., *Virginia Woolf and London: The Sexual Politics Od the City* (Chapel Hill and London: University of North Carolina Press, 1985)
Stalla, Heidi, 'The Play of Fact and Fiction in Virginia Stephen's "The Journal of Mistress Joan Martyn"', in *Virginia Woolf and Heritage*, ed. by Jane de Gay, Tom Breckin and Anne Reus (Clemson, SC: Clemson University Press/Liverpool University Press, 2017), pp. 190–5
Stephen, Leslie, 'Austen, Jane', *Dictionary of National Biography Archive*, 1885 <https://doi.org/10.1093/odnb/9780192683120.013.904>
Stephen, Leslie, 'Brontë, Charlotte', *Dictionary of National Biography Archive*, 1885 <https://doi.org/10.1093/odnb/9780192683120.013.3523>
Stephen, Leslie, 'Cross, Mary Ann', *Dictionary of National Biography Archive*, 1888 <https://doi.org/10.1093/odnb/9780192683120.013.6794>
Stephen, Leslie, 'Forgotten Benefactors', in *Social Rights and Duties, Volume II* (London: Swan, Sonnenschein & Co., 1896), pp. 225–67
Stephen, Leslie, *George Eliot*, English Men of Letters (London: Macmillan & Co., 1902)
Stephen, Leslie, 'Hours in a Library: No XVII – Charlotte Brontë', *The Cornhill Magazine*, 36.216 (1877), 723–39
Stephen, Leslie, 'Humour.', *The Cornhill Magazine*, 33.195 (1876), 318–26
Stephen, Leslie, 'National Biography', in *Studies of a Biographer, Volume I* (London: Duckworth & Co., 1898), pp. 1–36
Stephen, Leslie, *Sir Leslie Stephen's Mausoleum Book*, ed. by Alan Bell (Oxford: Clarendon Press, 1977)
Stephen, Leslie, 'Southey's Letters', in *Studies of a Biographer, Volume IV* (London: Duckworth & Co., 1902), pp. 45–85 <http://archive.org/details/studiesabiograp03stepgoog>
Stephen, Leslie, 'The Browning Letters', in *Studies of a Biographer, Volume III* (London: Duckworth & Co., 1902), pp. 1–35
Stone, Marjorie, 'Browning [Née Moulton Barrett], Elizabeth Barrett (1806–1861)', *Oxford Dictionary of National Biography* (Oxford University Press) <http://www.oxforddnb.com/view/article/3711?docPos=1> (accessed 2 March 2017)
Sullivan, Hannah, 'Autobiography and the Problem of Finish', *Biography*, 34.2 (2011), 298–325
Sullivan, Melissa, 'The Middlebrows of the Hogarth Press: Rose Macaulay, E. M. Delafield and Cultural Hierarchies in Interwar Britain', in *Leonard and Virginia Woolf: The Hogarth Press and Networks of Modernism*, ed. by Helen Southworth (Edinburgh: Edinburgh University Press, 2010), pp. 52–73
Sutherland, John, 'A Girl in the Bodleian: Mary Ward's Room of Her Own', *Victorian Literature and Culture*, 16 (1988), 169–80

Sutherland, John, *Mrs Humphry Ward: Eminent Victorian, Pre-Eminent Edwardian* (Oxford: Oxford University Press, 1991)

Sutherland, John, 'Ward [Née Arnold], Mary Augusta [Known as Mrs Humphry Ward]', *Oxford Dictionary of National Biography* <http://www.oxforddnb.com/view/article/36736?docPos=1> (accessed 19 May 2017)

Sutherland, Kathryn, 'Introduction', in *A Memoir of Jane Austen and Other Family Recollections* (Oxford: Oxford University Press, 2008), pp. xiii–xlviii

Sutherland, Kathryn, *Jane Austen's Textual Lives: From Aeschylus to Bollywood* (Oxford: Oxford University Press, 2005)

Tegan, Mary Beth, 'Training the Picturesque Eye: The Point of Views in Jane Austen's Persuasion', *The Eighteenth Century*, 58.1 (2017), 39–58

Todd, Janet, 'Who's Afraid of Jane Austen?', in *Jane Austen: New Perspectives*, Women & Literature (New York; London: Holmes & Meier, 1983), pp. 107–27

Trevelyan, Janet Penrose, *The Life of Mrs Humphry Ward* (London: Constable and Company Ltd, 1923)

Wah, Sarah, '"The most churlish of celebrities": George Eliot, John Cross and the Question of High Status', *Journal of Victorian Culture*, 15.3 (2010), 370–87

Wallace, Anne D., '"Nor in fading silks compose": Sewing, Walking, and Poetic Labor in Aurora Leigh', *ELH*, 64.1 (1997), 223–56 <https://doi.org/10.1353/elh.1997.0010>

Ward, Mrs Humphry, *A Writer's Recollections*, 3rd edn (London: W. Collins Sons & Co. Ltd, 1919)

Watson, Nicola, 'Homes and Haunts', in *The Literary Tourist: Readers and Places in Romantic and Victorian Britain* (Basingstoke: Palgrave Macmillan, 2006), pp. 90–117

Watson, Nicola, 'Introduction', in *Literary Tourism and Nineteenth Century Culture*, ed. by Nicola Watson (Basingstoke: Palgrave Macmillan, 2009), pp. 1–12

Wells, Juliette, 'A Note on Henry Austen's Authorship of the "Biographical Notice"', *Persuasions: Journal of the Jane Austen Society of North America*, 38.1 (2017) <http://jasna.org/publications-2/persuasions-online/vol38no1/wells/> (accessed 3 July 2020)

Wilson, Cheryl A., *Jane Austen and the Victorian Heroine* (Basingstoke: Palgrave Macmillan, 2017)

Wood, Alice, 'Modernism and the Middlebrow in British Women's Magazines, 1916–1930', in *Middlebrow and Gender, 1890–1945*, ed. by Christoph Ehland and Cornelia Wächter (Leiden: Brill Rodopi, 2016), pp. 39–59

Wood, Alice, *Virginia Woolf's Late Cultural Criticism: The Genesis of 'The Years', 'Three Guineas' and 'Between the Acts'*, Historicizing Modernism series (London: Bloomsbury, 2013)

Woolf, Leonard, *Downhill All the Way: An Autobiography of the Years 1919–1939* (London: The Hogarth Press, 1967)

Wynne, Deborah, 'The "Charlotte" Cult: Writing the Literary Pilgrimage, from Gaskell to Woolf', in *Charlotte Brontë: Legacies and Afterlives* (Manchester: Manchester University Press, 2017)

Zemgulys, Andrea, *Modernism and the Locations of Literary Heritage* (Cambridge: Cambridge University Press, 2008)

# Index

Angel in the House, 195
anger, 5, 26, 64, 68, 120, 130, 131, 186
  Charlotte Brontë, 30, 109, 120, 123–7, 129, 131
  see also Lady
Arnold, Matthew, 154, 158, 165, 179n
Ashton, Rosemary, 141, 142
*Athenaeum*, later *Nation & Athenaeum*, 9–10, 11, 51, 57, 78, 84, 157, 161
Austen, Jane, 3, 9, 22, 23, 24, 26, 29, 37–69, 75, 78, 79, 81, 82, 97, 119, 122, 138, 146, 147, 148, 152, 182, 192
  and Charlotte Brontë, 43–4, 64–5, 120, 122
  family biography, 3, 24, 29, 38–41, 42, 44, 52–3, 58, 64
  femininity, 37, 39, 43–4, 47, 49–50, 55, 63, 122, 124, 138
  juvenilia, 29, 38, 40, 54–6, 61, 62, 64, 150
  *Mansfield Park*, 45–7, 51
  *Persuasion*, 39, 48–9, 54, 57, 59–60
  proto-Modernism, 29, 38, 57–61, 63, 182
Austen-Leigh, J. E., *A Memoir of Jane Austen*, 3, 29, 38, 39–41, 42, 44, 58, 64, 82
autobiography, 16–18, 26, 27, 28, 30, 93, 99, 115–16, 141, 159–61, 182–96; see also Woolf, Virginia, biography: 'A Sketch of the Past'; 'Reminiscences'

Behn, Aphra, 26, 50, 63–4, 138
Bell, Angelica, 23
Bell, Clive, 188

Bell, Julian, 184, 189
Bell, Vanessa, 30, 139, 155, 157, 158, 160, 184–9, 194–5, 197n
Benson, E. F., *Charlotte Brontë*, 128–9, 135n
Black, Naomi, 6
Blair, Emily, 6, 29, 166–7
Bloomsbury, 11, 16, 145, 154
Bloomsbury Memoir Club, 183, 189
Booth, Alison, 3, 26, 76–7, 78, 146–7, 148
Bourdieu, Pierre, 12–13
Briggs, Julia, 94, 103
Brontë, Anne, 3, 109
Brontë, Branwell, 128, 135n
Brontë, Charlotte, 3, 5, 9, 13, 21, 22, 26, 30, 108–32, 138, 146, 147, 148, 152, 158, 175, 182
  and Jane Austen, 43–4, 64–5, 120, 122
  anger, 30, 109, 120, 123–7, 129, 131
  *Jane Eyre*, 44, 109, 112, 115–16, 119, 121, 123–4, 127, 131
Brontë, Emily, 3, 64, 64, 108, 122, 128, 134n
Brontë, Rev. Patrick, 129–31
Brosnan, Leila, 2, 11, 13, 113, 145, 157
Broughton, Trev, 189, 190, 192
Browning, Elizabeth Barrett, 22, 29, 74–5, 77, 90–103
  *Aurora Leigh*, 75, 90, 92–6, 100, 101, 102
  domestic tyranny, 29, 92, 97, 99, 100–3
  see also Flush (dog); Mitford, Mary Russell
Burney, Frances, 50, 64, 72n, 78, 119, 122

biography, 1, 3, 4, 6, 9, 12, 14–30, 38, 41–4, 48, 51, 52, 53, 57, 63, 75, 77–8, 81, 82, 84, 86–7, 89–90, 91, 93, 99, 108, 110–11, 112, 114–15, 116, 128, 129, 141–3, 145, 147, 151, 153, 161–3, 167, 170–1, 173–6, 182–96; *see also* character; New Biography; personality

Carlyle, Jane, 100–1, 102
Carlyle, Thomas, 25, 100–1, 186
Caughie, Pamela L., 102
Cecil, Nelly, 9, 128, 142, 157
character, 1, 3, 21, 23, 25, 27, 30, 39, 40, 41, 43, 63, 67, 68, 88, 89, 96, 114, 122, 143, 147, 151, 157, 162, 182, 194; *see also* personality
coarseness, 55, 67–8, 120, 132n
common reader, 9, 21
Corbett, Mary Jean, 5, 12, 13, 24, 30, 139, 158, 160, 162
*Cornhill Magazine*, 9, 19, 45, 76, 116, 137, 175
Cross, John, 141–2, 145, 151
Cuddy-Keane, Melba, 2, 11, 25, 115, 126

D'Albertis, Deirdre, 112
*Daily Herald*, 10, 77, 80, 150
De Gay, Jane, 37, 44, 48, 49, 51, 183
Dell, Marion, 5, 29, 78
Dickinson, Violet, 15, 17, 18, 155, 184
*Dictionary of National Biography*, 14, 16, 22, 25, 26, 44–5, 63, 74, 130, 137, 142, 145, 154, 167
disinterestedness, 164–5, 172
Duckworth, George, 139, 186
Duckworth, Gerald, 12, 47, 139, 186
Duckworth, Stella, 130–1, 183, 185, 186, 191, 195

Eliot, George, 3, 19–20, 21, 26, 27, 30, 63, 64, 119, 122, 140–53, 157, 159, 161, 163, 164, 165–6, 170, 172–3, 175, 176
 afterlife, 140–2
 eminence, 19–20, 143–4, 146–7, 152
 Victorian, 150–2, 161
Eliot, T. S., 10
Ellis, Steve, 4
Evans, Mary Ann *see* George Eliot

facts, 17, 18, 23, 25, 27–8, 49, 54, 62, 85, 87–8, 114, 116, 117, 122, 170, 182, 191; *see also* fiction; biography
fascism, 68, 97, 102, 165
femininity, 4, 8, 29, 30, 37–9, 43–4, 47, 49–50, 52, 55, 58, 62, 63, 66, 81, 94, 109, 111, 120, 122, 124–7, 138, 140, 142–4, 148–50, 151, 160, 171, 172, 176, 184, 185–6, 191, 195, 196
feminism, 4–7, 11, 12–13, 14–19, 22, 25–7, 29–30, 53, 57, 58, 66, 67, 68, 75, 78–80, 89, 109, 120, 123–5, 126–7, 129, 148, 152, 164, 165, 174, 175, 182, 184, 194
Fernald, Anne, 5, 6, 7, 9, 13
fiction, 1, 2, 9, 14, 15, 17–19, 22–4, 26, 29, 38, 41, 42, 43, 46, 48, 49–50, 52, 54, 57, 58–60, 62, 64, 66, 75, 78, 87, 91, 96, 99, 114, 115, 120, 125–6, 140, 141, 144, 147, 153, 155–7, 159, 160, 161, 164, 166, 170, 172, 173, 174, 175, 183, 184, 186, 191
Flush (dog), 29, 74, 75, 92, 96–102; *see also* Browning, Elizabeth Barrett; Mitford, Mary Russell
Forster, E. M., 52, 67–8
Fry, Roger, 27, 189, 190

Gaskell, Elizabeth, 29, 108
 *The Life of Charlotte Brontë*, 3, 25, 30, 44, 82, 109–17, 119, 121, 122, 124, 128, 129–31, 141
Gilbert, Sandra, 4, 123
Goldman, Jane, 72n, 97
Goldman, Mark, 2
Gualtieri, Elena, 2, 4, 11, 126, 165, 190
*Guardian*, 8, 113, 154, 156, 157
Gubar, Susan, 4, 123

Hare, Augustus, *The Story of Two Noble Lives*, 24
Haywood, Eliza, 49–50
high and low art, 11, 30, 58, 97, 113, 128, 138, 140, 170; *see also* Eliot, George; Oliphant, Margaret; Ward, Mary Augusta
Hill, Constance, 156
 *Mary Russell Mitford and Her Surroundings*, 13, 24, 75–90, 120
Hogarth Press, 10, 11, 22, 128, 190
Humble, Nicola, 2, 128
Huyssen, Andreas, 160

# Index

Hyde Park Gate, 15, 16, 80, 131, 139, 155, 159, 160, 183, 185, 187, 194
*Hyde Park Gate News*, 196

Ibsen, Henrik, *A Doll's House*, 82
impersonality, 1, 56, 60, 65, 109, 120, 147–8, 163

journalism, 3–4, 7–14, 17, 49, 75, 113, 114, 137, 140, 146, 147, 165, 166, 190, 196; *see also* Eliot, George; Haywood, Eliza; Oliphant, Margaret

Kaplan, Cora, 109, 121, 124

lady, 49–50, 54, 62, 67, 74, 76–7, 78, 79, 80–1, 82, 83, 85, 90, 112, 113, 118, 120, 126, 137, 138, 152, 158, 156; *see also* anger; femininity
Leavis, Q. D., 9
Lee, Hermione, 39, 130, 195, 198n
Lee, Sidney, 22, 25
Lee, Vernon, 139
Levine, George, 168
Lewes, George Henry, 39, 44, 112, 116, 122, 141, 142, 144–6
Lilienfeld, Jane, 109, 129, 130

MacCarthy, Desmond, 66, 72n
McNees, Eleanor, 165, 179n
McNeillie, Andrew, 4, 9, 10
Maitland, Frederic, 15, 17–18, 25, 184, 190
Mansfield, Katherine, 11, 48, 51–2, 56, 66
Marcus, Jane, 5, 109, 124, 127
Marcus, Laura, 25
mass culture, 11, 13–14, 160, 168; *see also* middlebrow; high and low art
Memoir Club *see* Bloomsbury Memoir Club
middlebrow, 2, 31n, 97, 128
Mitford, George, 29, 76, 77, 79, 80, 83, 84, 85, 86, 98, 100, 103, 120
Mitford, Mary Russell, 22, 23, 26, 29, 42, 74–90, 92, 93, 95, 97–103; *see also* Browning, Elizabeth Barrett; lady; Mitford, George; Flush (dog)
Modernism, 1, 2, 4, 9, 11, 14, 18, 22, 23, 25, 29, 38, 54, 57–9, 61, 63, 65, 96, 97, 109, 114–15, 120, 122, 138–9, 152, 159, 166, 182, 183; *see also* impersonality; New Biography
Moi, Toril, 12–13
Morley College, 15, 155

*Nation and Athenaeum* see *Athenaeum*
New Biography, 3, 4, 14, 17, 18, 22–5, 27, 29, 75, 84, 87, 151
*New Statesman*, 10, 54
Nicolson, Harold, 24
non-fiction, 1, 4, 9, 10, 87, 123, 140, 168, 182; *see also* autobiography; biography; journalism

Oliphant, Margaret Oliphant Wilson, 6, 13, 21, 30, 140, 153, 163–76
and George Eliot, 140, 172–3
*Autobiography*, 163, 170–4, 175

patriarchy, 5, 6, 29, 37, 44–5, 48, 57–8, 65, 66, 68, 74, 75, 78, 80, 82, 83, 89–90, 92, 101, 102, 118, 119, 125, 127, 129, 147, 162, 165, 169, 174, 182, 194
Payn, James, 76, 89
personality, 15, 18–19, 20, 22–3, 41, 63, 116, 118, 120, 121, 144, 151, 175, 191, 194
Peterson, Linda H., 77, 79, 82, 112, 113, 138, 140
Pouliot, Amber, 112, 119

Richmond, Bruce, 8, 10, 142, 145
Ritchie, Anny Thackeray, 29, 76, 78, 81–2, 143, 144, 174, 175, 176
Rosner, Victoria, 7

Sackville-West, Vita, 17, 23, 97, 129
Scott, Bonnie Kime, 89, 98, 99, 102
sexuality, 28, 49, 67, 93, 98, 102, 129, 169
Showalter, Elaine, 7, 83, 143
Silver, Brenda, 4
Simpson, Kathryn, 37, 48, 49
Sinclair, May, 11, 117
Smith, George, 112, 125, 128, 129
Smyth, Ethel, 68, 117, 129, 189
Snaith, Anna, 7, 17, 74, 83, 90, 92, 97, 101
Squier, Susan, 102
Stephen, Julia, 5, 16, 154, 160, 162, 183, 184, 185, 187, 191, 192, 195, 196, 198n
Stephen, Laura, 15, 94

Stephen, Leslie, 3, 6, 14–15, 16, 17, 20, 22, 25, 30, 37, 44–7, 53, 63, 76, 90–2, 94, 99–100, 101, 109, 110, 114, 115–16, 121, 125, 130, 131, 137, 140, 142, 144, 145, 147, 148, 154, 155, 168, 173–5, 183, 185–96
Strachey, Lytton, 25, 99, 157, 184
Sutherland, John, 157, 160
Sutherland, Kathryn, 40, 55, 58, 61

*Times Literary Supplement*, 8–10, 12, 21, 23, 41, 45, 48, 49, 50, 52, 67, 77, 78, 80, 93, 96, 108, 113, 115, 142, 145, 150, 157, 166, 167
Trevelyan, Janet Penrose, 155, 161–2, 173
tyranny, 29, 57, 69, 78, 92, 97, 99, 100–3, 129, 146, 170, 186

*Vogue*, 1, 2, 3, 4, 10, 11

Ward, Mary Augusta, 16, 21, 30, 140, 149, 153–63, 164, 165, 173, 176
  *A Writer's Recollections*, 159–61
West, Rebecca, 11, 66
Wood, Alice, 2, 10, 11, 25, 68
Woolf, Leonard, 10, 11, 51
Woolf, Virginia
  **Reviews and Essays:**
  'A Good Daughter', 77, 80–4, 89, 103
  'A Scribbling Dame', 48–50
  'An Imperfect Lady', 74, 77–80, 84, 89, 90, 118, 120, 126
  'Aurora Leigh' (1931), 92–7, 100
  'Aurora Leigh' (*Common Reader II*), 93
  'Charlotte Brontë' (1916), 9, 108, 113–18, 143
  '"Charlotte Brontë"' (1917), 108, 115
  'Fenwick's Career', 156–7
  'George Eliot (1819–1880)', 150
  'George Eliot' (1919), 9, 140–50,
  'George Eliot' (1926), 150–2
  'George Eliot' (*Common Reader I*), 142
    see also 'George Eliot (1919)
  'Haworth, November, 1904', 28, 108, 110–13, 118, 120
  'Hours in a Library', 114
  'How Should One Read A Book?', 24
  'Indiscretions', 1–4, 7–8, 191
  'Jane Austen' (1913), 9, 41–7, 114, 143
  'Jane Austen and the Geese', 48, 52–4
  'Jane Austen at Sixty', 57–61, 67, 125
  'Jane Austen' (*Common Reader I*), 61–3
  'Jane Austen Practising', 54–7
  '"Jane Eyre" and "Wuthering Heights"', 118, 120–2
  '"Maria Edgeworth and Her Circle"', 78, 156
  'Mary Wollstonecraft', 69
  'Middlebrow', 31n
  'Mr Howells on Form', 50–1
  'On Being Ill', 24–5
  'Outlines: Miss Mitford' (*Common Reader I*), 89–90
  'Personalities', 27, 30
  'Poets' Letters', 90–2
  'Professions for Women', 8, 30, 33n, 68, 163, 183, 190, 194, 195
  'The Art of Biography', 25, 27–8
  'The Compromise', 161–3, 164
  'The Decay of Essay-writing', 12–15
  'The Letters of Mary Russell Mitford', 89, 98
  'The New Biography', 4, 22–5, 27, 84, 87, 151
  'The Wrong Way of Reading', 24–5, 78, 84–9
  'Women and Fiction', 173, 194
  'Women Novelists', 118–20, 146, 167
  **Book-length Essays:**
  *A Room of One's Own*, 3–8, 12, 14, 21, 25–30, 38, 61, 63–7, 74, 89, 94, 108–9, 118–19, 122–9, 131, 138, 152–3, 165, 183, 194
  *The Common Reader*, 8, 10, 12, 28, 33n, 37, 58–9, 61, 63, 69, 87, 89, 108, 114, 118, 120, 142
  *The Pargiters*, 27, 96
  *Three Guineas*, 4, 6–8, 14, 25, 27–8, 69, 74–5, 83–4, 94–5, 102–3, 108, 109, 128–31, 138, 154, 162–8, 171–5, 183, 186
  *Women and Fiction: The Manuscript Versions of A Room of One's Own*, 63–4, 125
  **Biography:**
  'A Sketch of the Past', 8, 27–8, 30–1, 131, 139–40, 171, 182, 183, 184, 186, 188–96

'Impressions of Sir Leslie Stephen', 14–15, 23, 37
'Reminiscences', 30, 183–4, 184–8, 189
**Shorter Fiction:**
'Memoirs of a Novelist', 19–21, 22, 24, 30, 41–2, 143, 188, 193
'Phyllis and Rosamond', 15–18, 184
'The Journal of Mistress Joan Martyn', 15, 17–18, 21, 184
**Fiction:**
*Between the Acts*, 139
*Flush*, 22, 28, 29, 74–5, 90, 92, 96–103, 128

*Jacob's Room*, 23, 59, 77, 84, 87–8, 115
*Mrs Dalloway*, 9, 23, 60, 62–3
*Night and Day*, 20, 37, 48, 51–2, 66, 117, 158
*Orlando*, 17, 18, 22–4, 84, 93, 115, 188
*The Voyage Out*, 21, 37, 47–9, 60
*The Waves*, 67, 96, 97
*The Years*, 27, 128, 186
*To The Lighthouse*, 18, 162, 186

*Yale Review*, 10, 93, 96

Zemgulys, Andrea, 111, 118

EU representative:
Easy Access System Europe
Mustamäe tee 50, 10621 Tallinn, Estonia
Gpsr.requests@easproject.com

www.ingramcontent.com/pod-product-compliance
Lightning Source LLC
Chambersburg PA
CBHW070354240426
43671CB00013BA/2493